LONE MOTHERS, PAID WORK AND GENDERED MORAL RATIONALITIES

Lone Mothers, Paid Work and Gendered Moral Rationalities

Simon Duncan
Reader in Comparative Social Policy
Applied Social Studies
University of Bradford
West Yorkshire

and

Rosalind Edwards
Reader in Social Policy
Social Sciences Research Centre
South Bank University
London

First published in Great Britain 1999 by
MACMILLAN PRESS LTD
Houndmills, Basingstoke, Hampshire RG21 6XS and London
Companies and representatives throughout the world

A catalogue record for this book is available from the British Library.

ISBN 0–333–64452–2 hardcover
ISBN 0–333–64453–0 paperback

First published in the United States of America 1999 by
ST. MARTIN'S PRESS, INC.,
Scholarly and Reference Division,
175 Fifth Avenue, New York, N.Y. 10010

ISBN 0–312–22432–X

Library of Congress Cataloging-in-Publication Data
Duncan, Simon.
Lone mothers, paid work, and gendered moral rationalities /
Simon Duncan, Rosalind Edwards.
p.   cm.
Includes bibliographical references and index.
ISBN 0–312–22432–X (cloth)
1. Unmarried mothers—Great Britain.   2. Single mothers—Great
Britain.   3. Unmarried mothers—Employment—Great Britain.
4. Single mothers—Employment—Great Britain.   5. Working mothers–
–Great Britain.   I. Edwards, Rosalind.   II. Title.
HQ759.45.D85   1999
306.874'3—dc21   99–21783
                                                                                            CIP

This book is printed on paper suitable for recycling and made from fully managed and
sustained forest sources.

10   9   8   7   6   5   4   3   2
08   07   06   05   04   03   02   01

Printed & bound by Antony Rowe Ltd, Eastbourne

Contents

List of Figures

List of Tables

Acknowledgements

We have many people to thank. It is common practice to start with acknowledgements for academic support and to finish with thanks to family. However, we would like to start with our parents, none of whom made any direct contribution to the book. Ros's parents – Jean and Michael Joseph – provided her with longstanding opportunities to indulge in vigorous debate of political and moral issues, including those around lone motherhood. Simon's parents – Helen and Dunc – encouraged him to look.

The research project that provides the backbone of this book was fund by the Economic and Social Research Council (grant no. R00023496001). We would like to thank the members of the project advisory group: Graham Crow (Southampton University), Kieran Murphy (Gingerbread) and Bonnie Ure (London Borough of Southwark) for their support. Cilizia Armstrong-Gibbons, Joan Astill, Hope Banton, Laura Hart and Elizabeth Hibberts carried out interviews with groups of British lone mothers for us. Ulla Björnberg, Alina Tuvenäs and Sigrid Wall interviewed lone mothers and provided us with data for Göteborg, and Louise Gerber helped us with translating the scripts. Martha de Acosta organised interviews with lone mothers and provided us with data for Cleveland (USA). Claudia Neusüss interviewed lone mothers in Berlin, and she and Monika Zulauf provided us with data. Thanks as well to Tom Browne for his help in producing the SAR data, and to Simon Gleave for the LS data provided by the ONS. Terry Allen collated day care and employment data for our British case study area. Jane Pugh supported us throughout the project in drawing up maps and graphs and being ready to change and amend them in line with the evolution of the book. Thanks also to Annabelle Buckley at Macmillan for being patient with delays.

Many academic colleagues also provided us with opportunities to discuss our research, or commented on drafts of articles or chapters for this book. In particular, we would like to thank Frances Cleaver, Graham Crow (once again), David Donnison, Robert Eastwood, Susan Himmelweit, Diane Perrons, Fiona Williams, and members of the Women's Workshop on Family/Household Research. Final responsibility for the arguments here, or any errors or omissions, of course lies with us as authors.

1 Explaining the 'Problem' of Lone Motherhood: an Introduction

1.1 THE SCOPE OF THE BOOK: CONTEXTS, RATIONALITIES AND EXPLANATIONS

There are, proportionately, more lone mother families in Britain than in most other western countries, but British lone mothers are far less likely to be in paid work than their counterparts in countries such as Germany, Sweden and the USA. Why is this? Is it because British lone mothers do not want to work and prefer to live off the state? Or is it because their notions of 'good' motherhood mean they would rather stay at home? Do they want to go out to work but cannot because there is no available, or affordable, day care for their children? Or are there no jobs available or suitable for them? Or is it because the British benefits system makes it financially irrational for lone mothers to take up paid work? This book sets out to answer these questions. It focuses on how lone mothers negotiate the relationship between motherhood and paid work in the different social contexts of neighbourhoods, local labour markets and welfare states – contexts which present different sets of opportunities and constraints.

In addressing this range of contexts we are cutting across a British and North American debate that has become polarised between Fabian social policy and conservative new right views of lone motherhood. Despite their political differences, both tend to see lone mothers as a socially homogeneous, categorical group, and both see the national state as the dominant social actor. Arguably, the current 'New Deal' for lone parents in Britain, as proposed by newly ascendant 'New Labour', is using fashionable communitarian ideas as a vehicle to draw on both. Both sets of views also assume a particular notion of personal motivation, based on a neo-classical concept of individual economic rationality. In turn, this assumption supports a socially simplistic stimulus–response model of the relationship between human behaviour and social policy. It is assumed that if the national social policy stimulus is changed, lone mothers will respond

1

by changing their behaviour in an appropriate and uniform way. Thus mainstream social policy analysts propose welfare reform to alleviate the perceived constraints on economically rational behaviour. Changes to the tax and benefits systems should ensure that lone mothers are better off in paid work than they are living on benefits, and publicly funded day care provision should be increased to remove a fundamental block to lone mothers' uptake of paid work. The conservative new right also proposes changes in policy, seeking to remove the social threat they see in lone motherhood by removing state support to lone mothers. A reduction of benefits to lone mothers, for example, will force them into paid work, or dissuade them from divorcing or separating, or even from having children 'out of wedlock' in the first place. In this way both views lead to a form of social engineering. Through this debate lone motherhood also has taken a political significance far wider than the policy issues directly raised, particularly in Britain and the USA. It has become a symbol, and a means of political mobilisation, for rival discourses about the nature of the family and the welfare state. However, if the underlying assumptions of these views are incorrect – that personal motivation is a matter of economic self interest and that national states are the only important actor – then these policies are unlikely to have the desired effects. At best it will be a case of social engineering forcing people, unwillingly and hence inefficiently, into someone else's categorical box.

In contrast, this book takes an approach that highlights lone mothers' own variable understandings and capacities for social action, recognising that they live within particular social contexts, in accounting for how and why lone mothers do, or do not, take up paid work. This includes examining how lone motherhood is understood and analysed through public discourse, how lone mothers themselves understand the relationship between motherhood and employment, and what influence these understandings have on their uptake of paid work. We also examine how neighbourhoods, local labour markets and state welfare regimes provide opportunities and constraints for lone mothers in exercising these understandings. Throughout we compare the situation for British lone mothers, especially for selected social groups living in particular areas, with lone mothers in other countries, especially selected groups living in particular areas of Germany, Sweden, and the USA. Underlying our analysis is a concern with notions of rationality and motivation, where these are crucial to any explanation about how and why lone mothers make employment decisions. Rather than the neo-classical economics version of an individualistic, economic rationality (which is often assumed rather than explicit in much of the research and debate on lone mothers) we draw attention to what we call 'gendered moral rationalities'. These are collective and social understandings about what is the proper relationship between motherhood and paid work. Is it right that I, as a mother bringing up a child by myself, should try for a full-time job? What are my responsibilities, how will my behaviour affect my children? What do others expect from me, what do they see as right, and how will they treat me in consequence? Calculations about perceived economic costs and benefits will be important once these understandings are established, but are essentially secondary to such social and moral questions. We show how these gendered moral rationalities do not operate in any simple and uniform way for lone mothers, but are socially negotiated in particular local and national contexts. Our analysis is thus fundamentally contextualised. It is also fundamentally gendered, recognising that the overwhelming majority of lone parents are women who are mothers, who live in particular places and have relationships with other people, rather than ungendered 'parents' in some placeless, peopleless realm.

1.2 APPROACHES AND METHODS

Inside the Closed Box of Lone Motherhood

There is now plenty of information about lone mothers at the level of aggregate description. A large body of research describes the characteristics of lone mothers as a taxonomic category – their incomes, poverty rates, employment, use of benefits, housing tenure and so on – both in Britain and in comparative perspective. Often this research also breaks the category lone mother down into sub-categories, defined for instance by route into lone motherhood (divorce, never-married etc.) or by age or employment status. This sort of information is clearly very useful in indicating overall patterns, and we have drawn on previous research of this type in this book. Such research is often particularly necessary when a new area or concern is opening up, and this has been true of research on lone motherhood. Research can hardly start until basic information is established. After this stage, however, this sort of descriptive, taxonomic research becomes less useful. This is because the research concern changes from describing a new issue to attempting to understand how it is caused. Categorical research, focused on describing aggregate patterns, and based on taxonomic distinctions, is less effective in discovering social process – how and why these patterns have happened.

This is for two linked reasons. First of all, it is often inefficient to argue from form to process; the same process can produce alternative forms depending on the context in which it takes place – and viceversa. It is important therefore to access process directly, but categorical research is often unable to do this. We need to examine how, and why, some lone mothers take up paid work and others do not, rather than simply describe their characteristics after the event and then infer explanations on this basis.

The second problem with this type of categorical research is all the more severe because it often remains unrecognised. Research often proceeds as if the taxonomic group accurately delineates a social group, and hence also encompass similar social positions, social relations and social behaviour. This assumption is often quite wrong. Taxonomic groups, for example lone mothers distinguished as a particular parental form, are often different from the real substantive social groups which actually carry through social actions and relationships. It is not just that lone mothers are not a homogeneous or unified population, so that different social groups of lone mothers may behave differently. In addition it may not be lone motherhood in itself that is substantively or causally most important for their social behaviour. It may, for example, be membership of particular ethnic or class group, or location in a particular area, that explains why some lone mothers take up paid work and others do not. (The extreme example of the lone mothers among the British royal family makes the point here.) For instance, Black lone mothers in Britain are more likely to be in paid work than their White (or Asian) counterparts, especially for full-time jobs (see Table 1.1). Why is this the case? Similarly, as a taxonomic group, single (never-married) lone mothers show the lowest employment rates. But how far does this appellation disguise the fact that many are working class and live in local labour markets and neighbourhoods with poor job prospects (although even so Black single lone mothers have higher employment rates)? In turn, divorced lone mothers may be more likely to be middle class and to live in more favourable local labour markets and neighbourhoods. Underlying social divisions can remain unspoken, therefore. This is why, to use Andrew Sayer's memorable phrase (1984, 1992), research which is based on taxonomic groups is often, but unknowingly, using

Table 1.1   Lone mothers' uptake of paid work by ethnicity,* Britain 1991

Ethnicity	In paid work %	(of which full time) + %	No paid work %
White	37.7	(18.5)	62.3
African-Caribbean/ Black Other	57.1	(30.2)	44.9
African	55.9	(32.3)	45.1
Indian and Pakistani	23.7	(15.1)	74.3

* ethnicity defined as in 1991 Census (Black Other includes Black British and some small, miscellaneous groups)
+ including self-employed with employees
Source: 1991 household SAR, authors' calculations.

'chaotic concepts' – concepts which have little parallel with actual causal relations. 'Lone mothers' may be just such a concept.

For both these reasons – arguing from form to process, and the misidentification of substantive, causal groups – research based around taxonomic difference is in serious danger of neglecting process and of misappropriating cause. Rather, we need to go inside the 'closed box' (sometimes called the 'black box') of the category lone mothers and examine social differences and social behaviour within it. In this book we take a multi-layered context-action model for understanding the various dynamics and processes by which lone mothers do, or do not, combine motherhood and paid work. We therefore address both structural forms and the subjectivity and agency of lone mothers themselves, paying attention to the variety of social and material contexts such as social class, ethnicity and geographical location in which lone mothers are situated.

This discussion of research approach also has policy implications. Lone mothers are not an homogeneous group in terms of social characteristics, and it is not always lone motherhood that determines their behaviour. It is therefore extremely unlikely that, as a categorical group, they will hold similar views and respond to policy developments in similar ways. Unfortunately, this is the assumption held by both conservative new right and Fabian social policy analyses and proposals. In so far as more 'communitarian' approaches like the British 'New Labour' Welfare to Work programme draw on these perspectives, then the same mistake will be replicated. It may be that social policy needs to dispense with the chaotic concept 'lone mothers' altogether.

Extensive and Intensive Research – Mixing Quantitative and Qualitative Data

Going inside the 'closed box' of the taxonomic group 'lone mothers', and placing emphasis on direct access to process, has implications for research design and methods. These are usefully summarised by the distinction between 'extensive' and 'intensive' research (Sayer 1984, 1992). The former refers to research which aims to describe overall patterns and distinguishing features, for example the characteristics of a population. Taxonomic groups are the type of group studied usually (though not necessarily) using quantitative data from large scale surveys including official statistics. While producing representative description, this design is weak on explanatory power, that is on how something happens. Intensive research in contrast seeks to find out how a process happened by focusing on what agents actually do. It focusses on substantive process connections in causal, social groups rather than taxonomic groups. Taking a close-up look, it can better identify processes and mechanisms, going beyond simple association. It is often 'local' in that it deals with the complexities of social action in context, usually (although again not necessarily) employing in-depth case study and qualitative methods.

Each research design has different strengths and weaknesses, and are therefore more or less appropriate to different research questions. In this way they should be seen as complimentary. Unfortunately, and unhelpfully, they are usually regarded as lying in opposition to one another. This is particularly evident in the strict division often made between 'hard' quantitative, and 'soft' qualitative, data and methods (see Brannen, 1992). There are three problems here. First of all, the complimentarity of the two research designs is lost. Secondly, the reduction of research design (what the research is able to do) to techniques and methods (how the research is undertaken) in itself exacerbates the division. There is no necessity that a particular research technique or method is limited to either intensive or extensive research. Thirdly, and most unfortunately, there have been strong tendencies to privilege one design over another. Usually this has taken the form of seeing extensive research and quantitative methods as somehow superior, partly because of its associations with economic science, figures and machines, and men. Ironically, this is despite its weaknesses for explanation. A reaction by the excluded has been to privilege intensive, qualitative research, just because it has been particularly associated with feminist analysis, personal contact and women. Either sort of privileging further exacerbates the tendency for researchers to cut themselves off from complimentary research designs and to make unwarranted claims for their own.

In contrast we have 'mixed' research designs, methods and data. For some of the research we have used qualitative, secondary data in an extensive manner – for example in examining discourses about lone motherhood. At other times, where existing knowledge is sketchy, we have focused on extensive, quantitative data – as in our discussion of lone mothers in local labour markets. At the core of our empirical research, however, about how different social groups of lone mothers see paid work in relation to their responsibilities as mothers, we have combined intensive and extensive research designs, methods and data. This combination of research designs allows us to assess the generality of the qualitative interview information about lone mothers' social relations and understandings by using representative quantitative information as a check. Conversely, the interviews provide process explanations for the more descriptive information on lone mothers' characteristics found in quantitative data. This allows us to better link evidence on social process and cause (on how and why things happen) with evidence about social patterns (on what has happened).

The source for the extensive part of this core research was the 1991 British census. For information on lone mothers in local labour market areas, and in case study areas and neighbourhoods within them, we used the Local Base Statistics (LBS, providing census variables at District Council level) and the Small Area Statistics (SAS, giving the same information at ward and the even smaller enumeration district levels). Similar information was provided by our overseas collaborators for the German, Swedish and US case study areas. The major source for socio-economic information on different social groups of lone mothers was the Household Sample of Annonymised Records (SARs) and the Longitudinal Survey (LS). The former provides a one per cent sample of UK households in 1991,[1] including 11,388 lone mothers, and the latter follows a one per cent sample of individuals through census dates, including 6,496 lone mothers. The SARs and LS give two major advantages over conventional, area based census sources, such as the LBS and SAS (Dale and Marsh 1993; Openshaw 1995). First, analysis at the level of individuals avoids the 'ecological fallacy' of extrapolating individual social associations from aggregate spatial averages.[2] Second, the SARs and LS allow the creation of census categories, and the production of statistical outputs from them, in line with the needs of research, rather than having to rely on those predetermined by the Office of Population, Census and Surveys in their published output. We were thus able to produce census information for particular groups of lone mothers (subject, of course, to what was asked in the census). While the SARs provide 'snapshot' information for one census date in 1991, the LS provides longitudinal data between 10-year census periods.

The major source for the intensive part of the research consisted of 95 open-ended interviews with lone mothers. Typically, each interview lasted about one to one and a half hours, and covered the lone mother's feelings and understandings about combining motherhood and paid work, relations with other people in her social networks and her views about the local neighbourhood and labour market, as well as including factual circumstances about her life course and employment. We were not concerned with producing a statistically representative sample of the taxonomic population of lone mothers (having access to this through the census sources), but with sampling sets of lone mothers that we regarded as more adequately delineating substantive social – and thereby causal – groups. In other words, our selection of the sample of lone mothers for the intensive research was driven by an explanatory and theoretical logic. Altogether we interviewed members of ten groups of lone mothers. Between them these covered what we saw as important social divisions of class, ethnicity and culture (defined in terms of 'alternative' or 'conventional'), living in four different types of neighbourhood (innercity, gentrifying, peripheral social housing, and suburban), situated in different labour market areas and in different policy environments in Britain, Germany, Sweden and the USA. See Table 1.2 for details.

Social Divisions and Spatial Contexts

Previous work on lone motherhood, based on extensive research at a taxonomic level, has tended to downplay both the differences between lone mothers and in the contexts in which they live. In this study, aimed at investigating the processes by which some lone mothers take up paid work and others do not, both social divisions and spatial contexts assume greater importance. In terms of social divisions between lone mothers, we were primarily concerned with factors of class, eth-

Table 1.2 Interviewee characteristics by location and social group

Location and social group	Number	with paid work or full-time study (of which full-time work*)	with higher education	owner-occupiers	single mothers	with at least one child under 5
Inner City						
London:						
1. Younger African-Caribbean	9	5 (1)	–	–	9	8
2. Older African-Caribbean	10	6 (3)	1	–	10	4
3. West African	10	7 (–)	–	1	5	4
4. White 'alternative'	10	7 (3)	3	3	8	6
Cleveland, USA:						
5. Young, mainly White working class	10	8 (1)	–	2	9	10
Periperal social housing						
Brighton:						
6. White working class	10	3 (–)	–	–	8	7
Göteborg:						
7. White, mainly middle class	10	8 (4)	3	2	5	9
Gentrifying neighbourhoods						
Brighton:						
8. White 'alternative'	10	8 (2)	5	8	5	1
Berlin:						
9. White 'alternative'	10	8 (2)	4	–	9	4
Suburban						
Brighton:						
10. White middle class	6	3 (1)	2	5	3	3

* over 30 hours per week
Source: Interviews for authors' study, summer 1994.

nicity and 'conventionality'. As discussed earlier, much previous work on the uptake of paid work by British lone mothers, in focusing on characteristics such as housing tenure, educational level or employment experience, has an unspoken concern with social class issues.

However, as this remains at the level of the taxonomic group 'lone mothers', this concern cannot be effectively expressed or followed up. We attempt to investigate class divisions more explicitly. Our assessment of the interviewees' social class position included current or previous occupation, level of education and housing tenure. However, social class expresses social and cultural values as well as material achievements, while placing women in particular within classifications based on a combination of market and occupational variables is fraught with difficulties. This is partly due to the high proportion of women in part-time jobs within the British labour market (for White women at least) and, following occupational sex segregation, a considerable bunching of women in a few jobs. In addition, occupation does not capture style of life at home and in the neighbourhood, which are major sites where class understandings are shaped (see, for example, Abbott and Sapsford 1987; Harris and Morris 1986; Mirza 1992). We therefore also considered the class implications of lone mothers' lifestyles in particular neighbourhoods when ascribing class location. For the census analysis we used various social and economic proxy variables to assess class position, as well as the census socio-economic group classification.

Even less attention has been paid to the ethnicity of lone mothers, despite the fact that different ethnic groups have very different employment patterns. We focused on the differences between Black and White lone mothers because of the greater propensity, in Britain, of the former to take up paid work, particularly full-time work (see Table 1.1). For the British interviews, ethnicity was self-ascribed as African-Caribbean, west African and White as interviewers followed particular social networks (see below), while ethnicity in the census is also based on self-ascription in answering a specific census question. We also saw 'alternative', counter-cultural and feminist attitudes as another important social division between lone mothers. Feminist understandings of the social world can stress departure from traditional gender roles and family forms, and value independence from men (Gordon 1990), and thus may have an impact on lone mothers uptake of paid work. This was again operationally defined for the interview groups by following lone mothers' own social networks and ascriptions. There is no attitudinal information of this type in the census.

Where a social process takes place has considerable effect on how it takes place. This is another important theme in unpacking the closed box of lone motherhood, and in going further than taxonomic research. This is for two general reasons. First, the outcomes of social processes will be necessarily spatially differentiated as they interact with pre-existing and varying conditions. For instance, social policy changes allowing lone mothers to take up paid work more easily will have a differential effect in interaction with a pre-existing geography of job availability. Secondly, how social processes work will be spatially differentiated. For example, what lone motherhood means will be different in different areas, as people negotiate their identity in spatial varying social contexts, and hence these social policy changes will have different meanings and effects. In this way there are, in fact, no general processes like class, or gender – or lone motherhood – except in so far as these exist as abstractions in our minds (see Duncan, 1989a, 1998; Sayer 1985). Social processes do not float around in some ethereal dimension located somewhere above the real world.

Once the importance of spatial variability is admitted, then comparative research becomes a priority, both in describing variations and in building up an explanatory account of how social processes can vary and how they are differentially caused. Research on lone motherhood has indeed paid increasing attention to comparative differences, but only in a particularly partial way – the focus is limited to social policy differences at the level of the national state. This limited view neglects other spatial contexts where variability is important, for example between local labour markets and neighbourhoods. Thus variations in lone mothers' uptake of paid work at these scales in Britain are just as marked as between different countries. Most towns have their 'little Swedens', neighbourhoods where most lone mothers have paid work, as well as their 'little Irelands' where most are at home. Similarly, in 1991 only 16 per cent of lone mothers had jobs in Knowsley (a District Council of large social housing estates outside Liverpool) compared to 60 per cent in the Ribble Valley District Council (centred on the old cotton town of Clitheroe) little more than 30 miles away. And in closing off other spatial contexts, this limited view of comparative research also closes down examination of other social processes. What are those processes operating in local labour markets, and in neighbourhoods, that can produce such huge differences within the same national state policy regime?

The over-emphasis on the national state in comparative research on lone motherhood, as in other areas of social policy, probably relates to the centrality of the Fabian tradition, where a benevolent state is seen as the only effective actor. (Sometimes events conspire to refashion this image to a malign state, as with one view of Thatcherism.) This view is prolonged because of the undertheorisation of spatial difference in social policy. In turn this neglect of difference supports a taxonomic approach to lone motherhood. This is always the same, it is just state policy which differs. To redress this 'spatial deficit' in social policy, and to provide a a sense of 'place' to research on lone motherhood, we need to turn to the considerable body of work in geography and sociology showing how social processes operate at other scales and in other contexts. In the global market, international divisions of labour are spatially differentiated on regional and local scales. These 'spatial divisions of labour' distribute different types and numbers of jobs to different places. They are also highly gendered (Massey 1984, 1995; Walby 1986). Enduring regional and local cultures around gender and work interact with the geographical set of opportunities and constraints for paid work provided by the spatial division of labour; thus in some areas mothers are seen as also being paid workers, in others purely as homemakers. Both the expectations and the possibilities for lone mothers to take up paid work will differ markedly, therefore. At the neighbourhood level, lone mothers are often embedded in social networks, giving people a sense of identity and defining situations communally as well as individually. Particular discourses can circulate in different neighbourhoods about the nature of lone motherhood and of divisions of labour, providing another set of opportunities and constraints for lone mothers' uptake of paid work.

In this research we take account of these spatial contexts in two ways. First of all, we centre particular chapters on lone mothers in neighbourhoods (chs 3 and 4), in local labour markets (ch. 6) and in welfare states (ch. 7). Secondly, however, our interview data is explicitly set within particular national, local labour market and neighbourhood contexts. These provide another logic for taking samples so as to represent substantive social, causal groups. In Britain (see Table 1.2), four sets of interviews were carried out in the contiguous boroughs of Lambeth and Southwark, in Inner London. This is an extreme exemplar of an inner-city, which in 1991 contained the highest concentrations of unemployment in London (itself containing one of the largest concentrations of unemployment of any major city in the industrial world), and high concentrations of people on income support and Black ethnic groups. Social housing and private renting predominate over owner-occupation. There is also a high proportion of lone mothers. Another three sets of interviews were undertaken in

Brighton and Hove, on the south coast. This is in many respects a more 'average' area, with unemployment levels somewhat above the national level, a low proportion of Black ethnic groups, and most housing in owner-occupation. Lone motherhood is about average for the country as a whole. In one respect, however, this area (or at least parts of it) is different from much of the rest of Britain – it is a centre for 'alternative' styles of living.

Within these contrasting local areas the interviews were also set within four different neighbourhood types – disadvantaged inner-city, gentrifying inner-city, peripheral social housing, and middle-class suburbs. Disadvantaged innercity areas have a long history, in Britain, of being categorised and stigmatised as impoverished, deprived, and even dangerous, places (see Stedman-Jones 1971). Currently, there is poor access to housing for the majority on low incomes, with high house prices and shrinking private renting, and this has led to their concentration on residualised public housing estates nearby to pockets of conspicuous consumption and gentrification. Deindustrialisation and the collapse of manufacturing has led to a deskilling and a lack of jobs, while partial employment replacement in service and distribution sectors has increased social polarisation. High income jobs are taken by commuting or gentrifying professionals, with a 'semi-visible army' of low paid, often short term, workers (Williams 1995). Young school leavers, middle-aged and elderly men, Black and Asian groups, and the unskilled, are most affected by unemployment. Women tend not to be so severely affected, but still live in multiply deprived neighbourhoods. For our British interviews the four Lambeth and Southwark groups mostly lived in neighbourhoods of this type (Table 1.2).

Some innercity neighbourhoods have been subject to gentrification – the process whereby elements of the 'new service class' of professional and managerial workers, with shared lifestyle and 'yuppy' consumer preferences, move into previously decaying areas and in so doing displace poorer, working class households (Butler 1997; Savage 1995). Some areas show a more 'marginal gentrification', with lower income gentrifiers, and smaller and less presentable housing. Downwardly mobile middle class groups, especially woman-headed households who have been marginalised from the labour market through, for example, lone motherhood, are concentrated in such neighbourhoods. In both, changing gender relations have been identified as crucial to the gentrification process, and these neighbourhoods always show rapid increases in women's employment levels, especially in professional and managerial jobs. This is partly because of the possibility of shorter journeys to work for women combining employment with domestic responsibilities, but also because concentrations of like-minded people offer both a cultural identity, and emotional and material lifestyle support, for those attempting to establish new forms of gender relations. Gentrifying areas thus also encompass 'alternative' feminist or counter-cultural views. In the British sample, the Hanover area of Brighton was taken as the case study of this type of marginal gentrification (see Table 1.2).

Peripheral social housing estates have come to rival innercity areas in being recognised as sites of multiple deprivation. In contrast with innercity areas, however, they usually contain low proportions of minority ethnic groups. They are peripheral in both physical and social senses, in being located on the outer edges of cities and towns (thus, with long travel to work distances), and in containing concentrations of poorly educated, and socially excluded groups, with high levels of unemployment and reliance on benefits (Hall 1997). Such estates were often built as dormitory housing areas during the 1950s and 1960s, and usually have no local economic base of their own, as well as a lack of retail, recreational and social facilities. On the other hand there is usually good access to green space, and some have good housing. While many such estates generate strong community pride, residents – as in inner-cities – can often feel stigmatised. Moulscoomb in Brighton was our case study of such an area (see Table 1.2)

Suburban middle class areas are also situated on the fringes of cities and towns, and also have a predominantly White population. Their social and class position is quite different, however, with high concentrations of home-owning, nuclear and elderly households, with low rates of unemployment, reliance on benefits and disadvantage. Unlike the other three neighbourhood types, there are below average rates of lone motherhood. Suburban neighbourhoods represent, socially and physically, the social aspirations of the 'conventional' middle class. Often built during the inter-war period, they accommodated lifestyle and consumption patterns requiring low density single family houses with gardens, which could also be used as a financial investment (Hudson and Williams 1995; Butler 1997). Suburbs also represent an 'ideology of domesticity' with highly segregated gendered division of labour (Madigan et al. 1990). Even now poor public transport, a paucity of local jobs, and lack of material and social support mean that women can find it difficult to combine paid work and domestic responsibilities, or become socially marginalised if they do. In our

British interviews Patcham and Westdene in Brighton was the exemplar of this sort of area (Table 1.2).

We also interviewed groups of lone mothers living in Germany, Sweden and the USA where each is conventionally taken as exemplars of a particular type of welfare state regime (Duncan, 1995). Such regimes develop different sets of social policy in expressing their particular conception of the relationship between individuals, families, states and markets. These different conceptions and sets of policies are gendered, with different implications for the positioning of men and women, not least for lone mothers. While no one country presents a pure case of any regime and countries may straddle or move between them, the USA is generally regarded as a type case of the Liberal welfare state regime. Here social policy is used to uphold the market and traditional work-ethic norms, with modest and means-tested benefits aimed at a residualised and stigmatised group of welfare recipients. Lone mothers are stigmatised as 'mothers on welfare'. Germany is the type case of the Conservative welfare regime where states intervene to preserve status differences – including those of traditional gender roles and family forms. Lone mothers become peripheralised as mothers without male partners. In Social Democratic welfare state regimes, where Sweden is a type-case, social policy reforms which de-emphasise the market are extended to all classes, with equality at the highest standards rather than minimal needs. Both men and women – including lone mothers – are seen as independent worker-citizens who independently support themselves through participation in the labour market.

The interview groups in these countries were also chosen to represent particular social groups and neighbourhood types, and so allow comparison with the British groups. The German sample was of 'alternative' lone mothers in Kreuzberg, a gentrifying inner-city area in Berlin, the Swedish group from Björndammen in Partille commune, a peripheral high-rise housing area near Göteborg, and the US sample was from Near West Side, a disadvantaged inner-city area in Cleveland, Ohio. See Table 1.2.

Accessing Lone Mothers – Enumeration, Snowballing and Networks

Having chosen to focus research on particular social groups of lone mothers, the next task was to actually find information about them. For the extensive research based on census data, this was in principle a simple operation using computerised or published data sets, if sometimes intricate and time-consuming. The LBS and SAS data could be accessed via the Census Dissemination Unit, and the SARs from the Census Microdata Unit, both at Manchester University, while the LS data was available from the Social Statistics Research Unit at City University. It should be remembered, however, that the census is just another survey, subject to common problems. In particular, there was considerable underenumeration in the 1991 census, with an estimated 1.2 million people (2.2 per cent) missing (Simpson and Dorling 1994). This underenumeration was especially marked in inner cities, with as many as 20–25 per cent of men in the 20 – 34 age group missing. Fortunately, the underenumeration rate in the inner cities was much less for young women, at about 5 per cent, although there is some evidence that minority ethnic households were less likely to register the existence of young children and especially babies. The practice of 'imputation' (that is including some of the missing through 'reasonable' guesses by census officers) should be considered unreliable for social attributes. One of the strengths of the census is its large numerical base, but even so the SARS and LS can soon reach very small sample sizes with fine disaggregations, and some of our analyses suffer from this problem. Similarly, there are definitional problems, for example some census variables define lone mother families in purely household terms (the presence of child/ren and one adult), others in family terms (they are related), some count concealed lone mother households (where she is not head of the household), others do not. Not surprisingly, therefore, estimates of the number and type of lone mothers vary. Official and census definitions are also notoriously variable between countries (see Bradshaw et al. 1996).

What constitutes a lone mother family was also an issue for the interview work. The cut-off age for dependent children in British Official Statistics is either under 16, or from 16 to (under) 19 in full-time education. However, in the interviews we limited the cut-off point to 13. Beyond this age children are overwhelmingly regarded as being no longer in need of adult supervision before or after school, during conventional working hours, or in school holidays. Indeed, the majority of British parents see children over 11 years as old enough to look after themselves (Ford 1996), and the age cut-off for the British child care costs disregard for the in-work benefit family credit is also 11. Another definitional issue is whether or not lone mothers live with other adults. Here we followed the official British definition of living without a spouse and not cohabiting, in that we interviewed mothers responsible for their children on a daily basis and not living with a male partner.

However, a few of the lone mothers in our sample lived with other adults (their own parents or lodgers). This is an issue we will pick up again in looking at the social support available to our lone mothers.

The lone mothers interviewed for our study were accessed by snow-balling within their social networks, and in this sense (in interaction with our interviewers) they categorised themselves. The dangers of 'unrepresentativeness' in snowballing noted in the methods literature (for example, Lee 1993) were minimised in that we were conducting theoretically-based sampling, and in that we could position the snow-ball samples within representative census data on lone mother characteristics by social group and area. Moreover, the snowballing method matched our concern with the part played by lone mothers' social relations, including neighbourhood networks, in their uptake of paid work. Indeed, generally motherhood is never purely family-based, but extends to social networks and neighbourhoods (Bell and Ribbens 1994; Everingham 1994).

Previous experience had alerted us to the difficulties in reaching Black lone mothers in particular, and that they could make decisions about whether or not to take part in research in consultation with others in their social networks (Edwards 1996). Thus, for most of the social groups of British lone mothers we employed interviewers (largely mature undergraduate students) who were part of the groups and locations we had identified: younger and older African-Caribbean, west African, and both White 'alternative' groups. Drawing on people from groups or communities to themselves act as researchers has a long history (Finch 1986). Interviews with the remaining British groups (White working class 'estate' and middle class 'suburban') were carried out by one of us, working through more formal community or neighbourhood services or contacts, and those for our cross-national comparisons were carried out in a similar fashion by university researchers in each country.

The process of snowballing to lone mothers in this fashion proved illuminating in itself. Generally, people's social networks may be tied to particular neighbourhoods or may be more dispersed geographically, and this is often related to socio-economic resources and to gender. For example, travel for women can be a more difficult undertaking than it is for men, and mothers of young children can be especially tied to, or embedded in, their neighbourhoods (see Pickup 1988; Bell and Ribbens 1994). Thus, in some instances our interviewees, and their social networks, were strongly based in a relatively tightly defined area (for example, the White working class 'estate' group of lone mothers in

Brighton), while others were somewhat more dispersed (for example the White 'alternative' group living in London). This difference also has implications for their experiences as lone mothers.

The links between lone mothers in an area, crucial for our snow-balling approach, revealed an important aspect of lone mothers' social relations. In most cases, access and snowballing was easily achieved – lone mothers tended to know other lone mothers living locally. The 'snowballing maps', detailing how we reached a group of interviewees and who knew whom, for the younger African-Caribbean lone mothers and White 'alternative' group in Brighton (see Figure 1.1) illustrate this. (They also illustrate the embeddedness of our interviewers them-selves in these networks.) In one case, however – the White middle class 'suburban' group in Brighton – it proved difficult to reach lone mothers and to persuade those who were contacted to take part. Firstly, many did not want to associate themselves with a 'stigmatised' group of 'lone' or 'single' mothers. (This was despite the fact that we used the term 'mothers on their own', in describing the research to them.) Secondly, it was difficult to snowball out to other lone mothers from those who were interviewed as they did not know, or mix with, other lone mothers. Members of local agencies operating in this subur-ban area, such as schools, social service or health organisations took some persuading to help, equally fearing stigmatisation in approaching women as 'mothers on their own'. Thus we did not reach our target of 10 interviewees for this group (see Table 1.3). Their 'snowball map' (see Figure 1.1) illustrates the more fractured process in comparison with the other two groups. In themselves, these differences in access via snowballing lend support to our argument that variability in local contexts and of lone mothers within them need to be addressed.

Our practical concern with snowballing through social networks also mirrors some of the more abstract theorising about the direction of current society. The proliferation of individuals grouping together with chosen (rather than ascribed) like-minded and similar individuals is often pointed to as a feature of the (post) modern times in which we live. This principle of 'homophily' means that sub- or counter-cultural values and networks can develop around features of identity, including ethnicity, sexuality, sexual politics or political stance. For right wing the-orists wedded to the concept of an 'underclass', such counter-cultures contain a threat to society's traditional values (for example, Mead 1986; Murray 1990, 1994). Those on what might (perhaps simplistically) be characterised as the 'old left' can also take a negative view, seeing such developments as fracturing society and thus also mass political action

Younger African-Caribbean, (Inner London)

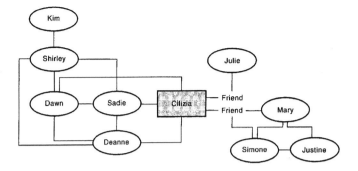

White 'alternative' middle class, (Brighton)

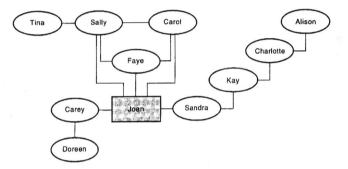

White 'suburban' middle class, (Brighton)

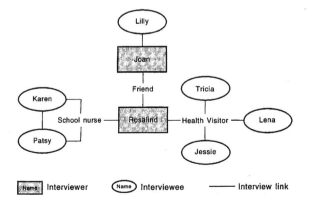

Figure 1.1 Snowballing maps: selected groups 1994

(for example, Bauman 1995). For those taking (again, simplistically) a new left or high modernist perspective, however, these network groupings are a positive movement in the face of an individualistic postmodern capitalism (for example, Beck 1992; Maffesoli 1995). Much of this debate is carried out at an abstract or populist level. In contrast, our research around lone mothers' social networks has a much more concrete aim, in seeking to identify what 'homophily', if it indeed exists, practically means for lone mothers and their uptake of paid work.

1.3　THE STRUCTURE OF THE BOOK

Chapter 2 begins with an examination of political and popular discourses around lone motherhood. These both inform and reflect policy developments, and shape interpretations of what lone mothers should do. They therefore provide an important context within which lone mothers live their lives. Not only do particular discourses about lone motherhood gain legitimacy in a national context, where different nation states can assume different discourses, but there are variations in the dominance of some (and marginalisation of other) perspectives over time. In addition, these discourses can be differentially held by particular social groups, and within particular social networks and neighbourhoods.

Chapter 3 continues by focusing on the variable nature of lone mothers' lives as lived within particular neighbourhoods, interacting with kin and friends in social networks. This includes variations in lone mothers' uptake of paid work, where geographical and social group differences are often coterminous. We examine this in the context of debates about social capital and its relationship to economic behaviour. What becomes clear is that distinctly moral understandings about the 'right' course of action to take, in combining motherhood and paid work, underlie lone mothers' access to such capital and hence also their variable uptake of paid work.

Chapter 4 follows this up by demonstrating these moral understandings in action. Variations in the uptake of paid work are reflected by systematic differences between social groups in their views, values and motivations towards combining motherhood and paid work. We distinguish between three main 'ideal types' of these gendered moral rationalities: 'primarily mother', 'mother/worker integral' and 'primarily worker'. These gendered moral rationalities do not operate according to the assumptions of individualistic 'rational economic man'.

Rather, they are negotiated socially within the context of social groups, social networks and neighbourhoods.

Chapter 5 continues this analysis by using extensive data from the census. It first checks and extends the information on the differential uptake of paid work by different social groups of lone mothers by using the 1991 SAR data. The chapter then goes on to assess how these patterns may change over time, using the LS data for 1981–91. For any level of human capital or individual constraint, Black lone mothers in Britain showed a higher rate of full-time work, and usually had higher rates of employment overall, than their White counterparts, and these differences were stable or even emphasised over time. The results support the gendered moral rationalities explanation for these differences, as advanced through the interview evidence in chapter 4. They also suggest that the 'new right' response to lone motherhood is misplaced.

Chapter 6 turns to constraints for lone mothers set up by the variable supply of jobs. Even if lone mothers hold gendered moral rationalities that are compatible with their uptake of paid work, jobs have to be available if they are to do this. Debates about lone motherhood are often couched in terms of 'getting lone mothers back to work', but jobs of the right sort, or even any sort, may simply not be there for lone mothers to take. Furthermore, the type and number of jobs are differentially distributed through local labour markets, and it is at this scale that lone mothers actually have access to jobs. These different local labour market characteristics also interact with local cultural understandings of what social role women are expected to hold. Where lone mothers live, therefore, has considerable implications for their employment prospects for both cultural and economic reasons.

Chapter 7 examines the dramatic differences in lone mothers' relative poverty and employment rates in different welfare states. We argue that conventional categorisations of welfare state regimes are inadequate in accounting for these differences and develop a 'gender-fare' categorisation of welfare regimes that more adequately reflects the positioning of lone mothers. We use this to examine the economic position of lone mothers in welfare state regimes, focusing on the three major available income sources – benefits, maintenance and employment. However, as the previous chapters have shown, lone mothers are not simply positioned by welfare state regimes or gender contracts – they also position themselves.

Chapter 8 examines the critique of conventional economics, and in particular the model of rational economic man, in explaining economic decision-making in general and of lone mothers in particular. The importance of this model is greater than its ostensible status as a rather bizarre economic theorisation would suggest because it extends far outside neo-classical economics, if often implicitly, into the realms of social policy and everyday politics. The logic of the critiques advanced is to instead employ social and moral definitions of rationality in understanding decision-making – a position also reached by our own empirical investigation of lone mothers' uptake of paid work.

Finally, *Chapter 9* addresses the implications of the book for current social policy. We argue that 'welfare to work' needs to be replaced by a locally sensitive 'welfare and work' programme, and that in so doing New Labour's increasingly conservative, conformist and moralistic version of communitarianism would be transformed to a more pluralistic, voluntaristic and socio-economic version.

Overall then, this book demonstrates that the issue of lone mothers' uptake of paid work is much broader and deeper than allowed by previous studies, which so often concentrate on the closed boxes of decontextualised individual variable-based correlations or national policy regimes. Rather than being underpinned by an individualistic 'rational economic man' framework, leading to a simplistic view of lone mothers' responses to social policy developments, the process of lone mothers' uptake of paid work is shaped by variable but intensely moral social processes, at all levels, concerning the compatibility of motherhood and paid work. Lone mothers' actions are not simply governed by economic cause and effect, but by the moral rationalities they use to interpret the world – how they contemplate, interpret and act within their environment.

NOTES

1. Two SARs were produced; the Individual SAR with a 2 per cent sample of individuals, and the Household SAR with a 1 per cent sample of households. We used the latter, although smaller, as the Individual SAR was, at the time we undertook the research, unable to distinguish adequately between lone mothers and co-residing daughters over 15.
2. For example, in Britain there is a high correlation for census areas between the percentage of Black residents and the level of 'deprivation'. To deduce from this that being Black induces deprivation is an ecological fallacy – most Blacks are not deprived while the substantial majority of the deprived are White. Individual level data would expose this error. See Openshaw 1984, Fieldhouse and Tye 1996.

2 Understanding Lone Motherhood: Competing Discourses and Positions

2.1 INTRODUCTION: LONE MOTHERHOOD AS A DISCOURSE

Lone motherhood is not neutral and apolitical; it is shot through with political and moral evaluations (Silva 1996). Britain provides a good example. In 1993, 'the year of the demonisation of lone mothers', lone mothers found themselves vilified by right wing politicians and the popular media as threats to the fabric of social order. Supposedly, they were rearing delinquent children while scrounging benefits and housing off the welfare state, and thus forming a dangerous under-class. Attempts were made by voluntary groups and others representing lone mothers to counter this portrayal and insert, or reinsert, a public image of lone mothers as women who were struggling to do their best in constrained and unfavourable circumstances. Lone motherhood was again a focus during 1996 as part of a national debate about British society's 'moral values', again conducted by politicians and the media. Lone mothers were one of several groups highlighted as an example of where these values were somehow going wrong. Towards the end of 1997 lone mothers were again in the news. This time debate centred on whether 'sticks' or 'carrots' were required to move lone mothers off welfare dependency and into paid work, following the new Labour government's benefit cuts and welfare-to-work strategies for lone mothers. In all these cases lone motherhood was used as a concrete symbol, or rallying point, for wider debates about the nature of society and how the state should react.

These political and moral discourses about lone motherhood provide one important context within which lone mothers live their lives. Generally, discourses both name and make sense of social relationships and behaviour. In assigning meaning and causes to situations and actions, they shape the ways we think of, and react to, aspects of the social world. However, all discourses are not equal, for institutional and social structures enable some discourses to be more

23

influential, or considered more 'natural' and legitimate, than others. The views of powerful social groups within society are more likely to gain legitimacy. Conversely, the perspectives of subordinate groups are likely to be marginalised (see Foucault 1976). In particular, the more dominant often receive backing and sanction in the form of state legislation. In this way the dominance of certain discourses about lone motherhood not only affects how it is understood, but also helps to set parameters on how individual lone mothers should act, and on how the state should intervene. In turn, state policies towards lone motherhood – and families in general – interact with popular and political perceptions to provide another reference point for the formation of discourses about lone motherhood.

Discourses are not only unequal, their importance also varies over time, space and social group. For example, lone mothers in the USA are often seen as immoral scroungers undeserving of social support (de Acosta 1997) while in Germany lone mothers are seen more sympathetically as a social problem, requiring social support, rather than as an undeserving scroungers. This is still an ambiguous status, however, where German lone mothers are portrayed as 'deviant' in terms of prescribed family forms (Klett-Davies 1997). In contrast again, public discussion in Sweden tends to see lone mothers as just another family form, receiving social support on the same basis as any other family (Björnberg 1997). It is also notable how it is chiefly in the English speaking world of liberal state welfare regimes that lone motherhood enters debate as a wider political symbol.

There are also shifts over time within any national context. Different discourses and terminologies can gain ascendancy, and others can become marginalised (Lewis 1995). For example, in Britain during the 1960s the concern was with the social problem of deviant 'fatherless families', who required special treatment. But by the 1970s and 1980s the underlying assumption became one where the needs of 'one parent families' were not fundamentally different from other families, they simply had 'extra' needs. More recently, as we have seen, the emphasis has changed again, where 'single parents' are more likely to be seen as 'anti-family' welfare scroungers (Song 1996). Everyday life, however, and the social meanings involved in it, is not just conducted at the national and 'public' level. Rather, the meaning and characterisation of lone motherhood can differ across social locations? – from one social class, ethnic group, age group, and neighbourhood, to another – depending on the context from which it is perceived. Locally available understandings in social networks and neighbourhoods, in localised socio-economic and cultural contexts, can also inform different interpretations – and these can become locally dominant even if they are marginalised in wider debates.

In the rest of this chapter we detail the diverse ways in which lone motherhood is understood at these different contextual levels. We begin, in section 2.2, by identifying the four main interpretive discourses through which lone motherhood may be viewed, using evidence largely from Britain but also referring to the other case study countries of different welfare state regimes (Germany, Sweden and the USA). The details of our evidence may date, given shifts in the potency of particular discourses. None the less, these shifts will take place within the framework of the major discourses we identify. These national discourses (and the state policies associated with them) provide one, generalised, context in which lone mothers negotiate their lives. Section 2.3 goes on to examine the views held by the different social groups of lone mothers in our interview sample about these political and popular discourses. However, as we have argued, this national level is not the only level at which discourses about lone motherhood operate. Section 2.3 thus examines the lone mothers' perceptions of which discourses are influential in the neighbourhoods in which they live, and which can affect their views about what they should do. This section also shows how discourses that are muted at a national level can have far more resonance in particular local contexts. Finally, in section 2.4, we examine the meaning of lone motherhood for the lone mothers themselves, living in the different local and national discursive contexts. We show how they draw on varying configurations of the four main discourses we have identified to understand their lives and the issues involved in their decisions about taking up paid work or not.

2.2   THE FOUR DISCOURSES AROUND LONE MOTHERHOOD

What we see when we look at lone motherhood depends as much on the particular configuration of the discourse that guides our gaze, and shapes our reports, as it does on the concrete 'object' and facts of our scrutiny. In Britain the socio-political debates about lone motherhood have become polarised between two major views. In one discourse, lone mothers are seen as a threat to society, both morally and financially; they are formative members of an underclass that has no interest in providing for themselves in legitimate ways. In the other discourse, lone mothers are seen as a social problem; they want to take up paid work to better provide for themselves and their children but external constraints in the form of the structure and nature of the welfare state prevents them from doing so. However, in addition to these 'social threat' and 'social problem' discourses there are two other main identifiable discourses on lone motherhood. These are firstly a view of lone motherhood as one of a number of diverse choices in a general social move towards 'lifestyle change' in family life, and secondly a view of lone motherhood as an 'escape from patriarchy', where women seek to live their lives without control by men. These four discourses can be characterised as in competition with each other in defining the meaning and causes of lone motherhood. However, while there are strong distinctions between the discourses, they are not completely separate but can overlap and combine in particular aspects of their construction, as depicted in Figure 2.1. Thus two very different discourses, those of 'social threat' and 'escaping patriarchy', are in some ways rather similar, appearing as opposite sides of the same coin. This conceptualisation is in contrast to Lorraine Fox Harding (1993a, b) who also identifies four positions from which lone motherhood is viewed, which she terms 'alarm', 'concern', 'beneficial effects' and 'liberation'. These bear some similarity with our own analysis. However, Fox Harding poses her identified positions – or, in our terms, discourses – along a continuum, which only allows for points of overlap at an immediately adjacent point. Furthermore, she interposes what she calls a 'notional', 'value free position' between her 'concern' and 'beneficial effects'. This assumes an ability to take a neutral, purely objective perspective on lone motherhood – in effect, a position outside of meaning. This is not sustainable. Nor is 'objective' necessarily the same as 'neutral' – the most extreme position may in fact be the more realistic. While the nature of lone motherhood as conceived and perceived through one discourse can differ substantially from its nature as seen in another discourse, the relative efficacy of either cannot be settled by reference to some supposedly neutral and objective position (see Gubrium and Holstein, 1990, on family discourses generally). Any meanings and interpretations attached to the 'facts' of lone motherhood are – and will be – guided through our tacit understandings about the nature of social relationships, particularly those between men and women.

We now deal with each of the four major interpretive discourses on lone motherhood and their underlying assumptions. We illustrate how

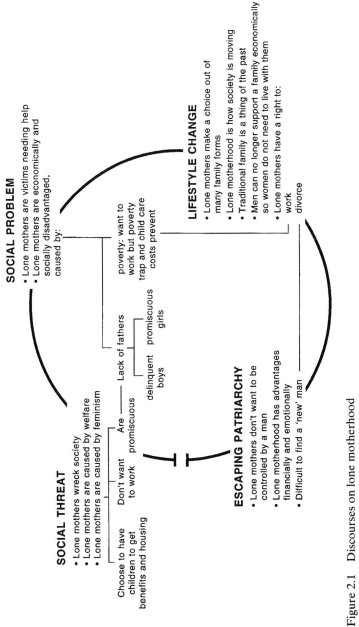

SOCIAL THREAT

- Lone mothers wreck society
- Lone mothers are caused by welfare
- Lone mothers are caused by feminism

Choose to have children to get benefits and housing

Don't want to work

Are promiscuous

Lack of fathers

delinquent boys

promiscuous girls

SOCIAL PROBLEM

- Lone mothers are victims needing help
- Lone mothers are economically and socially disadvantaged, caused by:

poverty: want to work but poverty trap and child care costs prevent

LIFESTYLE CHANGE

- Lone mothers make a choice out of many family forms
- Lone motherhood is how society is moving
- Traditional family is a thing of the past
- Men can no longer support a family economically so women do not need to live with them
- Lone mothers have a right to:
  work
  divorce

ESCAPING PATRIARCHY

- Lone mothers don't want to be controlled by a man
- Lone motherhood has advantages financially and emotionally
- Difficult to find a 'new' man

Figure 2.1 Discourses on lone motherhood

these discourses are used as a conceptual framework to understand perceptions of lone motherhood, and show the variability in the potency of discourses according in our case study national contexts.

a) Lone Motherhood as a Social Threat

This discourse links into the underclass theory of social structure which has developed in the USA in particular, but has recently gained influence in Britain – although it also has roots in a longstanding British 'social pathology' view of the poor (Macnicol 1987, Morris, 1993). The underclass theory posits that, in spatially segregated areas, there is a developing class that has little stake in the social order, is alienated from it and hostile to it, and thus is a major source of crime, deviancy and social breakdown. In turn, this links into a conservative new right view of the welfare state, which is viewed as encouraging dependency on 'welfare' and hence leading to the collapse of both the traditional family and the work ethic. An underclass has developed, the argument goes, because the welfare state has perversely altered the parameters for making rational economic decisions; it is no longer rational for some individuals to live in nuclear families or to take up paid work. This 'immoral' rationality is culturally reproduced in the everyday life of underclass ghettos (see Murray 1994).

Lone mothers are then seen as active agents in the creation of this underclass. In Britain, young single (never-married) mothers have been pointed to as the central culprits, but elements of a racialised discourse, highlighting Black lone mothers, are now emerging – as has long been the case in the USA (Song and Edwards 1997). In both countries, these lone mothers are said to choose to have children to gain benefits and then, supported by the state, they choose not to get a job. Their sons, assumed to be without male authority or roles, are thus seen as drifting into delinquency, crime and the drug culture, while their daughters learn to repeat the cycle of promiscuity and dependency. The fathers of these children – without the 'civilising' influence of 'the family' – supposedly lapse into inherent aggressive selfishness.

Academic versions of the social threat discourse tone down the emotive signifiers somewhat (see, for example, Segalman and Marsland 1989; Murray 1990; Morgan 1995). Popularising versions use emotional symbolism more fully, with socialists and feminists targeted as supporting lone motherhood and thus social breakdown (see Mann and Roseneil 1996 for review). The American academic

Charles Murray, in particular, has been given a platform in the British broadsheet 'quality' newspaper, *The Sunday Times*. During 1993 especially, there were regular 'wedded to welfare' and 'babies on benefits' stories and cartoons in the media, displaying raw prejudices. We give one example here:

> It is becoming increasingly clear to all but the most blinkered of social scientists that the disintegration of the nuclear family is the principal source of so much unrest and misery ... It is not just a question of a few families without fathers; it is a matter of whole communities with barely a single worthwhile role model. (*The Sunday Times*, quoted in *Search*, 16.6.93)

Similarly the tabloid newspaper *The Sunday Express* (13.9.85) claimed, under the banner headline 'The ethnic timebomb', that: 'Almost six in 10 black mothers are bringing up children on their own, urged on by our benefit system.' This disregards the fact that Black lone mothers are more likely to be in employment, especially full-time, than their White counterparts (see chapter 8). The recent emergence of a focus on Black lone mothers in the British mainstream press is also linked to broader social concerns – through exotic media explorations of Black family life, White people can vicariously play out their fears about social breakdown and relationships between men and women (Song and Edwards 1997; see also Mann 1994 for a similar point about middle class observers in relation to the underclass).

The strong association between lone motherhood, racial issues and perceived threats to the social order is dominant in the USA partly because Black people are seen as a threat from 'within'. Hence stigmatising Black (African-American) lone mothers can be linked to a restructuring of the already minimal US welfare state as a whole. Rather, it is Hispanic people who are associated with the threat from 'without' (as with the notorious Proposition 187 voted through in the 1994 November mid-term elections in California, removing welfare benefits from the children of illegal immigrants). In Britain, however, the conception of lone motherhood as a threat to the social order from 'within' has sat uneasily alongside a long held conception of Black people as a threat from 'without' (Phoenix 1996). To place a spotlight on Black lone mothers, until recently, would have concentrated attention on immigration policy rather than the welfare state.

Notions of lone mothers as a social threat can, therefore, be used as a vehicle for a restructuring of the welfare state that goes beyond this particular group alone. In Britain the underclass social threat discourse was taken up by sections of the Conservative Party when in government (1979–97). Although those on the libertarian new right took a laissez-faire approach to rising lone motherhood (for example, Willetts 1993), the neo-conservative wing stressed 'a return to family values' and castigated the role of the welfare state in providing housing and benefits, and hence encouraging single motherhood. For example, Stephen Green, Chairman of the Conservative Family Campaign stated: 'Putting girls into council flats and providing taxpayer funded child care is a policy from hell' (quoted in *The Observer*, 14.11.93). Such polemic illustrates the way lone motherhood has been used to legitimate far-reaching changes in the British welfare state. For example, amendments to the homelessness legislation were posed as putting an end to supposed 'queue jumping' by lone mothers, but diverted attention from a reduction in entitlement to permanent housing for all types of families or persons accepted as homeless (Carter and Ginsberg 1994). Some strands of an underclass discourse are also discernible in the communitarianism underlying the new Labour government's ideas about a 'stakeholder society' (Driver and Martell 1997). The long term unemployed, which includes lone mothers, are placed as having no stake in society, 'family values' are stressed as the key to a 'decent' and crime-free society, and an element of coercion is required to reintegrate the 'stakeless'.

Those who promulgate a view of lone motherhood as a threat to society campaign for policies that do not encourage or reward such 'self-damaging conduct'. Thus in Britain the new Labour government (elected in 1997), using a communitarian stance, has implemented the previous Conservative government's proposal to remove the extra allowances available to (new) lone parents on both the universal Child Benefit payment and on targeted income-related benefits. Other policy disincentives to lone motherhood promulgated by those who hold a social threat view include restrictions on payments to lone mothers who have more children while receiving benefit (now a practice in some US states, see de Acosta 1997); and making grandparents responsible for both lone parent and grandchildren (as is theoretically the case in Germany, see Klett-Davies 1997). There are also suggestions that young single mothers on benefit should be placed in hostels where their sexual relations and children's upbringing can be supervised, so as to enforce 'good behaviour' (see Zulauf 1997), as indeed happened in most countries in the past when lone motherhood was posed as grossly pathological or 'sinful' (see McLaughlin and Rogers

1997 for Ireland). This is an idea currently being refloated in Britain, with the communitarian new Labour government linking hostels with job training. Encouragement and reward for traditional male bread-winner/female homemaker married couples is also stressed within the social threat discourse, with policy proposals to redress the supposed benefit bias towards lone parents (a reason given for new Labour's benefit cuts). Other policy proposals in this mould include tightening up the divorce laws so that fewer lone mother families are created in the first place, as well as placing 'moral' family education (rather than sex education) on the school curriculum (for example, Davies 1993).

Scapegoating lone mothers in this way, and emphasising their active role in the creation of their own situation and, concomitantly, the breakdown of society, allows those of communitarian and conservative new right persuasions to sidestep a difficult choice. They avoid making the choice of seeing lone mothers as homemaking mothers or, instead, as paid workers. This also avoids contradicting their attacks on mothers who go out to work as also creating future ills for society, where day care is characterised as producing aggressive and depressive children who do less well at school (for example, Morgan 1996). In contrast to this view of lone motherhood as a self-created threat to the social order, the next discourse sees lone mothers as victims of externally created constraints and in need of help.

b) Lone Motherhood as a Social Problem

The view of lone mothers as victims of society posits that they should get more help, not less. Here, it is external social circumstances that are seen as placing both lone mothers and their children in econom-ically and socially disadvantaged positions. Stress is laid on the 'facts' whereby, in Britain, the majority of lone mothers (just over 50 per cent) are 'mature' divorced, separated or widowed women, rather than young single mothers. Within this discourse, there is no under-class in the sense of a self-reproducing distinct part of society who stand outside cultural, political and economic norms. In the USA, for example, the noted sociologist William Julius Wilson, although accepting notions of an underclass largely composed of Black lone mothers and other 'ghetto poor', argues this is a product of the spatial and industrial restructuring of capitalism, with Black women in inner-city areas having difficulty in finding a male partner with stable employment (Wilson 1989). Thus, within this discourse, there are a growing number of people in poverty, and any underclass has been 'thrown out' of society, rather than having willingly removed itself. The economic and social causes of this marginalisation are beyond the control of those they affect, where shrinking the welfare state only makes the problems worse. Lone mothers are just one of several groups affected by these processes (Morris 1993), and they do the best they can in unfavourable circumstances.

According to this social problem discourse, lone mothers want jobs, but they are simply prevented from taking them by the lack of affordable day care and the poverty trap. Indeed, recent British surveys show that as many as 90 per cent of lone mothers who are not in paid work say they would like a job, with over half saying they would take a job immediately if day care were available (Bradshaw and Millar 1991; Marsh and McKay 1993). Overall, lone mothers' estimates of the wages they would accept were extremely modest, so it is not expectations of a high wage that keep them out of the labour market (Marsh and McKay 1993).

In order to create more favourable circumstances for lone mother families, proponents of the social problem view of lone motherhood argue for changes in the benefit and day care systems. Lone mothers will then be enabled to get paid work and escape both poverty and state dependence. British social analysts often point to comparative evidence on supportive state policies in countries where there is a high uptake of paid work by lone mothers (such as Sweden's 70 per cent uptake) to bolster such arguments. (We critically discuss this argument in Chapter 7.) Advocates of this view argue that, at a minimum, day care costs should be taken into account when calculating the Income Support disregard or Family Credit payments (the former is the 'safety net' benefit payable to lone mothers and others who are not in paid work, but who currently can earn up to £15 per week, the latter a benefit payable to parents with dependent children who have low paid jobs). There should also be increases in lone parent top-up on benefits (Burghes 1993). In 1994, an earnings disregard for formal day care costs was made available to all parents claiming Family Credit, but at a level that would not even cover the full-time care of one child (and updated in 1997 – see Chapter 3). Nevertheless, this measure suggests that the social problem approach retained a foothold in British policy-making circles, despite the growing prevalence of the social threat discourse at the time. Other policy suggestions under this discourse include measures to encourage lone mothers to pursue training and higher education (see Chapter 5 for a critical discussion).

This social problem discourse continues to influence British policy through the new Labour government's 'welfare-to-work' strategy for lone mothers, in so far as this stresses training and advice. There is some support for 'after school' services but little in the way of expanding day care provision outside school, although there have been calls for the establishment of a public day care system that matches other west European levels (see Chapter 3). It is argued that not only would lone (and other) mothers be able to take full-time jobs, but that the system would soon pay for itself in terms of lower benefit outlay and higher tax income (see, for example, Cohen and Fraser 1991; Holtermann 1992). Thus, within this discourse, policy debate over day care in Britain is expressed in terms of mothers' access to the labour market, rather than social and educational benefits for children (Edwards 1993). This is in contrast to many other European countries, where the benefits to children are regarded as just as important as mothers' access to the labour market.

The social problem view of lone motherhood is dominant in much of the social policy academic discipline, among practitioners (such as social workers and health visitors), and the British liberal establishment (such as church leaders). The major lobby group for lone mothers in Britain, the National Council for One Parent Families, have also taken this line (see Song 1996; Song and Edwards 1997). This constituency reflects a Fabian political inheritance of enlightened state intervention. While such intervention was seen as thwarted during the 18 years of new right Conservative government (1979–97), there has been renewed lobbying for intervention with the advent of the new Labour government and support for the 'carrot' aspects of its welfare-to-work strategy.

Seeing lone mothers as a social problem is still central to the formation of state policy in Germany. In this conservative welfare state regime, pro-natalist policies and a concern with children as the future generation requiring integration into society mean that lone mothers are largely regarded as poor and overworked objects of sympathy, especially in being part of an 'incomplete' family. (There is some evidence that economic restructuring and cuts in public expenditure are leading to elements of the social threat discourse taking hold, particularly in relation to minority ethnic groups, Klett-Davies 1997.) In Britain, however, the liberal 'social problem' viewpoint became the perfect foil for those on the new right in lambasting the excesses of the 'permissive leftists' of the 1960s. Perhaps because of this intellectual and political inheritance the social problem discourse has fragmented in Britain. The lines upon which this break up occurred take us deeper into debates on the causes of social disadvantage for both lone mothers and families in general.

That British lone mothers and their children are more likely to be socially disadvantaged is not in dispute. Analyses of the National Child Development Study data (a major survey that follows the lives of all babies born in one week in 1946 and 1958) reveal that the children of the lone mothers in these samples were more likely to be unemployed, less well-qualified, suffer illness, and die earlier (for example, Elliott and Richards 1991; Kiernan 1992). However, this is hardly surprising when most of these families were also among the poorest. Indeed, Swedish evidence suggests if there is any difference between the children of lone mothers and those in couple families with the same social and economic circumstances, it is that the former are the more mature and self-sufficient (Björnberg 1992; Lassbo 1994). In other words there is no inevitable association between lone mothering in itself and poor outcomes for children (Burghes 1994). This may well be a case of analysts confusing taxonomic associations with social cause (see Chapter 1, p. 4–5).

The inevitability or otherwise of lone motherhood in itself leading to disadvantage, rather than merely being contingently associated with it, is still in dispute in Britain – and indeed this is the issue over which the British social problem discourse has fragmented. One stance is associated with the distinguished British sociologists A. H. Halsey and Norman Dennis (erstwhile supporters of the Labour governments in the 1960s, but more recently writing for the right wing think tank, the Institute for Economic Affairs). They argue that it is because lone parent families do not follow the 'norms of the traditional family' that children suffer (for example, Halsey 1993). The absence of fathers not only causes social disadvantage but, because of the lack of an authoritative paternal role model (as with the social threat discourse), also results in social deviancy, crime and hooliganism (Dennis 1993; Dennis and Erdos 1993). Thus, within this strand of the discourse, social policy changes seeking to bring lone mothers into the labour market will not have much effect on the fundamental cause of disadvantage: the lack of fathers. Rather, policies are required that reinforce traditional families, such as a 'parent wage' for mothers who look after their pre-school children at home (where in practice fathers would not fulfil this role). This would supposedly remove any financial incentive for 'pulling out' of a relationship. A legal 'Family Covenant' stating parental responsibilities, and extensive family conciliation and advice services have also been put forward as bolstering traditional families (Young and Halsey 1995).

While the emphasis on the absence of fathers and a desire to reinforce traditional families clearly links in with the conservative new right espousal of lone mothers as a social threat, it does not totally collapse into it. This is because, in such an 'ethical socialist' view, marketisation has been erroneously extended to the social world of partnerships, families and childrearing, replacing non-monetary moral codes. Halsey views Margaret Thatcher (the iconic 'free market' Conservative prime minister during the 1980s) as 'a major architect of the demolition of the traditional family' (Halsey 1993, p. 129; see also Young and Halsey 1995). According to Dennis, market values were extended even to sexual relations, with a high priority being given to 'sexual excitation' and the encouragement of a 'please myself sexual conduct' (Dennis 1991a, b). Here, one might detect an undercurrent of older, socially more powerful men seeking to regulate the private lives of economically weaker, younger women: freedom in markets normally leaves older White men in control, but freedom in sexuality does not. For Halsey, Dennis and others like them, the ideal is a return of the political left to an ethical socialism, with its historic mission 'to spread the values of the family throughout all the relationships of society' (quoted in *The Observer*, 14.11.93). Indeed, there is some resonance of this within new Labour communitarianism (Driver and Martell 1997). Such views ignore two points (particularly raised by the 'lone motherhood as escaping patriarchy discourse' outlined later). First, the 'traditional' father was and is often markedly uninvolved with his children (for example, McKee and O'Brien 1992). Indeed, some 'absent' fathers can have closer involvement with their children than they had previously as part of a two parent family (Smart and Neale 1996). Second, some fathers are violent or abusive – a reason given by 20 per cent of British lone mothers for the breakdown of their relationship (Bradshaw and Millar 1991) – so that their absence is surely a bonus. Indeed, conflict between parents prior to separation or divorce seems to most affect children's educational and social adjustment, rather than the separation itself (Elliott and Richards, 1991; Burghes 1994; Kiernan 1997 for Britain, Lassbo 1994 for Sweden).

An alternative view prioritises poverty rather than family, and this view is buttressed when we remember that most lone mother families are created by divorce or separation, rather than the single mothers who are central to the 'fatherless' version. Even Norman Dennis

(1993) accepts that any statistical associations between 'fatherlessness' and crime and delinquency have to be seen in the context of time and place. In the 1940s and 1950s, as in the National Child Development Study (NCDS) data base so often used, single mothers were a much smaller group who already tended to come from the most disadvantaged sections of society. They were mostly young White women from the poorest working-class families, often with poor social networks and education. So, controlling for class, income and housing, Elsa Ferri (1976) has shown that children from lone parent families in the 1958 NCDS sample did no worse than other children in educational performance. Lone motherhood as such does not cause disadvantage, but poverty does (see also analyses by Burghes 1996; Lambert and Streather 1980; and Utting 1995).

Nevertheless, if poverty is part and parcel of lone motherhood, then within western Europe it is a particularly British phenomenon. The dominant academic view argues that this is the result of poor social policy-making. As one leading British academic social policy researcher put it:

> The family form is changing rapidly. Social policy has failed to recognise the change and the least useful thing to do now is to start stigmatising the victims of these changes.   (Prof. Jonathan Bradshaw, *The Guardian*, 13.10.93)

However, the very notion of '*the* family form' would be challenged by those who believe there is not, and should not be, one family form. This brings us to the third discourse on lone mothers.

c) Lone Motherhood as Lifestyle Change

Both the social threat and the social problem discourses portray lone motherhood in an essentially negative way: the former views lone mothers as actively choosing to be anti-social, while the latter places lone mothers as passive victims. The lifestyle change discourse puts lone mothers into a more positive position. In this view, important social shifts are indeed emerging, but not through the action of states and governments. Rather, people's choices about how they live their lives in families and relationships are changing in a context of overarching economic, cultural and social change at a global level. At worst, the resultant plurality of family forms should be accepted; at best, they should be welcomed; but they are certainly not to be feared.

Proponents of this view can point to historical research showing that the assumed 'traditional family' never was that standard, normal or successful; it was created in particular historical circumstances and has a rather short history (cf. Lewis 1989a, 1992b). Current trends are not some epoch-shattering development and there was no golden age of family life – it was just one other form. Some emphasise more recent changes based on a new 'individualisation', where we embark upon one love project after another in a search for the perfect sexual and emotional relationship (Giddens 1991; Beck and Beck-Gernsheim 1995). Either way, there is little chance that government policy can reverse such deeply embedded processes. As the Deputy Director of the left wing think tank the Institute for Public Policy Research put it, '1990s women are not going to give up on the right to earn a living and 1990s men and women are not going to give up on the right to divorce' (quoted in *The Guardian*, 13.10.93).

As we noted in our discussion of the social threat discourse, those on the libertarian new right can share such views (for example, Willetts 1993). In Britain, popular appeals to a lifestyle discourse were signalled by the launch of the monthly glossy magazine *Singled Out* in 1995, aimed at the 'lone parent' market and covering all aspects of their lives, from holidays and cookery to financial and legal matters. The failure of the magazine to survive its first year of publication may signal the lack of an audience who either accept such 'lifestyle' appeals or relate to the category 'lone parent', or simply that lone mothers were too poor to afford the cover price (at just under £2).

To some extent, elements of the lifestyle discourse overlap with the social problem view. Lifestyle changes are seen as inevitably creating specific social problems, particularly as social institutions take some time to adapt. Marriage and taxation laws, for instance, will be outmoded, and social welfare legislation generally will address past problems. Thus policy recommendations are similar to those put forward in the 'poverty as causal' version of the social problem discourse; with social policy being developed so as to allow lone mothers to take up paid work and escape poverty. Day care provision is also seen as decisive in this view.

However, the element that differentiates this discourse from the social problem view is a 'post-modern' or, more accurately, 'reflexive modernist' emphasis on 'family' as a fluid and changing concept, and on the creation of new norms for daily life and relationships (Beck and Beck-Gernsheim, 1995; Cheal 1991; Giddens 1991). The spotlight is taken off lone mothers because they are simply one part of wider diversities in family forms and gender relations. Some proponents go so far as to stress the value of current changes compared with a stultifying and traditional family past. The influential British sociologist Anthony Giddens, for example, presents an argument that may seem rather romanticised to many British lone mothers:

> in experiencing the unravelling of traditional family patterns ... individuals are actively pioneering new social territory and constructing innovative forms of familial relations ... Individuals are actively restructuring new forms of gender and kinship relations out of the detritus of preestablished forms of family life. Such restructurings are not merely local and they are certainly not trivial.   (1992, pp. 176–7)

Or, in a similar vein, according to leading German sociologists Ulrich Beck and Elisabeth Beck-Gernsheim:

> The nuclear family, built around gender status, is falling apart on the issues of emancipation and equal rights, which no longer conveniently come to a halt outside our private lives. The result is the quite normal chaos called love. If this diagnosis is right, what will take over from the family, that haven of domestic bliss? The family, of course! Only different, more, better: the negotiated family, the alternating family, the multiple family, new arrangements after divorce, remarriage, divorce again, new assortments from your, my, our children, our past and present families.   (1995, p. 2)

In this view, then, policies should aim to create better conditions for all families in the context of changing circumstances, such as shortened working hours and comprehensive leave arrangements for parents. This is much the case in Sweden, where this discourse can be argued to have been most influential. Lone mothers are incorporated in universalistic state policies concerning paid work, parenthood and families, while in everyday and popular discourse the category 'lone parent' is hard to distinguish. There is an emphasis on enabling equality of living conditions regardless of family form. (Although Björnberg 1997 suggests that recent economic and political change encourages seeing lone mothers as a social problem.)

The lifestyle discourse and its policy recommendations take the emphasis off lone mother families, who are simply one element in broader social change. However, such policy changes mean facing up more squarely to changes in gender relations and the power of women visà-vis men. Indeed, Beck and Beck-Gernsheim (1995) point to the rising number of lone mothers in Germany and elsewhere as, in large part, due to women's greater participation in the labour market and the breakdown of traditional divisions of labour. It is precisely this issue of treating women as equal citizens with independent economic and sexual power, with its threat to established relations, that helps fuel the social threat discourse. It is also the issue that fuels the fourth, and final, discourse.

d) Lone Mothers as Women Escaping Patriarchy

One of the reasons for the restructuring of family forms, central to the lifestyle discourse described above, is the change in gender relations – or even the 'gender revolution', as some feminists have called it. They argue that the 'lifestyle change' thesis does not take account of continuing inequalities between men and women (or of ethnicity and class), and is little more than 'the contemporary angst of the chattering (middle class, educated, city dwelling) classes' (Leonard 1996, p. 838). Rather, women are said to be no longer willing to accept control over their lives by individual men. Other social changes, such as access to paid work, contraception, divorce and so on, give them the means to effect this (Phillips 1991). Some feminists argue that all this means is that private patriarchy – control by husbands or fathers – is merely replaced by public patriarchy – subordination to men in paid work and politics (for example, Walby 1990). From this perspective, while Swedish women may have made some important material gains and escaped dependence on individual men, they are merely 'second class men' subject to patriarchy by other means (Acker 1992; Langan and Ostner 1991). Nevertheless, whatever judgment is taken, the implication remains that lone mothers are women attempting to escape patriarchy.

Describing such changes as a 'gender revolution' also implies that while women have changed – or at least their expectations have – men have not (Hochschild with Machung 1989). Cohabitation and marriage is increasingly likely to lead to break-up and divorce, therefore, where both partners have different ideas of what their relationship involves. So while women very rarely 'choose' lone motherhood, once in this situation they can find advantages in it. They value their independence, making their own decisions about their lives, even if they do so in relative poverty (Bradshaw and Millar 1991; Dean and Taylor-

Gooby 1992; Graham 1987; Shaw 1991). Similarly, while many continue, ideally, to see life with a male partner as preferable, this is not understood as any man. The trouble is that the right sort of man, sharing their expectations about gender roles and relations, is not available. Indeed, past experience can be with inadequate, abusive or violent men (see Bradshaw and Millar 1991 for Britain; Mädje and Neusüss 1994 for Germany). Lone motherhood is thus seen as one way by which women can escape the immediate patriarchy of coupledom.

In Britain, this view become apparent in some of the campaigning against the Child Support Act (CSA) 1991 (for example Campaign Against the Child Support Act 1993; Wages for Housework 1993). The CSA attempts to ensure that absent 'parents' – overwhelmingly fathers – take financial responsibility for their children, and financially penalises lone mothers who do not name the father/s of their child/ren. Within the escaping patriarchy discourse, the CSA can be regarded as representing an attempt to enforce a relationship with a male 'head of household' (the absent father) even where he is not physically in situ. The patriarchal political establishment, acting through the state, is threatened by the growing independence of women; especially that of lone mothers, who have shown that women and children can live their lives without men.

This discourse finds inspiration in radical feminism, where marriage, the family and heterosexuality are identified as major sites of women's oppression. As Christine Delphy and Diana Leonard put it:

> What a husband gets from a wife is her hours of work and personal servicing. He saves money on goods produced and consumed at home, and gains time he would have had to spend on work for himself and his dependents or for the market if he did everything himself. He also gets personal support and ego-boosting, a pliant sexual partner, and children if he wants them. What men get from marriage is different, therefore, from what it costs women. Putting it crudely, what men get from marriage is 57 varieties of unpaid service, whereas the institution of marriage and the family restricts and (ab)uses (married and unmarried) women in all areas of their lives. (Delphy and Leonard 1992, p. 260, see also Barrett and McIntosh 1982)

This discourse can also share some of radical feminism's policy prescriptions, such as more support for women to leave violent men and set up separate households, and (more contentious) wages for housework. It also returns us to the social threat view with which we started this 'circular' discussion of discourses on lone motherhood. Yes, the traditional family is breaking up, but now it is not young women who are the threat and who are to be blamed – rather, it is men who are the problem.

e) The Potency of the Discourses

Lone motherhood can serve to highlight social expectations about gender roles and relations because of its assumed deviancy from idealised social norms. Discourses about lone motherhood, therefore, can play a particularly powerful role. This is especially the case in Britain, and the USA. In Germany and Sweden lone motherhood plays less of a symbolic role. This is partly because of the way in which particular discourses fit into the wider discourse and policy arena of particular types of welfare state regime. The social threat discourse nestles easily into a liberal regime where welfare is stigmatised, and has had increasing influence nationally in Britain and is dominant in the USA, although it is still strongly challenged by the social problem view that was dominant from the 1940s to 1970s in both countries (de Acosta 1997; Lewis 1995; Song 1996). During the 1980s and early 1990s especially, in both cases, the contradictions of a liberal state regime and an overtly conservative new right government, exacerbated by changes in women's roles and expectations, gave the social threat view particular resonance. Changes in government in both countries seem merely to have replaced overt new right views with implicit, or communitarian right, views with possibly much the same effect. The social problem discourse melds well with a conservative regime with the accent on status differentials, as in Germany, while the lifestyle discourse accords better with a social democratic regime, with gender equality an overt aim, and has been dominant in Sweden since the comprehensive policy reforms of the 1940s.

The women-escaping-patriarchy discourse has little fit with any welfare state regime, and has little influence on policy-making. However, as the next section shows, discourses that are muted or subordinated at the national level can nevertheless hold potency for particular groups of lone mothers living in particular neighbourhoods, affecting their views of themselves and their integration into society. As we argued in the introductory chapter, it is important to unpack 'closed boxes' if we are to understand lone mothers' uptake of paid work, and examining diversity is just as crucial in the area of discourse. Unfortunately, most research up to now concentrates on discourses at the national level, with the implication that policy-makers and the media are the only effective actors. An important dimension of lone mothers' action is thereby neglected.

2.3 LONE MOTHERS' VIEWS OF THE DISCOURSES

Views of National Discourses

The dominance of particular discourses about lone motherhood nationally are a significant feature of life as a lone mother. Indeed, one survey (McKendrick 1997) found that just under a third of lone mothers rated 'other people's attitudes' as very important to the quality of their lives. Our interviews were carried out with the British lone mothers in the summer of 1994, just after the furore in the media about the moral and financial threat lone mothers posed to society. Unsurprisingly, across all social groups, our interviewees were very aware of this social threat discourse and, overwhelmingly, considered this was how they, as lone mothers, were generally viewed in Britain. They referred to portrayals of themselves as: 'going from one relationship to another', 'responsible for delinquent children', 'sit[ting] their kids in front of the telly to go off and enjoy themselves', 'don't want to work', 'get pregnant to go on the state', 'scrounging off welfare', 'just having babies to get flats' – sometimes with anger in their voices.

The younger group of African-Caribbean lone mothers, and also to some extent the 'alternative' White lone mothers living in London, were particularly aware of the notion of a 'class apart' (that is the underclass) as an important element in the social threat discourse:

> They're [lone mothers] viewed as a very low class set of people. They're not viewed like they got any brains. They think lone parents just want to live off the government and have children to get a flat or whatever, and they ain't got no ambition. (Kim – younger African-Caribbean lone mother)

Particular categories of lone mothers were also seen as being singled out for particular criticism. The categories identified here could bear a relationship with the lone mothers' own situation, either in terms of similarity or difference. Thus, for example, the White working class group of lone mothers, mainly young themselves, tended to refer to young lone mothers as being subject to censure. Similarly, Black lone mothers often felt there was a racialised aspect to the castigation of lone mothers:

> Being Black does make a difference if you're a single parent. I think we're looked down on more … being a single parent you're a burden anyway, and being Black is even worse. I think they expect more from us. I think that sometimes they think we're scrounging from them, more than a White single parent might have that pressure put on them … Because they think it's the majority of us that are doing it. (Annette – older African-Caribbean lone mother)

In contrast the White middle class group of lone mothers could also refer to young, single mothers (that is unlike themselves) as being the problem. Comments made by one of the White middle class lone mothers living in a suburban area of Brighton, in her fourties and separated from her husband, illustrate how this group of lone mothers could attempt to distance themselves from those 'other' lone mothers who fuelled the social threat discourse:

> [Lone mothers] are typecast, very much so. Oh, very negative … I mean you get your, I don't know, young sort of 18, 19 year old single mum with, you know, a half caste baby. I don't really care what people think, but people do think – we get classed as the same, but people think differently of her than they might of, say, me. (Karen)

Concomitantly, particular categories of lone mothers were regarded as more 'acceptable', such as those who were divorced or were in employment.

White middle class lone mothers living in suburban areas appear to feel quite endangered by the social threat discourse and any association of it with themselves. This 'othering' had concrete implications, not only for their lives as lone mothers in the neighbourhood in which they lived (see below), but also for our research. As we noted in Chapter 1, we had particular difficulty in reaching White middle class lone mothers living in the suburban area of Brighton because they did not wish to associate themselves with research focusing on 'lone mothers'. In contrast, those from other groups could more easily see taking part in the research as a chance to have their say and 'put the record straight' in the face of political and media onslaughts. Indeed, the government and media were pointed to as particularly active in promulgating the social threat image of lone mothers from which the White middle class, suburban, lone mothers wished to distance themselves:

> Lone parents get blamed for lots of things that's happening anyway, but they created it, the government. (Pattie – older African-Caribbean lone mother)

> The press hound you. There have been a couple of really negative documentaries on telly. A load of women sitting around smoking fags and drinking tea. It came over very badly and didn't help at all. (Sharon – White working class lone mother living in Brighton)

Given the timing of our interviews and the context of a liberal welfare state regime, it is unsurprising to find that the British lone mothers felt that the social threat discourse circulated nationally, especially amongst policy-makers and the media. Concomitantly, we might expect that lone mothers' views of prevalent discourses in the other case study countries will vary in accordance with welfare state regime. Indeed, this was the case – with some pertinent exceptions.

For the Swedish lone mothers, living in a context where state policies support a lifestyle discourse, comments that lone motherhood was viewed as a normal part of life were extensive. For example:

> In the past it was almost a bit shameful [to be a lone mother]. Now it's more or less the opposite, it's not bad to be a single mother, it's quite normal. (Emma)

> Perhaps, yes, all people feel sympathetic or something, they understand how it is ... that you get by with the house budget and food, there's no room for more. (Agnetta)

Yet, the Swedish lone mothers' also saw strong elements of a social threat discourse at the national level. In this they made comments similar to the majority of lone mothers interviewed in the USA, who were living with a quite different, social threat, view of their situation. Compare Ulla, living in Göteborg, to Pam living in Cleveland, Ohio:

> It's terrible what you hear, that single mothers' children turn into criminals, that's what you see and hear in the newspapers and on TV, I think. Anywhere there's trouble, single mothers are in the picture.

Well, a lot of people would say we're a problem because so many single mothers are nowadays getting on welfare and having more welfare than they could go getting a job.

It may well be that economic and political change are changing the view of lone mothers in Sweden, as Ulla Björnberg (1997) suggests, and that lone mothers themselves are feeling this.

Similar changes in Germany may be encouraging a shift from a nationally dominant and sympathetic 'social problem' view towards the 'social threat' discourse (Klett-Davies 1997). Certainly the lone mothers living in Berlin portrayed the German government as not really wishing to offer policy support to lone mothers – as one said: 'in terms of financial security ... no-one is really paying much attention, and especially those in government'. They also emphasised a stigmatising morality in the German national discourse. While there were strong elements of the social problem discourse in their assessments, this was often experienced as patronising. In particular, distinctions were drawn between east and west German views on lone motherhood, with the former being regarded as more favourable:

I think we were much more progressive in the GDR [former East Germany], everything is much more conservative here. I mean it starts with the fact that single parents are given a youth services counsellor who is expected to tell you what to do. I'm sure that those counsellors can be helpful to some mothers, say in making sure the fathers make their payments. But if so, then you could go there and ask for help. But I can't accept someone telling me what do, I'm 32 years old. In the former GDR there wasn't anyone who told you what to do or what decisions to make, and the mother was seen as completely competent. (Eva)

None of the lone mothers saw any elements of an escaping patriarchy discourse circulating in any national context. However, while this discourse may be silent in how lone mothers think they are regarded by others nationally, it can be important for how they think they are seen by people in their neighbourhood. Furthermore, this discourse often has a special relevance to their own perceptions, helping them to understand the nature of lone motherhood as they themselves experience it. We turn next to the neighbourhood context in which the lone mothers lived. As several of the lone mothers pointed out, in discussing how they were viewed: 'It depends very much where you live, very much'.

Views of Neighbourhood Discourses

While the lone mothers may have felt that the social threat discourse was dominant or influential in the national contexts, this was not necessarily how they perceived the climate in the diverse neighbourhoods in which they lived. We will be describing the character of these neighbourhoods in more detail in the next chapter. Here, however, we discuss how comfortable the lone mothers felt, living as lone mother families, in their particular area.

The seven groups of British lone mothers were, as we outlined in Chapter 1, living in a diversity of areas in the contiguous inner London boroughs of Lambeth and Southwark, and the south coast city of Brighton. Of the four groups living in London, the younger African-Caribbean group were concentrated largely on public housing estates in central Lambeth. They felt that there was mainly a lifestyle discourse on lone motherhood circulating within their neighbourhood, arising out of the prevalence of lone mothers in the locality and amongst their social networks:

> Oh, [people are] so used to us! There's so many, including people that were married and they're divorced now. It's just become a way of life though, innit. It's just like everything else. They just accept you for what you are.   (Simone)

However, some felt that the high proportions of lone mother families could also fuel the social threat discourse:

> They think God, man, rah, you know what I mean. It shouldn't be happening. But it is happening and that's the way it is.   (Shirley)

The older African-Caribbean lone mothers also lived in public housing, but this tended to consist of smaller pockets rather than large estates, mainly in south Southwark. Consequently perhaps, they felt that the social threat discourse was stronger in their neighbourhoods than the younger group did. Many said they tended not to mix with people living locally. As we shall see later in this chapter, such differences in the perception of older and younger African-Caribbean groups carried over into how they experienced lone motherhood themselves. The west African group of lone mothers, largely living in council housing in north Southwark, were very reticent about voicing an assessment of prevalent local opinions about lone motherhood, a typical response being: 'No comment'.[1]

The White 'alternative' lone mothers were scattered across the centre and north of Lambeth and Southwark, largely living in public housing but some were buying their own house. Like the younger African-Caribbean lone mothers, in the lifestyle discourse mode, they mainly felt that lone motherhood was so common locally that it did not merit particular attention. Where they had felt censure, those who mentioned it associated such problems with the fact that they had children with a Black father and/or they were middle class women living in a working class neighbourhood, rather than their lone motherhood. Class or ethnicity were more important than lone motherhood (see Chapter 1). These situations could lead them to 'keep themselves to themselves' locally:

> Well, I'm not accepted in this community because I'm not from here ... I'm considered a middle class person as soon as I open my mouth ... I think it's to do with class and culture and race ... You get used to the looks, as in White people give you looks, Black people give you looks. I mean you get called golliwog lover. (Theresa)

A fall in income and a move into public housing (which has become increasingly economically and socially residualised in Britain) consequent to divorce, separation or cohabitation breakdown, is not uncommon for middle class lone mothers (Bradshaw and Millar 1991; Crow and Hardey 1991).

In contrast, the White 'alternative' group of lone mothers clustered together in a gentrifying area of central Brighton, mostly in owner-occupied housing, overwhelmingly felt that the lifestyle discourse on lone motherhood held sway in their neighbourhood, with any small elements of the social threat discourse confined to older people. Thus they felt very supported locally, and we shall follow the implications of this for their lives in the next chapter. The lifestyle discourse was also overwhelmingly considered the main local view of lone motherhood by the White working class lone mothers concentrated on a large, peripheral Brighton council estate. However, unlike the 'alternative' Brighton lone mothers, most added that they drew their support from family rather than other local lone mothers, and again we explore the consequences of this in the next chapter.

In stark contrast again, the White middle class group, mainly in owner-occupied housing and scattered across the suburban north of Brighton, largely felt that lone mothers were viewed locally as 'social threats', but that these threats lived in public housing areas such as the estate where the White working class lone mothers were housed – rather than in their neighbourhood:

> I do find that there aren't any other single parents, that I've come across certainly, which is sometimes a bit frustrating ... I don't know for sure, but the consensus of opinion is that there are lots of single parents there [the local public housing estate] who have unruly children. And I've been at school meetings where it has been said 'we don't want our children mixing with all those single parents because this is a nice area and we don't have those sorts of people'. And then I stick my hand up. And they're very apologetic, 'oh we don't mean you', because I'm a nice single parent, I'm the exception. People know me and they're talking about those *other* single parents that they read about in the tabloid press. (Lena – her emphasis)

Thus, the 'othering' of lone mothers by many of the White middle class group was mirrored by the attitudes of those around them locally, and our interviewees could not draw on support from other lone mothers locally in the face of such attitudes because they did not know each other. Lone motherhood is a feature of families in these suburban areas, as the census data shows, but despite this lone mothers remain hidden from each other. This separation meant that they could feel all the more isolated from, or uncomfortable with, the 'traditional' nuclear families they saw all around them. As one reported:

> Since I've been a single mum people have, oh, what? Whereupon they chatted when we [herself and her husband] came here, now it's, you know, total back turn. It's dreadful, it really is. (Karen)

Whilst angry about the national social threat view of lone mothers, most of our sample felt more comfortable with the general opinion in the neighbourhoods in which they lived. (Apart from the White middle class suburban lone mothers and, to an extent, the older group of African-Caribbeans.) Interestingly, much the same is the case for the lone mothers living in Germany, Sweden and the USA. All three groups saw the lifestyle perspective as dominant in their neighbourhoods, especially amongst younger people, based on the prevalence and normality of lone motherhood locally. It could, though, co-exist with elements of a social threat view. It appears that a high proportion of lone mothers in an area can engender or reflect both discourses. For example:

> My neighbourhood? There's lots of us. It doesn't make a difference, no. I mean you kinda look bad a lot, you know, by older people. (Janice – a White lone mother living in Cleveland, Ohio)

The Berlin and Göteborg lone mothers also thought that there were elements of an escaping patriarchy discourse in circulation locally:

> [Lone mothers are not seen] in a negative way, rather the opposite. They think it's fantastic that although I have such young children I was able to get away from something that didn't work ... You don't need a man. (Emma – a White lone mother living in Göteborg)

Thus the escaping patriarchy discourse, although silenced at national levels, does begin to be voiced at the neighbourhood level in some national contexts. It becomes much louder and extensive when we look at the discourses subscribed to by the different groups of lone mothers themselves.

2.4 LONE MOTHERS' OWN DISCOURSES

The Definition of Lone Motherhood

All the lone mothers interviewed as part of our research fell within our definition of 'lone motherhood' – that is, they were bringing up dependent children, at least one of whom was under 13 years, without a permanent male partner living with them. They obviously saw themselves as part of our project's remit, or at least acceded to it in that they were willing to take part. However, they did not necessarily consider themselves 'lone mothers' and most of the British interviewees used the term 'single parent' (with the exception of the suburban group). This conception was usually bound up with their understanding of themselves as carrying all, or the main, responsibility for bringing up their children (an understanding with important implications for their uptake of paid work, see Chapter 4). For example:

Yes [I think of myself as a single parent]. I've brought [my son] up
from a baby. I've got up for him, changed him, fed him. If it wasn't
for me I don't know where he'd be. His father's no good.   (Grace –
a White working class lone mother)

I think of myself as a lone parent because I am bringing up two children by myself. I support them, I buy everything for them. I look
after them and, quite frankly, I am on my own. And what this means
to me is that I've just got to take care of them and bring them up in
the best way I can by myself.   (Kim – a younger African-Caribbean
lone mother)

Several lone mothers in the 'alternative' groups, in London and
Brighton, stressed that they preferred the term 'single' to 'lone' because
the latter had negative implications. In a challenge to the social threat
discourse, they were proud of managing without a male partner:

I would say single parent. Lone parent has the implication of lonely
and it doesn't sound very positive. It just sounds sad. And single
parent is a celebration of being single, I can do it on my own.
(Charlotte – a White 'alternative' lone mother living in Brighton)

Nevertheless, a couple of the lone mothers in these groups, perhaps in
the lifestyle discourse mode, said that generally they did not like
'labels', including that of 'single parent' or 'lone mother'.
    Again with the exception of the suburban lone mothers , there were
at least a couple of women from each group who said that they
thought of themselves as just a 'mother' or a 'parent'. They usually
explained this conception of themselves in terms of involvement on
the part of their children's father/s and/or extensive support from
others in their social networks:

I don't think I'm bringing [my children] up on my own as such. I
mean their dad is there, although we're not living together. But I
mean if I didn't have a dad at all, if he wasn't around, I didn't know
who he was, then yes, I would class myself as a lone parent. But I
know who he is and I know where he is, and he is always here.
(Sonia – a younger African-Caribbean lone mother)

In contrast, most of the suburban group said that they only acknowl-
edged themselves as lone mothers sometimes, when reminded of the

fact – such as when claiming income support or treated differently by neighbours – even though they all felt solely responsible for their children. Rather, they preferred not to think of themselves as lone, or single, mothers because of the negative image the category carried for them. This was a result of the pervasive social threat view of lone mothers in their neighbourhood, resonating with national political and media representations.

A similar pattern was shown by the German, Swedish and US groups. All (with the exception of three Swedes and one American) considered themselves lone mothers and associated this with responsibility for their children. The few who rejected the term, similarly, explained this as related to the involvement of their children's fathers or other adults. Several of the lone mothers in Berlin, while also stressing such involvement, still thought of themselves as lone mothers, however.

The involvement of their children's fathers in their lives (for good or ill), as well as support from family and/or friends (see Chapter 3), was an element in the mix of discourses expressed by the lone mothers in talking about what being a lone mother (or mothering without a permanent male partner) meant to them. It was also significant in the lone mothers' assessments of their similarity or difference to 'other' lone mothers (whether they thought of themselves as such or not). Both of these understandings echoed the four main discourses around lone motherhood we initially identified in this chapter, and we now turn to them.

The Meaning of Lone Motherhood

The lone mothers' understandings of being a lone mother did not fall simply into any one of the four main discourses on lone motherhood as we have discussed them above, either as social groups or individually. Rather, they wove together elements from the whole range of perspectives in understanding their experiences. Although this might appear incompatible when looked at in the abstract, it made sense to them within their everyday lives. There were, nevertheless, particular configurations and balances of the discourses within the combined accounts of each of the social groups of lone mothers. These are shown diagrammatically in Figures 2.2 to 2.5.[2]

The escaping patriarchy discourse we identified earlier in this chapter was not a strong feature in the discourses around lone motherhood circulating nationally nor, for the most part, in the neighbourhoods in which the lone mothers lived. However, it features more strongly in how lone mothers understood their situation for themselves. This is especially evident for the older African-Caribbean, White working class and London alternative groups of lone mothers. While there were differences between these three groups in the balance between discourses, all their accounts were dominated by a combination of the escaping patriarchy and social problem discourses (see Figure 2.2). They particularly stressed not having to produce meals for a male partner, how difficult it was for them financially, the lack of a social life and, amongst the older African-Caribbean group, difficulties in finding day care for their children:

> It's a very difficult job. No official rest time, break time. It's ongoing and it's so diverse. You name it, I have to do it ... financial restraints ... and the expense of child care means I'll have to wait until they're both at school for a job ... [But I have] freedom to cook what I want when I want. Just to get up and go out with my children when I want to. I can have friends home when I want to, I don't have to consult anyone.   (Elaine – an older African-Caribbean lone mother)

> Lack of money, I mean that's the obvious one. Maybe loneliness at night, you know, once the girls have gone to bed. Sometimes I wish someone would come and knock on the door and have a chat ... [But] I enjoy the freedom. If we want to all go out somewhere we can all go out, rather then when we get back he's coming home and he wants his tea. It's just an easy feeling.   (Donna – a White working class lone mother)

While the White alternative group of lone mothers living in London focused strongly on the benefits of life without having to take account of a male partner, and indeed were particularly proud of managing on their own, they also expressed worries about this in terms of the effects on their children. In other words, the social threat discourse held more purchase for them than it did for the older African-Caribbean and White working class groups:

> I think probably becoming a single parent I've had to become very very strong, and I think I've gained an enormous amount of strength as a person ... I've always felt quite independent, but I tell you what I do like about being a single parent is my home is my home, and I actually feel at the moment that I don't ever want to

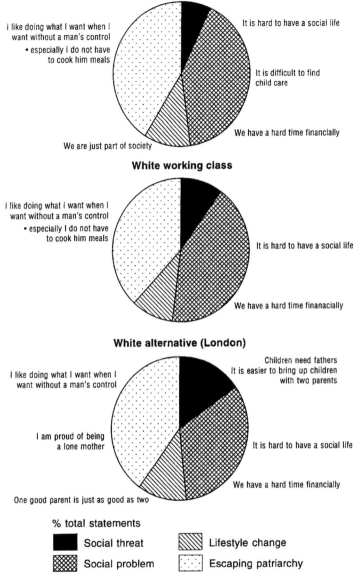

Figure 2.2 Lone mothers' own views about lone motherhood: escaping patriarchy and social problem discourses dominant

live with a man again! ... [But my children are] mixed race, for them to grow up from a single parent family, there's such a negative expectation of them, and I think that is one of my biggest fears for them ... I get depressed about things like oh, is it going to be really damaging for them not living with their father.   (Susan – a White 'alternative' lone mother living in London)

There were also some differences between the London White alternative group and the older African-Caribbean and White working class lone mothers, in that the latter two groups largely saw themselves as similar to 'other' lone mothers. (Amongst the few who saw themselves as different, for the older African-Caribbean lone mothers this was because of a lack of financial support from the father/s of their children.) In contrast, the White alternative lone mothers from London perceived differences between themselves and other lone mothers, in terms of involvement on the part of their children's fathers or other adults, but also in terms of being in employment (for those who were, see Chapter 4).

The lifestyle discourse assumed more importance in the accounts of the west African, younger African-Caribbean and White alternative lone mothers from Brighton (see Figure 2.3). However, there were again variations in the ways they combined the perspectives. The west African group of lone mothers were likely to perceive a similarity between themselves and 'other' lone mothers. Along with the older African-Caribbean and White working class lone mothers discussed above, the social threat discourse held little purchase for them. Rather, the lifestyle perspective was combined with a focus on the social problems they faced as lone mothers, especially in terms of maintaining any social life, and, like the African-Caribbean groups, the availability and expense of day care for children making it difficult for them to get a job.

The younger African-Caribbean lone mothers balanced the lifestyle discourse with understandings of themselves as being better off without men (escaping patriarchy), together with elements of a social problem perspective. They saw themselves as a normal part of society and enjoyed not having to organise their lives around a male partner, being able to bring their children up in the way they wanted to and just as competently, or more competently, than if the children's father was living with them:

Me personally, I think that if the parent's morals are good and their discipline is okay, the children shouldn't be brought up no different

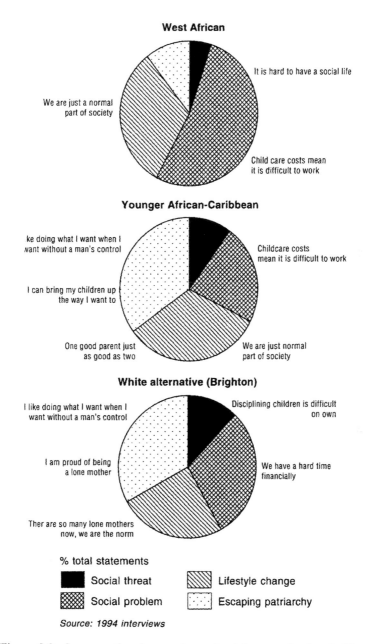

West African

It is hard to have a social life

We are just a normal part of society

Child care costs mean it is difficult to work

Younger African-Caribbean

ke doing what I want when I want without a man's control

Childcare costs mean it is difficult to work

I can bring my children up the way I want to

One good parent just as good as two

We are just normal part of society

White alternative (Brighton)

I like doing what I want when I want without a man's control

Disciplining children is difficult on own

I am proud of being a lone mother

We have a hard time financially

Ther are so many lone mothers now, we are the norm

% total statements

Social threat

Lifestyle change

Social problem

Escaping patriarchy

Source: 1994 interviews

Figure 2.3   Lone mothers' own views about lone motherhood: lif change discourse more dominant

with a lone parent than if it was with two parents there ... I mean it doesn't matter to me if a father figure is there or not. At the end of the day the mother is always lumbered with the child. The father doesn't really take them and the father can walk out at any time. (Kim)

Despite this, in discussing the similarities and differences to other lone mothers, several stressed that they were different because (in a reverse of the differences expressed by the older African-Caribbean group) the fathers of their children were still involved in their lives:

No, because I have got a partner and he is doing some things for me. Like he does give me money for my children, you know, and he does look after them once in a while. So we have got something there, but he's just not there full time. Most [other lone mothers] are different because, as far as I'm concerned, like the mothers that I know I've not seen their partners around. (Sadie)

These differences between the older and younger African-Caribbean groups may simply result from their age, or more precisely differences in their social networks and in who offered them support. In turn, these may have contributed to differences in their experiences of lone motherhood (see Chapter 3). However, like their older counterparts, the main feature of this group's discussions of the problems centred around the obstacles to their taking up paid work, especially in the form of the cost of day care.

The voicing of concern about day care and paid work by the Black groups contrasts to the White lone mothers in Britain. This is not to say this was not an issue for the latter; rather they did not raise it in discussing problems associated with being a lone mother. This difference is quite significant in terms of the findings, from both intensive interview research and extensive census data, that we will be discussing in relation to the uptake of paid work amongst lone mothers from different ethnic groups in Britain (see Chapters 4 and 5).

The lifestyle discourse was also important in the understandings of the White alternative group of lone mothers living in Brighton, a perspective they saw as holding sway in the neighbourhood in which they lived. As with the younger African-Caribbean lone mothers, they combined this view of themselves as 'just a normal part of society' with escaping patriarchy and social problem discourses. In relation to the latter, again like the younger African-Caribbean lone mothers, they hardly ever mentioned difficulties in socialising as a problem. This is notable, and can be linked to the strong local support networks, including other lone mothers, in which both groups were embedded (further discussed in Chapter 3). Similarly, as with the younger African-Caribbean lone mothers, and like their counterparts in London, these lone mothers saw differences between themselves and other lone mothers in the amount of involvement on the part of their children's fathers or other adults, and in having a job (for those who did – see Chapter 4). Unlike their London counterparts, though, the Brighton alternative group tended to balance this with comments about the shared 'ups and downs' and financial hardship of life as a lone mother:

> I think I'm lucky in that I have more support from their father [than other lone mothers]. I'm in the same position as many, yes, also. It's hard to run a household and bring up children on your own, you're at a material disadvantage. But their dad is a big help.   (Faye)

In contrast to all the other social groups of British lone mothers, the White middle class suburban group is distinct in terms of the lack of any perception of their lone motherhood that resembled a lifestyle perspective (see Figure 2.4). The rainbow of family forms and normality of lone motherhood did not exist for them.

Like other groups, the White suburban middle class lone mothers combined escaping patriarchy and social problem views. But unlike the other groups, the problem of financial hardship as a lone mother was hardly mentioned. Indeed, being better off financially and mostly living in owner-occupied housing were part of the differences they saw between themselves and other lone mothers.

> I think probably I'm different ... One tends to think of lone parents, you know, being stuck in a grotty flat or bedsit ... If you're only getting £60 a week plus your rent being paid, I mean how else can anyone live, you know, if they don't have family to support them financially or whatever.   (Jessie)

In addition, the social threat discourse held a special purchase in their perceptions of their lone motherhood, just as it did with their assessment of neighbourhood attitudes:

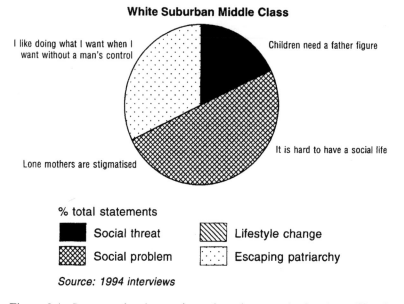

Figure 2.4   Lone mothers' own views about lone motherhood: no lifestyle change discourse

I mean [my daughter's] father, I mean we still see him perhaps once a week or every couple of weeks. But he hasn't got much say in what I do sort of thing. It's me that's the main person ... [But there are] things like I think when [my daughter] gets older and she comes home with things like homework, if there's only me and she's doing something I haven't got a clue about, there's not the father's side. You know what I mean. Cos I always had great respect for my dad.   (Lena)

The British lone mothers live in a particular national discourse and policy context that might be expected to produce a focus on financial and day care problems, and on the stigma of lone motherhood (although we have seen that this was far from the only focus for them). Perhaps for lone mothers in national contexts where lone motherhood is more supported, financial and day care problems are less in evidence in their accounts of the meaning of lone motherhood for themselves? The German, Swedish and American groups of lone mothers held similar discourse mixes, largely focusing on the escaping patriarchy and social problem discourses, although each group lives within quite different national contexts (see Figure 2.5). In this they resembled the older African-Caribbean, White working class and London White 'alternative' British groups. We have seen that elements of an escaping patriarchy discourse first appeared in the German and Swedish lone mothers' assessments of prevalent discourses in their neighbourhoods. This view came through even more strongly in their own views – as it has done for all the groups of lone mothers, in all national contexts.

Within the escaping patriarchy discourse, the White 'alternative' lone mothers in Berlin were notable in expressing a pride in managing alone, particularly akin to that expressed by the British White 'alternative' groups. It was also accompanied by similar social threat concerns about the consequences for their children to those expressed by the London group. Additionally, the Berlin lone mothers saw differences between themselves and 'other' lone mothers, including around the involvement of their children's fathers or other adults in their social networks. The Göteborg lone mothers also felt different from 'others', but this time concerning either a lack of involvement on the part of their children's fathers or, conversely, the involvement of the fathers, as well as support from family or friends:

> What's different in my case is that the fathers don't have the children every other weekend. Yes, that's the difference. (Gunilla)

Indeed, fathers relating to their children is a particular concern, and more of a norm, in Sweden, more than in many other countries (Arve-Peres 1994).

The Berlin lone mothers particularly stressed obstacles to taking up paid work. However, they did not concentrate on problems of day care availability, as with the Black groups in Britain, perhaps because the neighbourhood in which they lived was well served with such facilities (as we discuss in the next chapter):

> Well, the problem is that [lone mothers] can only work part time or at the most 30 hours a week ... you don't have enough energy for a 40 hour work week ... And they really do make it difficult, very difficult ... it's cheaper and easier for the authorities to keep the status quo rather than offer some programmes. And usually the retraining programmes start at eight in the morning or even at seven, and with a child it's really difficult. (Martina)

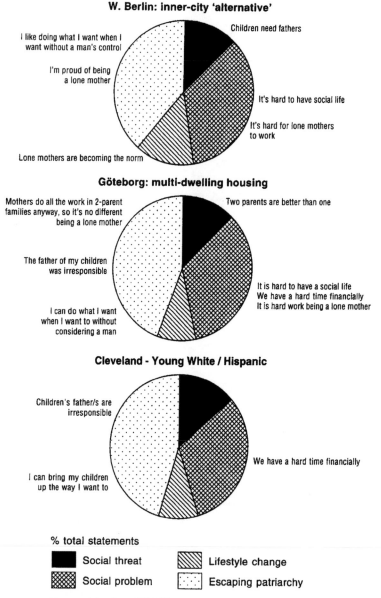

Figure 2.5 Lone mothers' own views about lone motherhood: Germany, Sweden, USA

The other two groups, in Göteborg and Cleveland, in contrast stressed the problem of financial hardship, rather than obstacles to paid work. Both these groups had good access to day care if they wanted it. The Swedish lone mothers particularly lived in the context of a nationally pervasive system, where most lone (and other) mothers work and, unlike the German lone mothers, more than 30 hours work a week is the norm. The American group also had day care available to them as part of a neighbourhood educational and training programme directed at teenage mothers – thus looking for employment was not an immediate priority for most of them. Additionally, also within a social problem perspective, the Cleveland lone mothers, like the younger African-Caribbean and Brighton White 'alternative' British groups, rarely mentioned difficulties in maintaining a social life. Again, we can relate this to their embeddedness in local social networks (see Chapter 3). However, unlike these British groups, they stressed their similarity with 'other' lone mothers in having ongoing responsibility for their children and the general 'ups and downs' of life as a lone mother:

> We probably all go through the same things, hard times and good. (Viv)

The discourses around the meaning of lone motherhood, as sub-scribed to by the varying social groups of lone mothers in different national contexts, show a complex weaving together of a diversity of elements. A few of them stressed that they did not think of themselves as, or were unlike, 'other' lone mothers because there was involvement from their children's fathers or support from others in their social networks. Nevertheless, all talked about the experience and meaning of bringing up children, wholly or mainly on their own, in terms of a particular balance of the four discourses elaborated at the beginning of this chapter. Thus, they can see their lone motherhood, variously, as a configurations of: (i) potentially creating problems for their children in growing up 'without' a father, (ii) difficulties in managing financially, taking up paid work and/or having a social life; (iii) just a normal part of the lifestyles they see around them; and (iv) being able to do things and make decisions without being constrained by a male partner.

For most of the lone mothers then, whatever the national context, the meaning of lone motherhood was rooted in the realities of their daily lives, rather than merely being informed by prevalent political and popular discourses. This reality was shaped by the national policy context (including provision of day care support and benefit structures). However, perhaps more importantly, it was also shaped by the neighbourhoods in which they lived and the social support, or lack of it, they received at this level.

2.5 CONCLUSION

In this chapter we have examined the ways in which particular discourses form different frameworks for understanding the phenomenon of 'lone motherhood'. Such discourses are spoken and written expressions of ideas that, together with politics and social practice, constitute the explicit or implicit meaning of 'lone motherhood'. Importantly, we have illustrated how these expressions and practices differ according to social context, providing different layers of meaning within which lone mothers live their lives and take action.

Drawing on textual material and analysis of policies, section 2.2 identified four main discourses around lone motherhood: as a social threat, a social problem, as part of lifestyle change, and as an escape from patriarchy. While the material we have reviewed here may date, further developments will be constituted largely within this analytic discourse framework. We have shown how particular discourses have gained legitimacy within different national contexts, in terms of both popular and political rhetoric, and have resonance within particular welfare regimes. These nationally prevalent understandings and policy regimes provide one context for lone mothers' lives and actions, of which they are certainly aware, as section 2.3 shows. However, we have also shown that these national level discourses are not simplistically adopted or adhered to by lone mothers. Rather, discourses around lone motherhood also differ by neighbourhood and social group within any national context. It is at this level that alternative ideas about the meaning of lone motherhood, not dominant nationally, can have more influence. For example section 2.3 shows that being a lone mother in the suburban north of Brighton, where lone mothers are firmly placed as 'other' by the locally prevalent social threat discourse, can feel quite different to being a lone mother on the peripheral public housing estate nearby or in an 'alternative' area, where lone mothers are largely viewed locally through the lens of the lifestyle and escaping patriarchy discourses. Where a social threat discourse predominates in both national and neighbourhood contexts, lone mothers can feel isolated and stigmatised. Where nationally dominant social threat or social problem discourses are challenged by lifestyle and escaping patriarchy discourses circulating within the neighbourhood context, lone mothers can feel accepted and empowered.

Moreover, for lone mothers themselves, the framework of discourses around lone motherhood is drawn on in overlapping and flexible configurations according to the realities of their lives. As we saw in section 2.4, whether or not lone mothers want to conceive of themselves as part of this category is informed by discourses around lone motherhood, and they can bring together elements from different, perhaps even contradictory, discourses according to their material and social situation. For example, White middle class groups of British lone mothers (both 'alternative' and suburban) could combine positive evaluations of the benefits of life without a male partner (escaping patriarchy) with worries about the implications for their children (social threat); White middle class suburban British lone mothers did not draw on the poverty aspect of the social problem discourse in the same way as other groups; Black lone mothers were far more likely to draw on the day care barrier aspect of the social problem discourse than other British and national groups; and finally groups of lone mothers who were embedded in neighbourhoods with a supportive lifestyle discourse did not draw on the barriers to social life aspect of the social problem discourse.

The lens through which lone mothers view their situations is therefore shaped both by the national media and policy context, and by the material and social context of the neighbourhoods in which they are located. Thus the overall lesson from our analysis of discourses around lone motherhood is that context is crucial. We now turn in the next chapter to examine in more detail one of these contexts – the material and social contours of the neighbourhoods in which our groups of lone mothers lived, including the social networks in which they were embedded.

NOTES

1. It is difficult to know why the west African lone mothers were particularly unwilling to comment on views about lone motherhood locally. The interviewer was nervous about pursuing any of their answers to questions and her demeanour may have inhibited the interviewees.
2. The pie charts illustrating the lone mothers' own views about their lone motherhood were generated by extracting all the opinions they

expressed about their situation (as it related to their lone motherhood) during their individual interviews and grouping together statements that were similar (and allowing for contradictions within one account). Groups of statements were then collated as a whole for each social group of lone mothers.

3 Lone Mothers in Neighbourhoods: Material Contexts and Social Capital

3.1 INTRODUCTION: NEIGHBOURHOODS AND SOCIAL CAPITAL

In this chapter we examine the social nature of lone mothers' lives as lived within particular neighbourhoods, as they interact with kin and friends in social networks. In other words, we look at what some theorists call 'social capital'; that is, those features of social organisation, such as norms, values, expectations and networks of social support, which facilitate co-operation and trust between people for their mutual benefit. In turn, these features are seen as decisive in enhancing – or undermining – the economic health of localities and of those living within them. Indeed, without strong local traditions of active reciprocal engagement, embodied in social networks and dominant norms, state economic and social initiatives are thought likely to fail. Stocks of social capital, as collective action, thus tend to be self-reinforcing and cumulative – the more social capital an area has, the more it will generate and the more prosperous it will become. Conversely, the less social capital an area has, the less it will generate, and the poorer it will become. According to this view the individualism and pursuit of self-interest so beloved of free market theorists is in reality an economic dead end; rather, it is collective ties of social and civic trust and mutuality which are the key ingredients of economic prosperity (Putnam 1993a, b; Fukuyama 1995; Wann 1995; see Chapter 8 for further discussion).

Applying this view to lone mothers, it would no longer be their individual personal resource characteristics (that is, their human capital) which is crucial for their economic behaviour, and hence whether or not it is economically rational for for them to take up paid work. Rather, it is how lone mothers' social capital is developed, and how their human capital is socially supported or constrained, that influences their economic behaviour. Furthermore, different ethnic and social class groups, living in particular areas, are said to have enhanced or reduced, facilitatory or obstructive, social capital (see Wilson 1989; Putnam 1993a, b). Thus, the classical liberal economic and social policy emphasis on individuals is misplaced; it is social capital that needs fostering or rebuilding. In this way, theories about the workings of social capital have clear overlaps with ideas of both the 'underclass' and communitarianism, as discussed in the previous chapter in relation to discourses around lone motherhood. Notions of social capital are also clearly related to the overlap we identified in Chapter 1 between social divisions of gender, class and ethnicity with cultural and material issues of marginalisation and social aspiration, and with the nature and physical location of neighbourhoods. If the social capital you can draw on helps to define who you are, what your resources are and hence your economic prospects, then where you live and who you know will be a major factor in shaping lone mothers' differing ability to take a job.

This issue has not been explored to any great extent in studies of lone mothers' uptake of paid work, where the research focus has remained on national policy frameworks and lone mothers' individual attributes. This focus will therefore miss a crucial – maybe *the* crucial – explanation for lone mothers' varying uptake of paid work. In this chapter we therefore examine the varying nature of lone mothers' social capital in particular neighbourhoods. We begin, in section 3.2, by describing the material differences in the neighbourhoods in which the lone mothers interviewed for this research lived, and which contribute to the quality of their lives. One of the features of these local material and social landscapes is the extent to which lone mothers take up paid work. Section 3.3 maps and compares this for the British case study areas. Indices of individual human capital do not account for the employment variations found, and this leads us to turn to social capital type explanations. First, in section 3.4 we examine the role played by child care in enabling the interviewees to undertake paid work. Both the use different groups made of formal care, and the extent to which they could rely on on informal child care support were important parts of their 'social capital'. Finally, section 3.5 examines the nature of the interviewed lone mothers' social networks – the lubrication of social capital in practice. We discover that these links, and the nature of social capital, are not so straightforward as they at first appear.

3.2 THE NEIGHBOURHOODS

Different neighbourhoods show a whole gamut of social and economic variations, as so well established by the 'urban ecology' research tradition, with different dimensions of advantage and disadvantage (see Savage and Warde 1993). However, few commentators explicitly examine the significance of the neighbourhood environment for lone mothers' lives, despite evidence that lone mothers' limited mobility and restricted time budgets mean that their lives are often focused on their place of residence (Parkes and Thrift 1980; Winchester 1989), and that this environment is not a passive context but an active influence on the quality of lone mothers' lives (McKendrick 1997). This influence, as we discussed above in terms of social capital, may be decisive for lone mothers' economic behaviour. Certainly 'underclass' theory, discussed in Chapter 2, would see neighbourhood as crucial – for 'underclass' culture is viewed as being re/produced within particular neighbourhoods by particular social groups.

Some of our case study areas held strong 'underclass potential' in these terms – there were high numbers of lone mothers and minority ethnic residents, with high numbers living on state benefits in inner-city areas and in public, local authority, housing estates. The underclass debate can be regarded as one extreme, if an overly politicised and moralistic one, of social capital theory. Thus we would expect these neighbourhoods to possess low social capital. The inner-city areas of the south London boroughs of Lambeth and Southwark, and the Near West Side in Cleveland, Ohio, could be seen as clearly falling within this category, as could the peripheral public housing estate of Moulsecoomb in Brighton. Other case study areas provided less obvious 'potential' in the terms posed by underclass theory, and presumably therefore more in the way of potential social capital. The residualised outer-city estate of Björndammen in Partille, near Göteborg, the 'alternative' inner-city neighbourhood of Kreuzberg in Berlin , and the gentrified central area of Hanover in Brighton, fall into this group. Finally, one area would provide no underclass 'potential' at all in these terms: Patcham and Westdene in the suburban north of Brighton. An affluent, middle class and respectable neighbourhood, it would be expected to possess high stocks of social capital.

As we shall see, however, this assumed association between the ascribed social (dis)advantage of an area, and the level of social capital available to lone mothers living within it, is misleading. Yet again, we need to unpack a 'closed box' of taxonomic association to discover those actual social processes by which lone mothers have access to, and can use, different sorts of social capital. We begin this process by describing the characteristics of the neighbourhoods in which the lone mothers' lived, and their views on living in them, as a prelude to examining what this meant in terms of access to social resources.

The Inner-city Neighbourhoods in London and Cleveland

The contiguous inner London boroughs of Lambeth and Southwark, and Near West Side in Cleveland, Ohio, are both extreme or classic inner-city ares. Both have been subject to economic decline and restructuring, with shifts from skilled work in manufacturing (especially for men) towards more polarised professional and low skilled employment in business and personal services (with greater employment opportunities for women) and both show concentrations of unemployment, poverty and social deprivation – although both also show pockets of affluence as young professionals gentrify some particularly attractive and well-located neighbourhoods like Clapham in Lambeth or Ohio City in Cleveland. Both also show high levels of lone motherhood at around twice their national averages, with 44 per cent of families with dependent children in Lambeth and Southwark in 1991 and around 50 per cent in Near West Side. Both show a mix of ethnic groups; as many as 42 per cent of lone mothers are Black (African-Caribbean, 'Black other' and African) in Lambeth and Southwark, way above the national average of just over five per cent, while many lone mothers in Cleveland are African-American and Hispanic. They differ in that Lambeth and Southwark lie within Greater London, Britain's social and economic powerhouse (although much of this opportunity remains outside the reach of lone mothers) while Cleveland is a type-case, in the USA, of a 'rust-belt' city of former manufacturing preeminence, now in economic decline and with high levels of inner-city poverty.

The four London groups of lone mothers interviewed for our research were distributed in different neighbourhoods across Lambeth and Southwark. As Figure 3.1 shows, there are substantial variations in rates of lone motherhood within the boroughs at the smaller ward (electoral district) level. These variations largely reflect the local housing market where most lone mothers (84 per cent) live in public sector housing, and fewer live in the more prosperous wards, with more owner-occupation, in the south of the boroughs. There is also a variety

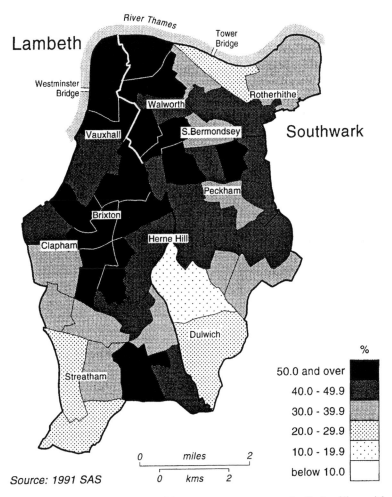

Figure 3.1 Lone parent families as a percentage of all families with dependent children, Lambeth and Southwark 1991

of voluntary agencies working in the two boroughs, some aimed at women or particular ethnic groups, and there is a relatively high provision of day care in British terms (but low in European terms).

In the *Brixton* neighbourhood, in the centre of Lambeth (see Figure 3.1 for this and subsequent London locations), lone mothers account for around half of families with dependent children. Housing consists mainly of large estates of blocks of public housing with some owner-occupation. The younger African-Caribbean group of interviewees were largely concentrated in this area, all but one of them living in such housing (the exception was in a housing association flat).[2] Thus, rather than having actively chosen to live in the neighbourhood, most felt that it was a case of 'it's where they [the local authority] put me'. Indeed, most were ambivalent about living in the neighbourhood, although nearly all had been lived there for a long time – sometimes all of their life. Most valued being surrounded by people they knew and who were friendly and, as noted in the Chapter 2, they felt that their family situation was regarded as quite 'normal' locally. The neighbourhood is also well served by shops and public transport, and a variety of clubs and leisure facilities, often with an ethnic specialisation where Brixton serves as one centre for African-Caribbean life in London. The younger African-Caribbean lone mothers valued this aspect of local life highly. At the same time Brixton is seen to suffer typical 'inner-city' problems. Several of the lone mothers felt that there were too many young people congregating in the streets, with a lack of safe play space for children, and also too much drugs and crime:

> The area's nice, everyone's nice and friendly. There's just things that are happening, too many kids hanging out, late parties, tramps on the side of the road, people selling crack to people in the street. That's awful.   (Deanne)

In the south of Southwark, in the Herne Hill and East Dulwich neighbourhoods, lone motherhood is less prevalent, with below 30 per cent of families falling into this category. The older African-Caribbean group mainly lived here and, like the younger African-Caribbean group, most had lived in their neighbourhood for a considerable period of time. In these areas housing consists of a mix of public and private renting with owner-occupation, but apart from one lone mother in housing association temporary accommodation, our interviewees all lived in the public housing. While several of the older African-Caribbean lone mothers held similar views to their younger counterparts about having little choice over where they had been placed by the local authority, they mainly liked their neighbourhood. The area contains several parks and sports grounds, and the lone mothers appreciated the facilities for children's play, although poor shopping facilities were also seen as a negative feature of local life. However, although some felt they had good friends and neighbours, others felt that they did not 'fit in'. This was in part related to the White, and to some extent middle-class and conventional family, nature of the neighbourhoods:

> Being a single parent, there's not a lot of single parents on this new estate ... There's a slight hint of racism. Apparently they objected to these houses being built. They objected that people from out of the area were coming in. (Annette).

The west African lone mothers were distributed across the north of Southwark, mainly in the Walworth and South Bermondsey neighbourhoods. Most had lived in the area for less time than the African-Caribbean groups. In these neighbourhoods, lone mothers and their dependent children form just under half of all families. Housing is mostly public renting, with some large estates, which is where the majority of the west African lone mothers had been 'put' by the local authority (two exceptions were an owner-occupier and a private renter). While public transport, shopping and leisure facilities is variable in this area, and there is little green space, the lone mothers chose to concentrate on the positive aspects of their neighbourhoods:

> It has a lot of good things, schools, playgroups, shopping complex. It has a lot of things. And nice people around. (Bunmi)

In contrast to the three neighbourhood based Black groups, the White 'alternative' interviewees were scattered across the central and northern area of Lambeth and Southwark, often in the neighbourhoods we have discussed above. Like the west African lone mothers, most had lived in their neighbourhoods for around 3–9 years and were in public housing (three were owner-occupiers and another was in a housing association flat). This group of lone mothers were far more critical of the areas in which they lived. Those in public housing often felt that they had been 'put' where their 'higher' social class background meant that they did not 'fit in':

> I think if I had a choice I would move further out of London. I don't think about it too much, I haven't got the choice! ... To a certain extent I view myself as quite different from other people. Just sort of – I suppose I think I've had a slightly better education possibly. I think I'm viewed very much as a snob really in my street, cos I don't

let [my daughter] out in the street, and shut the door and come in ... They think we're too posh.   (Hannah)

In contrast, those few who were owner-occupiers had, within their price range, chosen where they lived and spoke of the friends they had locally. Like the younger African-Caribbean lone mothers, the White 'alternative' lone mothers, while appreciating shopping, transport and other facilities, were concerned about crime and street gangs and the effects of growing up in such a milieu on their children. In addition, they referred to the poor schools available to them, and those with children who had a Black father worried about the racism their children suffered.

Near West Side, in Cleveland, comprises three 'old' inner-city neighbourhoods – Detroit-Shoreway, Ohio City and Tremont. In all three, housing is mainly two story, detached but closely built, wooden structures, both privately rented and owner-occupied with some pockets of public housing project buildings. All but two of the interviewed lone mothers were privately renting (both exceptions living with their mother and other siblings in owner-occupied housing). Unmarried and teenage lone motherhood is not unusual, with around one in ten teenage women giving birth (US Bureau of Census 1990) and half of our interviewees, scattered across the three neighbourhoods, were currently in their late teens, while the others had given birth aged 20 or under. Living among other young mothers, as noted in the previous chapter, made the lone mothers feel comfortable.

Although half the lone mothers had only moved to their neighbourhood in the previous year or so, this was often a move back after living elsewhere. Their return was because the Near West Side was where they felt their family and/or friendship support networks were situated, and this support was cited by some of them as the best thing about living in the area as well as reasonable rents. The area is well served by shops, parks and recreational facilities and even attracts tourists. A number of statutory and voluntary agencies serve the residents of the neighbourhoods, providing a range of education, health and social services, as well as job search and training schemes (one used by some interviewees), several targeted at particular minority ethnic groups. The downside, for the lone mothers, was crime, drugs and lack of safety. Crime rates were three times higher than the average for Cleveland as a whole and all three neighbourhoods have a reputation for being unsafe after dark, especially Detroit Shoreway.

Like some of the groups in our British case study areas, the Near West Side lone mothers worried about the negative influence of the neighbourhood on their children:

> There's a lot of drug dealers around the neighbourhood, young kids. I don't like that. Gangs, killing. I was right up on 47th when that girl got killed ... (Janice)

The Peripheral Housing Neighbourhoods in Brighton and Göteborg

Björndammen, adjacent to Göteborg – Sweden's second city, and Moulsecoomb on the edge of the seaside conurbation of Brighton and Hove (now a single local authority) on the south coast of Britain, are both typical peripheral housing neighbourhoods. Both areas have become residualised and associated with social problems. Moulsecoomb ward mainly consists of large estates, built in the 1930s and 1950s as a public housing answer to the central town slum problem. Much is semidetached, with only a few low-rise flats, and the more attractive houses have now been sold off into owner-occupation. As a whole the ward has a rate of lone motherhood around the Brighton and Hove average of 24 per cent in 1991 (in turn near the national average). However, lone mothers appear peripheral even within this peripherality, and the interviewees were housed in a particular stigmatised estate – the archetypical Moulsecoomb neighbourhood itself – where lone mothers constitute almost half of all families with children. Unlike the inner cities, lone motherhood in Moulescoombe (and in Brighton) is racially homogeneous – 99 per cent were White in 1991, as were all the interviewees. Björndammen, a like-sized area within the suburban commune of Partille has a similar origin, built in the mid 1970s as part of the 'million programme' when estates of flats were built to solve the post-war housing crisis. Björndammen also has a high concentration of lone mothers (35 per cent of families with dependent children) compared with Partille commune as a whole (10.9 per cent). However, while all the Moulescoomb lone mothers were working class, most in Björndammen were middle class. This may reflect the mixed tenure of Swedish social sector housing, and its lesser residualisation compared with Britain (Barlow and Duncan 1994). It also seems, however, that Björndammen offers more to its lone mothers than Moulescoomb, as we shall see. The two neighbourhoods differ, therefore, in that Moulescoomb is the more socially peripheral.

Like the local authority tenants in London, the Moulescoomb lone mothers mostly felt they had been 'put' in the neighbourhood rather than made a positive choice to live there. However, a few also mentioned that this was fine because they had local family ties. Most had lived in the area for some time. The friendliness of the neighbourhood generally, in addition to feeling comfortable in a situation where lone motherhood was not uncommon (see previous chapter), was mentioned by several. However, the neighbourhood not only has a poor reputation locally but was the site of national 'demonising' attention after the 'Wild Park' murders of two young girls in 1987 in open space next to Moulsecoomb. Most of the White working class lone mothers felt ambivalent about living in the neighbourhood because of its reputation and the potential effect on their children:

It's okay, but if I could move tomorrow I would, outside Moulsecoomb. It's the reputation it's got. When people say 'where do you live?' and you say Moulsecoomb they just think it's a shit area ... You got all these kids that swear and smoke, I just think it's really bad. For [my children] to grow up surrounded by young kids, ten, swearing at the mothers and smoking in front of their mothers, it's a bad influence. (Sylvia)

Child deprivation in the area is a concern to local statutory agencies, who have set up health, education and social projects providing activities and support to families, which several of the lone mothers referred to as a positive feature. There is also a sports centre. Shopping facilities on the estate are poor, however, comprising small parades of shops, and there is little in the way of day care provision.

There is also social service concern in Björndammen about poverty, overcrowded households, child and youth welfare, drug and alcohol abuse, as well as about women's mental and physical health, and concomitant sick leave from employment (Källstrom 1993). Indeed, social service agencies have begun a project to 'empower' women to 'better' their own and others' lives. Individual indicators reflect this areal pathology. The average income of families in Björndammen is significantly lower than in Partille as a whole, and lone mothers' average income is even lower. Similarly, while almost two-thirds of lone mothers in Partille (65.7 per cent) are in rented housing (public and private), this rises to nearly all (91.5 per cent) in Björndammen and all but two of the interviewees were in such accommodation (the exceptions being in owner-occupied and co-operative housing).

This picture of residualisation and stigmatisation may remind us of Moulsecoomb, but in other ways Björndammen is quite different. Partille itself has a significant employment base in manufacturing, service industries, and public sector employment, as does nearby Göteborg as whole, and unemployment is low. In contrast there is virtually no employment in Moulescoomb itself, and with the closure or downsizing of many manufacturing and transport workplaces in Brighton and Hove, the public and private service sectors now provide the bulk of employment. Much of this is part-time and low paid, and a significant part of these jobs are only seasonal or casual. Nor, unlike Moulsecoomb, was there any great sense in Björndammen of having been 'put' in the neighbourhood and none of the interviewed lone mothers mentioned social problems, or expressed any concern about negative influences on their children. The majority liked living in the neighbourhood and spoke positively of it, with only a few complaints about poor shopping facilities and the dullness of life in the suburbs. Several lauded the ready availability of good quality nursery provision and schools. Björndammen itself is built in small neighbourhood 'yards' organised around children's playgrounds and cycle ways, and most respondents also appreciated the lack of traffic, the area's safety, and the bordering woods and lakes (including a nature reserve). These were major reasons given for moving to the area:

> I felt I couldn't live there with the children in the middle of the city, there wasn't anywhere green ... So I put myself on the waiting list [here] and said I wanted a ground floor flat. And the nursery places were vital ... It's green and lovely and traffic-free and quiet and big open areas, and I think that's important for the children. Also there are a lot of children of their own age ... The car's outside, the nursery's in the yard, no distance to anywhere, so I haven't found any disadvantages [in living here], nothing that's bad.   (Beata)

As with Beata (above), the perceived prevalence of families with children was regarded as a positive aspect of neighbourhood life. Despite feeling somewhat stigmatised as lone mothers nationally, at the local level family forms were not such an issue for this group of lone mothers as it was for many of the British, US, and German groups. Although most had been in Björndammen for a relatively short period of time (three years or less), they largely felt well-embedded in local social networks and the friendliness of the area was also valued and another important reason given by several for moving to the area.

The 'Alternative' Neighbourhoods in Brighton and Berlin

Brighton and Berlin both have national reputations as the site of alternative, sometimes outrageous but always 'trendy', lifestyles. Within the former, it is the Hanover neighbourhood that epitomises this alternative, with hilly gentrified streets of 'period' terraced housing overlooking the fashionable centre of Brighton, with a reputation for containing a variety of left-leaning, university educated, liberal or 'alternative', middle-class groups. The remnants of some features of its former role as working class, inner-city area increases this attractiveness. Kreuzberg has a similar position, not far from the centres of both former west and east Berlin, and is a typical of the sort of metropolitan, inner-city neighbourhood that has long been nationally famed as a progressive 'alternative' area. There is a number of active politically oriented groups, a lively street life, with a plethora of small theatres, clubs and restaurants. Both areas have easy access to swimming pools, shopping, and transport facilities. However, Kreuzberg retains more typical inner-city features with relatively low average income, high unemployment and an ethnically mixed population, where Kreuzberg functions as something of a centre for Berliners of Turkish origin. Both also have high proportions of lone mothers at around two fifths of all families with dependent children.[3] In both areas the White 'alternative' groups of lone mothers we interviewed had access to a wide range of voluntary and community-based facilities, with substantial day care facilities in Kreuzberg and voluntary play schemes for children in Hanover. All appreciated living in neighbourhoods with an alternative atmosphere and high concentrations of lone mothers.

The Hanover interview group were owner-occupiers, apart from two who were renting privately, and had mostly been living in the area for between four to eight years. All the lone mothers very much liked living there. They specifically mentioned its location near to the sea, parks and shops, and the positive aspects of not 'standing out' as a lone mothers (see Chapter 2), and stressed the sense of community and strong local support networks:

> We moved here nine years ago. We chose it because the housing was inexpensive and we liked the feeling of the area, and we liked the house. I think it's brilliant. It has a very exceptionally good community spirit ... It's very supportive, it's relatively safe, and I think there's quite a high proportion of people who are in the same situation as I am. (Carey)

Like Carey, the 'feel' of the area – and the price of housing – was why most of the interviewees had moved to the neighbourhood.

Housing in Kreuzberg is mainly privately rented and all the interviewees lived in the turn of the century blocks of flats that are typical of the neighbourhood, and where rents are comparatively low. Most had been in the area for quite some time (from four to 15 years). The lively, alternative atmosphere and the comfortable feeling that they did not 'stand out', combined with good amenities, low rents, and the presence of friends in the area, were the main reasons the lone mothers gave for moving to the neighbourhood:

> I got the flat through a friend of mine, about seven years ago ... And the price of the flat, it was very cheap, and still is ... The atmosphere, the pubs, the night life, the atmosphere of the people who live here [appealed to me]. Colourful, all mixed up and not elitist. Alive. (Inge)

However, these positive assessments were balanced by concerns about traffic and pollution, and the safety of their children

> I've got everything here, my friends are here, all within three kilometres or so ... I do a lot with the kids here in the area, and I feel comfortable right here. There's a whole shit load of single mothers in this area ... And for me as a mother, I have all the shops right here, so if I want to I can get all the shopping done in an hour, not like living in the suburbs ... But Hermannplatz, it disgusts me, really, for the children, this incredible stress, the traffic. (Karin)

The Suburban Neighbourhood in Brighton and Hove

The three groups of lone mothers interviewed in Brighton were located in three distinct areas (Hanover, Moulsecoomb and Patcham/Westdene; see Figure 3.2) with quite different, almost type-case, reputations for trendy gentrification, deprived peripherality, and posh suburbanism respectively. Indeed, the lone mothers sometimes referred to one or both of the other neighbourhoods as contrasting exemplars to their own, as with Alison, living in Hanover:

> I like this area. I wouldn't like to live in an area where everywhere you went you were noticed as a single parent, like Patcham. Round

here quite a few are. I wouldn't like an estate or something, like out in Moulsecoomb, a council house ...

There are also significant ward level variations in the distribution of lone mothers in Brighton and these, as in inner London, reflect a constrained access to housing. Those areas with the higher rates of lone motherhood follow the distribution of local authority property (mostly in some outer wards like Moulescoomb) and the availability of cheaper owner-occupation and private renting in the central wards, as with Hanover. See Figure 3.2.

In contrast to the all the other case study neighbourhoods, therefore, the affluent suburban wards of Patcham and Westdene contain quite low proportions of lone mothers. Housing is overwhelmingly owner-occupied and detached or semi-detached. Indeed, all of our White 'suburban' interviewees were owner-occupiers, apart from one privately renting. Most had been living in the area for 10 years or more. There are some nurseries in the area, but, apart from the standard statutory health and education services, little in the way of voluntary facilities or other projects. The area is served by small local

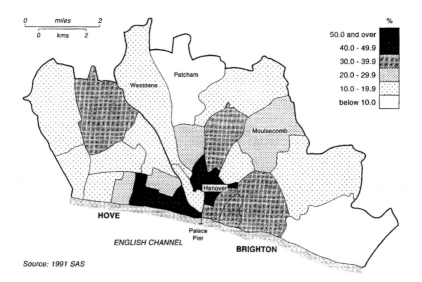

Figure 3.2   Lone parent families as a percentage of all families with dependent children, Brighton and Hove 1991

parades of shops and some public transport. The White 'suburban' lone mothers mostly liked living in their neighbourhood for material reasons, although they felt uncomfortable with the dominant 'social threat' view of lone motherhood held by people in the area (see Chapter 2). They stressed the standard of housing, the spacious gardens and, in particular, the 'good' schools nearby. Although the Patcham and Westdene lone mothers lived within a couple of miles of Moulsecoomb, each group lived in quite different conditions, held different concerns about the effect of living in their particular neighbourhood and, as we shall see, took part in quite different social relationships.

3.3 HUMAN CAPITAL, EMPLOYMENT AND SOCIAL CAPITAL IN NEIGHBOURHOODS

The various neighbourhoods we describe in the previous section provide a range of material contexts within which the lone mothers experienced their lives. Employment rates also vary across these neighbourhoods, sometimes quite dramatically. For example, in Brighton only 23 per cent of lone mothers were employed in Moulescoomb, compared to over 60 per cent in some affluent suburban wards, including Patcham. A first explanation of these varying employment rates would appeal to the varying human capital characteristics of the lone mothers within these neighbourhoods, linking in with the bulk of research (see Chapter 1) that sees lone mothers' personal and individual characteristics as determining their employment position. In this sense, then, the different neighbourhoods we described in the last section would just be containers of groups of lone mothers with different characteristics, because of the way the housing market works to distribute and concentrate people with different levels of human capital. What does this mean, however, for theories of social capital which imply that the neighbourhoods where lone mothers live should be more than just containers of atomistic individuals? In this view, in contrast, these individuals would be differentially embedded in different sorts of social networks in the different neighbourhoods, and it is this which should be decisive for lone mothers' desire and ability to take of paid work. We will now go on to evaluate these perspectives looking at employment rates, child care and social networking, using the British neighbourhoods as major case study areas.

Lone Mothers' Employment and Human Capital

Figure 3.3 maps both numbers of lone mothers and their rates of employment for both the British case study areas, and shows well the much larger number of lone mothers in Lambeth and Southwark. The figure also points to an inverse correlation between the two – the fewer lone mothers there are in an area, the more likely they are to be employed. This in turn reflects social class and housing tenure distributions. There are less lone mothers in more middle class, owner-occupying, suburban wards on the fringes of Brighton and Hove such as Patcham, or in the south of Lambeth and Southwark, such as Herne Hill. In these wards lone mothers are also more likely to be in employment. Conversely, those areas with more lone mothers are also those with more public housing and lower employment rates, like Moulsecoomb or Brixton (compare with Figures 3.1 and 3.2).

Housing tenure is correlated with social class, and is useful for estimating the social class attributes of lone mothers in Britain, where the other usual class index – employment status – is inadequate for this task when the majority do not have paid employment. Social class can also be taken as a rough measurement of human capital: the higher the social class of an individual the more likely that person is to have higher educational levels and superior job experience. Using these measures, the human capital school of explanation would seem to be most germane – higher average human capital in any area equates with higher employment rates for lone mothers. This is apparently confirmed by the graphs in Figure 3.4, which more closely presents the association between housing tenure, car ownership and employment rates. Car ownership can also be taken as a complimentary measure of household income and wealth, at least within areas with similar transport infrastructure (Fieldhouse and Tye, 1996). The more owner-occupation and car ownership in a ward, the more likely that lone mothers are in paid work.

There are, however, some substantial problems with this conclusion – some technical, some conceptual, and some empirical. Technically, Figure 3.4 is subject to all the problems of aggregate, spatial analysis. The lone mothers themselves may well hold a different tenure or car ownership than the average (census figures are available for lone mothers' tenure by ward, but only from a ten per cent sample which would give large standard errors). This may well be a factor in the lower association between tenure, car ownership and lone mothers' employment rate shown in Lambeth and Southwark (Figure 3.4b) –

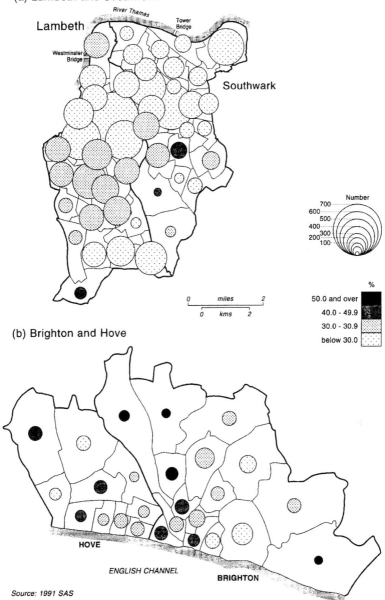

(a) Lambeth and Southwark

Lambeth

River Thames

Tower Bridge

Westminster Bridge

Southwark

Number
700
600
500
400
300
200
100

%
50.0 and over
40.0 - 49.9
30.0 - 30.9
below 30.0

0 miles 2
0 kms 2

(b) Brighton and Hove

HOVE

ENGLISH CHANNEL

BRIGHTON

Source: 1991 SAS

Figure 3.3   Percentage of lone mothers in employment, British case study areas 1991

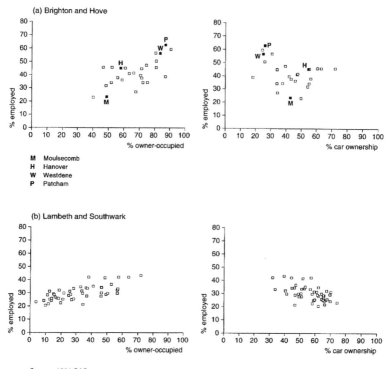

Figure 3.4   Housing tenure, car ownership and lone mothers' employment: British case study areas by ward 1991

there are low rates of owner-occupation and car ownership overall, and lone mothers themselves will probably not be among the owner-occupiers or car owners. Similarly, wards are large areas which aggregate different conditions, and spatial census variables are notoriously autocorrelated – that is they can show a statistical relationship simply because they co-vary over space as they reflect urban social structure. There may be no causal link at all between tenure and car ownership, as indices of human capital, and employment rates.

These technical problems link into an overall conceptual problem with the 'human capital' explanation – it may well be lone mothers' access to social capital which allows them access to paid work, and it is this which is causally effective. Access to social capital, which is not recorded in the census, may simply co-vary with housing tenure and car ownership, which are. This suspicion is heightened when we examine more closely the somewhat anomalous tenure/employment graph for Lambeth and Southwark (Figure 3.4b). Not only is the overall relationship less marked than in Brighton and Hove, but there are also a number of wards with much higher, or lower, employment rates than expected given their tenure average. Looking at these residual cases more closely, it seems that they are associated with ethnicity. Wards with a high percentage of Black lone mothers tend to show higher employment rates than expected. Some wards with a high percentage of White lone mothers also show high employment rates – but these are the middle class areas in the south of the boroughs. Wards with a high percentage of working class Whites, in public housing, show lower rates than those with a high percentage of similarly positioned Black lone mothers. Maybe this ethnic difference gives some sort of index of differences in social capital, and this also influences employment rate? The jury is still out.

This argument that the likelihood of lone mothers' employment does not simply reflect their level of human capital becomes all the more pervasive when we turn to the differential ward take-up of full-time work. Generally, it is full-time work which is necessary to offer lone mothers economic independence and sufficient income to support themselves and their children, and in this way it is full-time work which is crucial. Most part-time employment is inadequate in these respects (see Chapter 6). However, there is only an extremely weak relationship between housing tenure and car ownership, as indices of ascribed human capital, and the uptake of (full-time) paid work (see Figure 3.5). This operation was repeated for the more numerous, and much smaller, enumeration districts (1357 in total compared to just 74 wards), to check that it was not the large ward aggregation affect that was responsible for this result. Even then, however, the statistical association between housing tenure, car ownership and lone mothers' employment remains weak.[4] Figure 3.6, in mapping ward employment data, makes this same point more dramatically. There are large numbers of lone mothers in Lambeth and Southwark with apparently low levels of human capital and a high 'underclass potential' who none the less were in full-time work in 1991. It would appear that human capital, as measured by housing tenure, has little relationship with lone mothers' uptake of full-time work, and it is full-time work which is crucial for their economic independence.

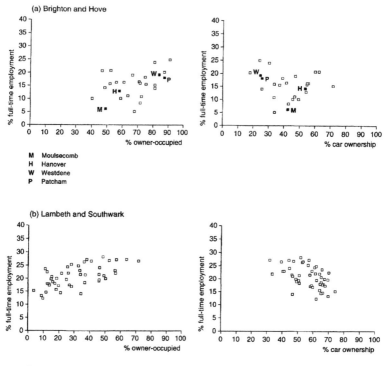

Figure 3.5   Housing tenure, car ownership and lone mothers' full-time employment: British case study areas by ward 1991

If levels of individual human capital do not explain the differential uptake of full-time work, can we therefore turn to differential access to social capital as an explanation? In following up this theme we first examine the nature of child care provision in the British case study areas. It may be that this acts as such a constraint (or opportunity where it is available) that human capital influences on lone mothers' ability to take paid work are simply overridden. On the other hand, access to child care may in itself be a reflection of access to social capital. We turn to this issue in the next section.

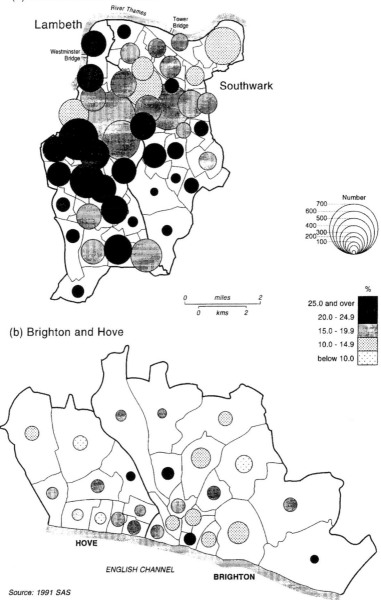

(a) Lambeth and Southwark

River Thames

Lambeth

Tower Bridge

Westminster Bridge

Southwark

Number

700
600
500
400
300
200
100

%

25.0 and over
20.0 - 24.9
15.0 - 19.9
10.0 - 14.9
below 10.0

0   miles   2
0   kms   2

(b) Brighton and Hove

HOVE

ENGLISH CHANNEL

BRIGHTON

Source: 1991 SAS

Figure 3.6   Percentage of lone mothers in full-time employment, British case study areas 1991

3.4   CHILD CARE, EMPLOYMENT AND SOCIAL CAPITAL

Uses and Preferences for Child Care

Lack of affordable day care provision is often cited as a severe constraint to British lone mothers taking up paid work (Bradshaw and Millar 1991; Bryson et al. 1997; Holtermann 1993), especially when compared to the situation in other European countries with much greater access, such as Sweden (Bradshaw et al. 1996, see also Chapter 7). Indeed, day care provision in Britain has long ranked amongst the worst in Europe (Cohen and Fraser 1991; Phillips and Moss 1989). Successive British governments have adopted a 'hands off' approach, arguing that they have little or no direct role to play in making provision to support employed parents. Moreover, again unlike many other European countries, there has rarely been much sense of the importance of good day care, and outside school provision in general, for children's social and educational development. (Although lone mothers can value such benefits: see Edwards 1993.)

Child care policy includes state provision of day and outside school care, as well as provisions giving parents the right to spend time caring for their children whilst protecting their employment and/or income rights. This is what Anette Borchorst (1990) calls 'political motherhood' – the social context that shapes how and under what conditions motherhood is carried out, and thus how it might be combined with paid work. In the British definition of political motherhood, parents are seen to be 'free to choose' paid work, and if they do so they must deal with the consequences themselves or in co-operation with their employer. In reality, it is mothers, not 'parents' who face this problem (Brannen and Moss 1991). In so far as state agencies are involved in day care provision, practices and interpretations vary in the 'local state' of elected local authorities, non-elected quangos and quasi-market organisations (Goodwin et al. 1993), while NGOs and commercial firms, often locally organised, also play a role in day care and outside school provision. This results in the development of a patchwork of formal public, private and voluntary sector provision and informal arrangements – all varying in terms of availability, type, quality and affordability, as well as location. (It also provides another example of our argument that we cannot only concentrate on national policy: see Chapter 1.)

Lone mothers living in different neighbourhoods in Britain will, therefore, have access to different types and amounts of provision, with implications for mothers' access to paid work (Bowlby 1990; Pickup 1983). How far does the differential pattern of local day care provision account for the differential uptake of paid work by lone mothers in the British case study areas?

At the time of the interviews, both Lambeth and Southwark had above national average levels of nursery places per capita, with places for 9.1 and 6.1 per cent of children under five (the normal age for starting school), compared with just 4.6 per cent nationally in 1994. Registered childminder places were however just 3.5 per cent in Lambeth compared with the average for England and Wales of 6.9 per cent and 7.4 per cent in Southwark. Adding these together, in Southwark there were day care places for 13.5 per cent of the under fives, in Lambeth for 12.6, compared with a national average of 11.5. Southwark also provided after school places for 12.5 per cent of five to seven year olds, compared with just 1.6 per cent nationally (figures were unavailable for Lambeth). In a British context, the two London boroughs are relatively well provided with day care, but of course the vast majority of young children living in the boroughs would be excluded, and in a wider European context these figures look puny. For example virtually all of the under sevens in Björndammen have access to formal day care (where seven is the school starting age).

Within the boroughs there were proportionately fewer local authority and voluntary sector nursery places in the southern wards, even though proportionately more lone mothers are in employment in these areas. Rather, nursery places are concentrated in the central areas of the boroughs, where proportionately fewer of the larger number of lone mothers have paid work. At first sight, the varying level of nursery provision does not seem to be associated with varying lone mother employment rates, and the patterns of use amongst the London interviewees reflect this. The African-Caribbean lone mothers who had full-time (over 30 hours per week) or long part-time (22–30 hours) paid work, and relied on formal day care provision to enable this, were more likely to use a childminder, while the west African and White 'alternative' lone mothers tended to use nursery provision for younger children. Many, however, relied on informal care. Some of those with short part-time (16–21 hours per week) or minimal part-time work (under 15 hours per week) used a mix of playgroup and after school care (and some informal care), but some also used a nursery place. In addition, four lone mothers were studying full-time and used nursery provision attached to their education institutions.

Brighton and Hove (as part of the county of East Sussex) also has above average nursery places but below average national levels of childminder provision, and hardly any after school places (Department of Health 1995). Again, the geographical distribution of places varies dramatically within the borough. Nursery provision tends to be situated in the more affluent suburban and the central areas of Brighton. In contrast, the peripheral public housing estate of Moulsecoomb has no nursery places other than through part-time provision attached to the local school, although some childminding places are located there. This pattern does suggest a link between day care provision and lone mothers' employment rates, but the vast majority of our Brighton interviewees did not use it. Only one (alternative) lone mother used formal day care, in the form of a childminder, to enable full-time work. The rest with paid work, whether full-time, long part-time or short part-time, used informal care.

While we have no way of judging patterns of day care use more generally by other lone mothers living in these areas, the use made by our interviewees does not particularly match local patterns of provision. For example, the younger African-Caribbean lone mothers had more nursery provision situated in their neighbourhood than did the older African-Caribbean group, but both tended to rely on childminders. However, we should not then assume that these groups tended to use the forms of day care provision they preferred and trusted. In fact, nurseries and after school provision were preferred amongst these two groups. This was because they were regarded as providing children with educational activities that developed their learning (including, in the case of nurseries, preparing children for school), a chance to mix and interact with other children and adults, as enhancing children's independence, and as providing stability. Childminders, in contrast, were regarded as more suspect. A constant refrain was that if you found a good minder it was fine, but that you had to be careful:

A childminder, that's what I use at the moment. I did try and find some after school care but I couldn't find any. It's okay if you've got a minder that you think is quite capable and who you can trust to look after your children ... My cousin had one and she didn't look after her child. She'd go and pick up her child, that child used to be dirty ... But child care, there's just no provision. Good after school clubs would make life a lot easier.   (Vivienne, an older African-Caribbean lone mother with full-time paid work)

Similar concerns were expressed about childminders (and, in fact, especially about registered childminders) by the White 'alternative' lone mothers in London, but in contrast they appeared to find it slightly easier to access nursery provision, which they preferred and trusted for the same reasons as the Black lone mothers. In contrast though, the Brighton lone mothers did appear to use the form of child care that they preferred and trusted – informal care.

The lack of formal day care provision in Britain means that, for the most part, British lone (and other) mothers tend to rely on family and other local support networks for child care (Bradshaw and Millar 1991; Ford 1996; Popay and Jones 1990; Thomson 1996). However, this is not only because of the lack of formal day care provision – it is also a matter of preference. Yet different notions of what constitutes acceptable and trustworthy child care has not been explored in terms of systematic differences between particular social groups of lone mothers.

Like many other lone mothers, the interviewees in this study received child care support from within their social networks. This was most often on an occasional basis to allow them to go out in the evening or away for a weekend, or simply to give them a break from practical responsibility for their children. However, in some cases this care took place on a regular basis and enabled the lone mother to take up paid work or study. Overall, lone mothers in the younger and older African-Caribbean groups tended to turn to female family members and their children's fathers for child care, but also some female friends, as did the White working class group. In contrast the White Brighton 'alternative' group mainly turned to female friends. However, these patterns did not always simply reflect the type of regular child care they would have chosen to use if they could.

All three of the Black groups of lone mothers said that they would rather use formal day care services for regular care – even those who were reliant on the care provided by family members, friends and children's fathers to enable them to work. For example, Kim, who worked long part-time hours and who relied on her youngest child's father and other family members to care for her children, said:

> I use the play centre for my oldest child, about three days a week and my niece after she's finished school, and sometimes my sister if she's not working will help out. I prefer the centre cos she needs stability in her life and to mix with other children outside the home … I would prefer something for the youngest like a playgroup or

nursery, but I need flexibility cos of my hours and you've still got to pay to keep that space open for your child.

The White suburban lone mothers felt that they would rather have a nanny or au pair for regular use, even in the two cases where, respectively, care by a family member and a friend allowed the mothers to work or study:

> If I could have it as I wanted it, without thinking about my daughter, I'd have a live out nanny, like my friend Dee. I wouldn't have any peace if she went to a childminder, I want one to one care. If I could employ a nanny I wouldn't have to compromise ... I don't trust babysitters and you can't tell friends to do things exactly how you want them!   (Jessie)

In contrast, the White Brighton 'alternative' lone mothers mainly used child care from female friends, and preferred that source:

> Child care for me is doing swaps with people, and the kids have their father and I have my mum. So that sort of child care's okay ... Mainly people that I know that have to have child care, they organise it themselves. They pay a friend or something. That way you don't have problems, your child can be with their friends.   (Kay)

In the case of four of these lone mothers, this preferred type of care (which for two was combined with care by family members) allowed them to undertake paid work.

The White working class lone mothers similarly preferred informal sources of care but, in distinction, family members as opposed to friends were often prioritised:

> I'd trust all my family with the kids, but not friends. They wouldn't do anything that would like upset me or – they know what I want sort of thing, and they would like stick to that. They wouldn't go off and do something with my kids if I told them not to. Like if I said don't take them out somewhere, they wouldn't go ahead and do it without my permission. They just all care and just love them anyway. We're a really close family anyway. Friends and that have got different ideas on some things, but whereas like all the family

like have all got the same sort of views on like different things. We all share the same views on things. (Lynn)

Marilyn Porter (1982) and Erica Wimbush (1986) found a similar preference for care from kin amongst similar groups of White working class mothers living in areas of Manchester and Edinburgh respectively. As for Lynn above, this preference and trust was often related to these White working class mothers' conceptions of what good mothers should do (an issue we examine in the next chapter).

There is a complex variation of local day care provision, use and preferences among the groups of British lone mothers. There is certainly no overall consensus about child care across the groups as a whole, but certain patterns have emerged. To simplify, there is a preference for, and trust in, formal day care provision by the interviewees in Lambeth and Southwark, but a tendency to prefer and trust informal care by the Brighton interviewee groups. These preferences occur in the context whereby there are proportionately more lone mothers in Lambeth and Southwark than in Brighton and Hove, where proportionately more lone mothers in Brighton and Hove have paid work, but proportionately more lone mothers in Lambeth and Southwark have full-time paid work. While access to child care may provide a constraint to lone mothers' employment in an absolute sense – they will be unable to work if they cannot find day care of some sort, this is not how care provision affects the take up of paid work in practice. Rather, lone mothers evaluate the suitability of different forms of care and, as the interviews showed, these preferences are underlain by moral ideas about what is best for children – an issue to which we will return in the next chapter

This conclusion implies that even if, in Britain, formal day care was to be made widely accessible, as recommended in much of the social policy literature, this might not significantly extend lone mothers' uptake of paid work. (A conclusion supported by the results of econometric studies; see Chapter 8.) What of the comparative situation in other countries, therefore, where often state day care is more widely available? At first sight it appears that those European countries with high levels of day care provision do usually have high levels of lone mother employment – Denmark, France and Sweden are often cited as examples. However, some countries show high levels of lone mother employment with low state provision (e.g. Austria) or vice versa (e.g. Belgium). It is also not clear which is chicken and which is egg. Paid work by mothers (including lone mothers) may simply

reflect different cultural attitudes about what women and men do –
maybe we should call this social capital – and the provision of day care
follows after. We discuss these issues more comprehensively in
Chapter 7. In this chapter we will describe how the interviewees in
Germany, Sweden and the USA – type case examples of different
welfare state regimes with different types of day care systems –
actually perceived and used these different systems.

In the USA, as in Britain, both federal and state governments have
rejected comprehensive publicly funded day care provision. None the
less there is some public provision, in particular areas, as a means of
tackling poverty and getting lone mothers off welfare and into paid
work. Thus overall there is a varied mix of public and voluntary sector
provision, as in Britain, but also a significant amount of private sector
franchised chain provision. Class and ethnic divisions in the use of different forms of provision are marked (Ginsburg 1992). In Cleveland
day care provision has grown in recent years – a mix funded by government and the voluntary sector. However, there are still places for
only 16 per cent of under sixes in the area. Several day care centres
provide early education programmes that attempt to boost disadvantaged children's educational and social development and thus their
future human, and maybe social, capital. The neighbourhoods of
Detroit-Shoreway, Ohio City and Tremont, in which the interviewed
group of young, mainly White lone mothers lived, each have several
day care centres and some run such programmes. Indeed, six of the
lone mothers were studying for a General Equivalency Diploma
(GED), equivalent to graduating from high (secondary) school, at a
local centre that also provided day care. However, only three of them
actually used the centre day care, the others relying on care by a
mother, a friend and a childminder respectively. The one lone mother
in this group who had paid work (full-time) relied on care by the
female cousin she lived with. Ideal preferences for regular day care
were also quite diverse amongst this group, however, ranging across
family members, nurseries, and nannies or au pairs. The lone mothers
who could have used the day care at the centre where they were studying, but did not, were among those who preferred informal care or
care in their own homes by nannies.

In former west Germany, national government has also taken no
direct responsibility for day care, and provision is similarly patchy and
uneven. Day care also functions more as a support for home-based
motherhood rather than being intended as a support for employed
mothers. Most provision is part-time and lunch is not provided. In the

former GDR, in contrast, significant levels of public day and outside school care supported (previously) high levels of mothers in employment, but since reunification in 1989 this is now collapsing. However Kreuzberg, despite its location in former west Berlin, is relatively well served with community organised nurseries (although not all offer full-time care) organised and supported by parents. These were used by two of the lone mothers to enable them to work long part-time (22–30 hours per week), one for minimal part-time (under 15 hours per week), and by another to study full-time. Of the remainder with paid work or full-time study, three combined school attendance with care by a childminder, and another worked long part-time hours during the school day. None of these mothers used informal child care to enable employment. Most said they preferred and trusted nursery care – although a couple stressed that they would prefer services that did not involve the sort of parental input required by the community nurseries.

In stark contrast, Sweden strongly promotes investment in public day care provision, both in nurseries and with registered childminders, with the current aim of providing a place for all pre-school children over 18 months. Day care can cover the whole working day and includes lunch and often other meals (sometimes night care is available). The responsibility for providing day care places rests with local government and thus there are still geographical variations in the extent of availability of day care (Dahlström 1993), as well as overlapping social class differentials in uptake (Broberg and Hwang 1991; Lewis and Aström 1992). However, lone mothers often have a preference in gaining day care places. Partille, and Björndammen within it, has good provision of nursery places and municipally salaried childminders. Indeed, purpose built nurseries were erected alongside the flats in the neighbourhood when they were built. Seven of the group of White lone mothers living in Björndammen were in employment, and one was studying full-time. Four of these used a local authority nursery to enable them to work full-time; two worked long part-time and used a local authority and voluntary sector nursery respectively; one used a local authority nursery to work part-time; and another used the nursery at the college where she was studying. Thus none of this group had to rely on their social networks for regular child care, and formal sources of day care provision were the most preferred and trusted.

The patterns of child care use and preference for the US, German and Swedish groups of lone mothers provide another indication of the complexity of the relationship between day care provision and the uptake of paid work. The understandings of particular social groups of lone mothers are a crucial meditating factor. In the Near West Side public services were provided for particular welfare-dependent groups, but they were not always taken up where potential users preferred and trusted other informal or home-based forms of child care. In Kreuzberg the form of local provision matched quite well with the use and preferences of the lone mothers, apparently because it was community organised (although some disliked the amount of parental involvement required). Finally, in Björndammen, there appears to be a good match between public day care provision and the use of, and preference for, formal day care (at least amongst the majority who wanted child care for their children – see Chapter 4). What are the lessons of this for British child care initiatives to enable more lone mothers to take up paid work?

Child Care: Building on Social Capital?

The preceding discussion of the use of, and preferences for, different sorts of child care indicates that the provision of day care services to enable British lone mothers to take up paid work, as advocated within the social problem discourse on lone motherhood (see the previous chapter), is a more complex issue than has often been recognised. British lone mothers did not simply want more child care – rather it was the type of care, and the sorts of people who would be looking after their children, that was crucial and this varied by social group. The same seems to be true for the German, Swedish and US lone mothers, despite quite widely varying levels of provision. This was related to their views and values about childrearing and the needs of their children (an issue we return to in the next chapter). Hence their evaluation of different sorts of care – and the trust they placed in different types of carer – also varied. Institutionalised responses to day care provision need to be creative to accommodate these differences if lone mothers are to be enabled to take up employment comfortably, rather than feel constrained to use services they do not believe are in the best interests of their children. In the latter case, of course, they may well prefer not to use what they see as unsuitable day care at all.

From a social capital perspective, a more creative and socially sensitive institutionalised child care response should build on the resources available within particular social groups and neighbourhoods. Thus, while the Black lone mothers in Lambeth and Southwark would especially welcome expansion of formal day care services, the White alternative lone mothers living in Hanover, Brighton, would find institutional support for already existing child care swops amongst friends more acceptable. Similarly, in Moulsecoomb in Brighton, projects to support care by family members, especially lone mothers' own mothers, would probably be more acceptable if lone mothers were to feel comfortable in delegating their responsibility for their children to others. Furthermore, if care by friends and family members is to be supported institutionally in Britain, it would help if the child care disregard on Family Credit (an in-work benefit) was extended to cover such informal care, rather than being available only for formal provision, as currently.

There is also some evidence from our interviews that teenage children (usually daughters but sometimes nieces) provide crucial child care support, before and after school, for working lone mothers with younger children. This is a 'variable' in lone mothers' uptake of paid work that has received little attention. Again, projects might be set up to support older children caring for younger siblings, or to widen involvement in child care support more generally to young people in an area. Indeed, on the latter scenario, some aspects of the current 'new deal' strategies for training unemployed young people as day care assistants – particularly young women – might be seen as just such a move. However, it remains unlikely that young people in general (as opposed to particular, trusted family members) would be seen as suitable carers by most mothers.

Moreover, there are problems with building on available social capital in this way. First is the problem of the supply of labour for informal child care. In Britain, during the 1950s and 1960s, a higher percentage of lone mothers were in paid work than currently. This was partly because many lone mothers, particularly those who were working-class and unmarried, lived in their own parents' homes, where their own mothers provided the child care that enabled them to work (Land 1994; Land and Lewis 1997). This arrangement followed traditional familial moral obligations. However, this situation no longer prevails. Lone mothers are unlikely to live with their parents and, moreover, their own mothers are now far more likely to be in paid work themselves and/or do not wish to undertake such caring (Brannen and Moss 1991; Cotterill 1994). Certainly, few of the lone mother interviewees in this study lived with their parents or other family members, and none of those few who did utilised this as a child care resource enabling them to take up paid work. It might be argued that employment rates for lone mothers' own mothers is also likely to vary by neighbourhood and social group, just as it does for the lone mothers themselves, and that where this is so initiatives could support the use of grandmother's labour for child care. Moulsecoomb is one example where both lone mothers and their mothers were largely without paid work. However, as Katarina Thomas (1996) suggests, the supply of family, kin and friends as a source of informal child care is not inexhaustible and may have already reached saturation point. Those family members and friends able and prepared to offer child care so that lone mothers may work probably already do so.

Secondly is the problem of the moral terms on which informal labour is provided. Even if family and friends are in a position to offer child care support, they may not be prepared to do so. This is because informal child care is located within moral frameworks about what are the 'right' circumstances in which to offer help with, or accept requests for, child care. Bill Jordan and colleagues' (1992) study of employment decisions by low income families (both couples and lone mothers) shows well the importance of complying with local network systems of values. Lone mothers on the largely White, deprived public housing estate studied held a stronger desire for paid work than part-nered mothers, but they were constrained in following this desire through into action in the face of a strong neighbourhood belief that mothers should prioritise caring for their own children and only 'fit in' paid work around this moral priority. Child care and other infor-mal support could be withdrawn if mothers transgressed these local norms. Similarly, Erica Wimbush (1986) has shown that the provision of support, including child care, can mean influence by the giver over other aspects of the recipient's lifestyle (an issue for some of our lone mothers – see Chapter 4). As Margaret Levi (1996) notes, social capital can also have a stultifying and dark side (see Chapter 8).

Thirdly, the promotion of informal child care has implications for gender and class inequality Building on informal social capital to provide child care and so enable lone mothers to take up employment is in fact predicated on the availability of a pool of women. Indeed, other than where children's fathers are involved in child care, it is overwhelmingly women – as family members, friends and older sib-lings – whom lone mothers rely on for informal child care. Any institu-tionalised moves to build on this form of available social capital will further 'naturalise' and reinforce the notion that it is women who take on the task of caregiving – the very reason why there are many more lone mothers than there are lone fathers in the first place. It is also likely that social class inequalities will become further entrenched, with working class women much more likely to take up low paid child care work.

This discussion implies that even if state investment and support for formal day care is the best option, especially if existing social inequalities are not to be further entrenched, this cannot be accomplished in a merely resource based, compartmentalised fashion. Attention needs to be paid to the variable context into which such services are to be introduced. This context includes different ideas about what is morally right and good for children. In neighbourhoods and amongst social groups where this is seen to be care by (female) family members or friends, formal day care services are unlikely to be taken up to any great extent – unless effort is put into demonstrating that day care is in children's best social and educational interests, rather than focusing on day care merely as a means of enabling (or forcing) lone mothers to take up paid work. This vital distinction is currently not a major feature in British policy development. Nevertheless, moral notions concerning children's best interests is in fact a crucial issue in understanding lone mothers' uptake of paid work, and we will examine this in detail in the next chapter.

3.5   LONE MOTHERS AND SOCIAL NETWORKS

As became evident in the discussion of lone mothers' child care support in the last section, their social networks are an important means through which social capital is in fact accessed and distributed. First, social networks are potential sources of material resources, and not only with regard to informal child care. For example, relatives and friends can offer short term accommodation (Holme 1985; Pahl 1985), and can provide financial and in kind help (Middleton and Ashworth 1997). Social networks are also significant in providing information about access to resources. For example, they have been found to play an important role in British mothers' search for job and day care (Brannen and Moss 1991; Callender 1987; Morris and Llewellyn 1991).

Secondly, however, social networks are significant in lone mothers' (and other people's) lives in a more ideological way. They imply people in groups; groups that define experiences and situations communally as well as individually. They give people a sense of identity and belonging.[5] As webs of social ties and relationships in which lone mothers (and others) are embedded, networks are the primary social environments in which perceptions and identities are constituted and negotiated. They are normative and moral, as well as material, features of the social landscape. As we noted in Chapter 1, it is these sorts of issues around identities, beliefs and network groupings that have been taken up by social theorists. There is also empirical evidence of the link between social networks and identities, as Linda Bell and Jane Ribbens (1994) show for mothers' networks within a particular locality. Thus, members of social networks can share beliefs and assumptions about what is right and wrong in particular contexts – including the uptake of paid work. This was evident in our critique of social capital and child care, when we discussed how informal child care support may be refused or withdrawn if local norms about what motherhood constitutes are transgressed.

A few studies have picked up these issues in addressing lone. mothers' uptake of paid work (see Cochran et al. 1990, Allan 1996). From this body of work we can draw two, linked lessons. On the one hand, lone mothers with close-knit, largely kin-based networks tend to hold 'traditional' views about the relationship between motherhood and paid work, supported by those networks. This type of network is mostly found amongst working class people. On the other hand, lone mothers with loose-knit, largely friendship-based networks tend to hold less traditional attitudes, and those networks support lone mothers taking up paid work. This type of network is largely to be found amongst middle class people. We will follow up this line of argument empirically in the rest of this section by examining the nature of the social networks for the interviewee groups of lone mothers, and assessing how these fit with their uptake of paid work.[6]

The lone mothers in our study placed considerable value on their social networks – at least those amongst them whom they considered supportive. Their networks were important to them as sources of support or of constraint, both practically and emotionally, most often (but not only) rooted in the neighbourhoods in which they lived. The composition of their networks, in terms of ethnicity, class, family form, economic status and so on, thus reflected the local neighbourhood social structures discussed in section 3.2 . They could also be a consequence of an individual lone mother's active search for 'like-minded' people, and thus also for the 'right' sort of neighbourhood for her. As we noted in Chapter 1, it is this grouping together of like-minded individuals that preoccupies commentators on our (post)modern times. It is also such groupings that are of interest to social capital theorists.

However, some of our groups of lone mothers were able to exercise more choice than others in where they lived, and thus how embedded they became in local social networks. Similarly, these social networks are not alike either in their nature or effects.

Working Class Groups

While immediate family members or other relatives were regarded as significant in their daily lives as lone mothers by women from all the social groups and neighbourhoods studied (as they are generally, see McGlone et al. 1996), this was particularly the case – as the literature suggests – for the working class groups. A few lone mothers even had family members living in their household or they lived in theirs, but despite the importance of family such household sharing remained rare.

Both the younger and older African-Caribbean groups in Lambeth and Southwark referred to their mothers, sisters and brothers as most important to them, along with the father/s of their child/ren:

[Important people] would be Donna, my eldest daughter, she's grown up now, and Dianne's [youngest daughter] father. And my aunt and her two children. And my brother, I see him quite often. (Ella, an older African-Caribbean lone mother)

Family members were spoken of in a positive way, in terms of practical, financial and emotional support. However, although some of the lone mothers felt their children's fathers also provided positive support, others felt that their involvement was important in an essentially negative sense, in that it was undermining or interfering.

The west African lone mothers in Southwark mainly referred to cousins and aunts as important in their lives rather than parents or siblings (perhaps as a result of more recent migration), but a few felt that no one was there for them as an important source of support. None referred to positive or negative involvement from the father/s of their child/ren as significant in their lives, although most felt that there was little in the way of anything from them at all.

The emphasis on family and relatives by all three Black groups, though, has to be placed in the context of wider networks which were friendship as well as family based. Within these wider networks, the young African-Caribbean lone mothers tended to mix more with other lone mothers, including as members of their families, than did the older African-Caribbean and west African groups. (As we saw earlier, there were relatively more lone mothers in the younger African-Caribbean group's neighbourhood than was the case for the other two Black groups.) Two of the younger African-Caribbean lone mothers' networks were particularly extensive in consisting of all the congregation of the church they attended, and whom they referred to as 'like a family'. The social networks of all three Black groups overwhelmingly contained people of the same ethnicity as themselves, although the older African-Caribbean lone mothers tended more to include some White people (again relating to the social characteristics of the neighbourhoods in which they lived). Ethnic homogeneity was a feature of all the other, White, groups of lone mothers too, with some exceptions amongst the 'alternative' lone mothers in London and Berlin.

The White working class lone mothers in Moulsecoomb also considered mothers, fathers, sisters and brothers as important in their lives, in providing them with practical, financial and emotional support, although a few also mentioned friends in this respect. For some, their wider networks were also strongly family based, but more often they contained both family and friends. Reflecting the social characteristics of the peripheral estate on which they lived, most mixed with both lone mothers (including as family members) as well as partnered mothers. Like the group of west African lone mothers, their children's fathers were usually not mentioned as playing either a positive or negative role in their lives, and most felt there was little from them at all.

The group of, mainly White, young working class lone mothers in Near West Side, Cleveland, like their White working class counterparts in Britain, spoke of family members (particularly mothers and sisters and brothers) as the most important sources of support in their daily lives. Three lived with family members (including the only two Hispanic women in this group). Unlike their British White counterparts however, this group of lone mothers tended to include the father/s of their child/ren as significant, although whether this was regarded in a positive or negative light varied. Their wider networks mainly comprised both family and friends, and (reflecting the social composition of the neighbourhood in which they lived) included a lot of other lone mothers, both as friends and family. Despite the diverse ethnic mix of the area in which they lived, this group's networks tended to comprise others of the same ethnicity to themselves – only the two who were of Hispanic origin, and those who had children with Hispanic fathers, having mixed ethnic networks. This group's networks could be said to be marginally less female based than in Moulescoomb.

Middle Class Groups

As the literature predicts, the White 'alternative' lone mothers in Hanover, Brighton, who were overwhelmingly middle class, referred to friends as significant in their lives. However, they also regarded family members (mostly their mothers), as well as the father/s of their child/ren (again with the latter as mainly unsupportive or interfering) as equally important in their lives:

> Their father [is important]. He lives in Hampshire. He has them every other weekend, they go there. I suppose my general circle of friends, I've got a lot of support through friends. My mother and step-father, they live just outside Brighton, and my sister who lives in Brighton. (Sandra)

For all this group their wider networks were friendship based, and, like the younger African-Caribbean lone mothers, the composition of their networks reflected the high proportion of lone mothers locally (including lone mothers amongst their family members for some), although many had partnered friends as well.

The group of White 'alternative' lone mothers in Lambeth and Southwark were a mixed group in terms of social class. As expected from the literature, family – largely mothers and sisters – were referred to as of chief importance by the working class women, while the middle class women cited female friends as significant (two having friends living with them as lodgers). The father/s of their child/ren were also seen as significant, although largely in the negative sense as unsupportive and interfering. Nevertheless, all the 'alternative' London lone mothers had a friendship base to their wider networks, which for several included Black people, especially those who had children with Black fathers. There were also class differences in the family forms of this group's networks, with the middle class women tending to mix more with other lone mothers as friends than other groups.

The White 'alternative' lone mothers in Kreuzberg, Berlin shared a stress on female friends as important in their lives with their middle class 'alternative' British counterparts in London and Brighton (and, again, two had friends living with them as lodgers). Like the London group, they were less likely to refer to family members as significant compared with the Brighton group. Their wider social networks were also mainly friendship based and contained lots of other lone mothers.

They mainly mixed with other White people, although a couple numbered people of Turkish origin amongst their friends (reflecting the ethnic composition of their neighbourhood). This group of lone mothers rarely mentioned the father/s of their child/ren as important in their daily lives.

Unlike the 'alternative' middle class lone mothers, the White suburban, largely middle class, group in Patcham and Westdene referred to their family, especially their mothers, as significant in their lives. However, there were two who (like the west African lone mothers) felt that no one was important to them in this way:

> There's no one. Well, I've got my niece, she pops in, not that often. She's not really here. (Patsy)

The reasons for this can be inferred from our previous discussion here and in Chapter 2. These include their own negative feelings about their lone motherhood and the predominance of a social threat view of lone motherhood locally, both sets of views situated within the context of a relative paucity of lone mothers in their neighbourhood (see also Brayfield 1998). These lone mothers' wider networks were most often a mix of family and friends, and overwhelmingly partnered. In contrast the mainly middle class group of White lone mothers in Björndammen outside Göteborg stressed that family members (mainly mothers, fathers and sisters) were most important in their daily lives. This is in distinction to suggestions that Swedish mothers networks are loose knit and friendship based (Cochran et al. 1990). These lone mothers overwhelmingly mixed with others of the same ethnicity, and had lots of lone mothers in their networks, including as family members. As we have said, the role of fathers is an issue of public concern in Sweden (including for our Swedish researchers), and the lone mothers also saw them as significant in their lives – overwhelmingly in a positive sense.

Social Network Composition and Uptake of Paid Work

Overall then, the interviewee lone mothers' social networks could be said to conform to the dominant theme of the social network literature, in particular with the working class lone mothers, whether White or Black or holding 'alternative' views, more likely to see family as significant in their lives. However, not all the middle class lone mothers were more likely to see their friendships as most important.

While this was the case for the middle class members of the White 'alternative' lone mothers in London and Berlin, the White 'alternative' group in Brighton tended to refer to a mix of family and friends, as did the Björndammen group, while the White suburban lone mothers in Brighton, if they regarded anyone as significant, also referred to family members. In addition, if we also consider the lone mothers' wider networks, the conventional distinctions tend to break down even further.

Furthermore, our study also challenges aspects of the literature linking social network composition and lone mothers' uptake of paid work. This is especially the case if we look at ethnicity. As we stated in chapter one, Black lone mothers generally are far more likely to be in employment, and to work full-time, than lone mothers from other ethnic groups. While we have no way of assessing the composition of the networks of Black lone mothers as a whole, our own groups – all largely working class – tended to be embedded in mainly kin-based networks. This sort of network is supposed to support 'traditional' views about the relationship between motherhood and paid work, but this clearly did not hold for the members of these groups who had either full-time or 'long' part-time paid work, or who were studying full-time (six women altogether). In other words these lone mothers were not just 'fitting in' paid work or study as the literature suggests. Similarly, the young lone mothers in Near West Side in Cleveland, despite their 'traditional' family based social networks, were mostly studying full-time in an effort to place themselves better in the labour market (although only one was in full-time paid work), while the family-based networks of the Björndammen mothers also co-existed with the majority in paid work. Nor did the largely female based networks of the Kreuzberg lone mothers seem to support notions of traditional motherhood, as suggested by Cochran and colleagues (1990), in that six were working long part-time or full-time hours and two were studying full-time. In contrast, although the White working class group of lone mothers in Brighton also tended to be supported by close-knit kin-based networks, none were in full or long part-time employment, and they did seem to adhere to more traditional patterns of motherhood.

Not only is there considerable current deviation from the supposed class-based general relationship between lone mothers' social networks and their uptake of paid work, but if we look back in time in Britain we find a reversed picture. As we noted earlier, during the 1950s to early 1970s the majority of lone mothers were in paid work, many full-time, but they were also closely embedded in kin-based social networks. Most lived with their own mothers who also provided the child care that enabled them to work – a situation, as we have said, that no longer exists. Of course, at that time, lone mothers made up a far smaller percentage of families with dependent children, and lone motherhood as a status carried far greater stigma. Mothers who had children out of wedlock especially were in a marginalised position that placed them outside the dominant norms of 'good' motherhood, focused around the norm of being a full-time homemaker. Married mothers largely did not take up paid work – a reason why lone mothers' own mothers were available to provide child care. Thus, compounding the stigma of being a lone mother with the transgression of being a working mother was a small step, perhaps even a price to pay. Importantly, it was a step that was obviously supported by those in the lone mothers' close knit social networks, as evidenced by their mothers' provision of child care. As lone mothers have become an increasing proportion of the population, and as the situation has become one that 'normal' mothers may face (especially given the rise in separation and divorce), they too have become subject to dominant understandings of mothers and their role – now incorporating part-time paid work (albeit with lone mothers still feeling varying senses of stigma, as we saw in Chapter 2).

Some of the work on lone mothers' social networks suggests that these vary between national contexts, in part influenced by state welfare regime conceptions of the roles of mothers and concomitant social provision (see Chapter 6). On the basis of case studies in particular cities in the same four countries we are examining in this study, Cochran and colleagues (1990), for example, suggest that British and German mothers as a whole tend to have more female-based networks supporting a 'traditional' mothering role (with the respective welfare regimes also organised around ideas of mothers as homemakers). In contrast, the networks of mothers in Sweden and the US tend to be more diverse in terms of gender, supportive of the uptake of paid work, and with the former being more friendship-based (with the welfare regime in Sweden – but not the USA – also supporting paid work). There is a danger here of assuming homogeneity within a national context. Certainly, we found that this picture did not hold for the varied groups of lone mothers we studied.

Thus, the relationship between lone mothers' social networks and their uptake of paid work is neither simply class-based nor static, and this is particularly clear if both ethnicity and the longer term historical

record are considered. We go on to examine the processes that underlie these differences in the next chapter.

3.6 CONCLUSION

In this chapter we have explored the variable amount and nature of
social capital available to lone mothers – their lives within particular
neighbourhoods, interacting with kin and friends in social networks,
and the availability of particular formal and informal resources. In
section 3.2 we detailed the characteristics of the neighbourhoods in
which our groups of lone mothers lived, including the distribution of
lone mothers, and the extent to which the lone mothers felt that they
'fitted in' locally, particularly in relation to their status as lone mothers
but also related to issues of social class and ethnicity. These are
important considerations in understanding the mechanisms of social
capital in terms of its links to material conditions and economic development. For example, the materially affluent suburban area of
Patcham and Westdene in Brighton, in fact seemed to offer lone
mothers low access to social capital. This was perhaps because they
were marginalised, as a stigmatised group, from what social capital
existed locally, however high its stocks may have been. In contrast, on
inner city and peripheral public housing estates, such as in Brixton,
London and Moulsecoomb, Brighton, social capital may be quite high
for lone mothers in terms of embeddedness in social networks, but
material deprivation is still widespread and offsets this. Here, local
social capital would appear to be in the wrong currency, at least in
terms of converting it to economic capital. It is more in the gentrifying
areas of Hanover and Kreuzberg that higher levels of social capital
seems to give better access to material resources.

We also examined the employment rates for lone mothers in our
British case study areas, in section 3.3. We demonstrated that there is
a significant anomaly whereby there are higher rates of full-time
employment amongst lone mothers in areas with lower human capital.
How does this link with social capital theories? Interestingly, some
social capital advocates associate mothers' increased movement into
the workforce with declining stocks of social capital, because it means
they supposedly have less time available for their own civic engagement, or for supporting that of their husbands (for example, Putman
1993b; and see Levi 1996 for a critique). Yet, as we saw in section 3.4,
in Britain at least, lone mothers largely need to have access to social

capital in the form of informal child care support from (female) kin and friends. This is not only because successive British governments have played a minimal role in directly developing formal day care provision to support employed parents, but also because some groups of lone mothers trust informal rather than formal child care sources (where theorists have identified 'trust' as an essential component of social capital). From a social capital perspective, such informal network resources should be fostered and developed. However, we argued that there are several problems inherent in this. The supply of informal child care may have already reached its optimal level, especially where more women are entering the labour market, and where preparedness to provide support is located within moral frameworks about what is the 'right' course of action for mothers. Furthermore, building on social capital can also mean building on social divisions and inequalities, in that it is overwhelmingly women who are trusted and relied on as carers.

In section 3.5 we moved on to consider other aspects of lone mothers' networks as social capital facilitating employment. Contrary to suggestions in the literature, the nature of these networks were not easily associated within simple and clear-cut class, kin/friendship or gender divisions. Rather, the social processes and mechanisms underpinning the relationship between social capital and lone mothers' uptake of paid work require unpacking. These processes and mechanisms, as we have indicated at various points throughout this chapter, comprise distinctly moral understandings about the 'right' courses of action to take. This unpacking is the concern of the next chapter.

NOTES

1. Ethnicity as self-defined in the 1991 Census. The 'African-Caribbean/Black' category includes both those counted as 'Black other' in the census, mostly of African-Caribbean or mixed White/African-Caribbean descent, but with several other miscellaneous groups included. 'Black Africans' are mostly west African.
2. Housing associations provide a form of social rented housing, but are outside local authority control. Quite often the rents they charge are higher than those for public, local authority, housing.
3. Exact figures are not available for Kreuzberg, but births to single, never-married, mothers amount to as many as 30 per cent of all births in 1995 – the highest rate of any district in former west Berlin (but far lower than rates former East Berlin which run from a 'low' of 40 per cent to a high of 53 per cent).

4. Correlation coefficients between the full-time employment rate and tenure variables (per cent owner-occupation, per cent private renting, per cent social housing) and for per cent no car were all in the 20 per cent range. For Lambeth and Southwark the coefficient for per cent Black lone mother was slightly higher.

5. See Allan 1996, Bagnell et al. 1997, Cochran et al. 1990 for reviews of the literature on social networks and the different theoretical perspectives within it.

6. We do not present here a detailed analysis of these networks in terms of size, density, duration, frequency, spatial distance, multiplexy, density, role composition etc.

4 Lone Mothers and Gendered Moral Rationalities: Orientations to Paid Work

4.1 INTRODUCTION

The neighbourhoods and social networks we examined in the previous chapter have been described as 'mesosystems' – it is these that link individual agency with social structures and institutions (see Cochran et al. 1990 for the relationship between the three levels). The relationship between structure and agency also features in debates about lone motherhood. The essential question here is the extent to which lone mothers create and make sense of their own lives within constraints that they have little or no power to alter.

Scott Lash, for example, has questioned the thesis advanced within the 'lifestyle' discourse (see Chapter 2), that individuals are increasingly and purposively exercising agency and breaking free from tradition and structure, by reference to a particular group of lone mothers:

> Just how reflexive is it possible for a single mother in an urban ghetto to be? ... just how much freedom from the 'necessity' of 'structure' and structural poverty does this ghetto mother have to construct her own 'life narratives'?   (Lash 1994, p. 120)

'Urban ghetto' lone mothers also feature in new right and some communitarian 'underclass' discussions, but in contrast they are now seen as agents who actively create their own marginalisation, and promote and perpetuate deviant norms and values. Those who have sought to defend lone mothers in the public debates we referred to in Chapter 2 have largely framed their responses within the 'social problem' discourse on lone motherhood, posing them as victims of external material constraints. Like Lash, they position lone mothers as without agency in order to emphasise structural and economic issues. This strategy, however, has its critics. Kirk Mann and Sasha Roseneil

108

(1996) argue that Lash and others are 'implicitly suggest[ing] that agency is something reserved for the well-off and educated' (p. 207), and 'believe that there are women living in situations of structural poverty who exercise agency' (p. 208).

Both sides of this 'structure–agency' debate can be seen to be correct at the same time, however. In other words, if we are to understand lone mothers' uptake of paid work, we need to look at both their agency and at the different structures and institutions that facilitate or constrain that agency. (And this is one of the overarching tasks of this book.) In this chapter we concentrate on lone mothers' own understandings and agency using interview information, examining how lone mothers socially negotiate understandings about their lives as mothers bringing up children without a male partner living with them, and about the extent to which mothering is compatible with paid work. This is complemented in the next chapter by an analysis of different lone mothers' employment positions using census sources. Subsequent chapters go on to address the social structural contexts of local labour markets and welfare states (Chapters 6 and 7).

Section 4.2 begins by examining social negotiations about motherhood and paid work, using the example of three lone mothers living within the context of particular neighbourhoods, and who interact with kin and friends in specific social networks. Drawing on these cases, and on data from the other British interviewees, section 4.3 goes on to develop a model of 'ideal types' of mother and/or worker values and orientations. We term these 'gendered moral rationalities'. We show how these gendered moral rationalities, in being socially negotiated, vary systematically amongst the different social groups of lone mothers. As a consequence we take issue with the model of individualistic economic rationalising that is a feature, implicitly or explicitly, of much mainstream research on lone mothers' employment. Rather, we show that lone mothers' agency in deciding whether or not to take up paid work is essentially concerned with what is best and morally right for themselves as mothers and for their children. Finally, in section 4.4 we assess some possible counterarguments – that gendered moral rationalities are determined by the different policy practices of welfare state regimes, that expectations of repartnership (with an implicit economic rationale of financial support or exchange) provide an explanation for lone mothers' employment behaviour, and that gendered moral rationalities merely provide post-hoc justifications for lone mothers' current employment position.

4.2 NEGOTIATING MOTHERHOOD AND PAID WORK: THREE EXAMPLES

In this section we detail the cases of three British lone mothers, each from a different social group and neighbourhood, and examine the processes involved in their respective social negotiations concerning the relationship between motherhood and paid work. Examining individual cases in some depth allows us to present the holistic character of the lone mothers' lives, to illustrate concrete aspects of the interaction between lone mothers' social networks and their understandings about motherhood and paid work, and to give due weight to their agency – as against concentrating on the institutional framework within which they are operating or simply reducing their lives to predetermined atomistic variables.

Sylvia – a White Working Class Lone Mother Living in Moulsecoomb, Brighton

Sylvia is 24 years old and has two children aged 2 and 3. She has been living on the public housing estate of Moulsecoomb, on the periphery of Brighton (see Figure 3.1), for just under two years. Her views on the estate's reputation as 'a shit area' were quoted in the previous chapter. Shortly after the family moved to the neighbourhood, her boyfriend (her term) left her and their children. Sylvia counterposes her situation with the social threat discourse on lone motherhood that she feels is the dominant view in society generally, but at the same time as she challenges this view of herself, she nevertheless confirms its depiction of feckless men:

> They think some of them [lone mothers] bring it on themselves, they just get pregnant just to get somewhere, just to get a flat and get moved out of home. But I mean I was living – I wasn't married to the bloke. He was just too selfish and wanted to be on his own. And I got stuck with the kids.

Despite enjoying no longer having to always prepare and cook evening meals, as her boyfriend had expected, Sylvia largely finds lone motherhood a negative experience:

> I'm on my own. I wish I wasn't, but I am. I'm a one parent ... I'd rather be living with a bloke or married to one than be like this. It's

lonely at night, you know what I mean. You're on your own and all you've got is the bloody telly. It is pretty lonely.

Sylvia's social networks are strongly family based. She knows that there are 'a lot' of other lone mothers locally, but says she does not mix much outside of her family because 'I'm a shy person'. She has little in the way of contact with her ex-boyfriend's family, but he usually comes to collect the children and take them out on Sundays. It is her own family who are significant in her life, especially her mother. Every day, Sylvia and the children go to visit her mother who, with one of Sylvia's sisters, lives on an adjoining small council estate. Her mother is a very important influence on how she thinks about her responsibilities to her children and the relationship between motherhood and paid work.

Sylvia left school with no qualifications, and before she had her children worked as a waitress. She said that she would like to return to paid work because, based on one of her sister's experiences, she thinks she would be better off if she took this course of action:

> I'd love to go out to work, I'd love to go back full-time … I think I'd be better off financially if I was working than I am now because I only get £68 a week on benefit. My sister gets £185 a week working in a nursing home and I think I could live off that.

There is, however, the problem of who would care for her children. Sylvia's preferred choice of child care would be one of her family but 'like my sister works, so she couldn't have them. And my other sister lives [outside Brighton] and she's got children of her own and she's married'. Sylvia cannot ask her mother, who is not working and would seem the ideal person, to look after the children because her mother strongly disapproves of mothers leaving their children and going out to work. What is more, in essence, Sylvia agrees with these views, although she regrets their extension to curtailment of her social life as well:

> My mum is a one parent and she thinks, like most old people, that if you have children you should be with them. You don't have children to bugger off and leave them with someone else is how she sees it. She didn't do it. Sometimes I agree with her. That's the idea, isn't it, of parenting, being with them, isn't it? Well I think it is. Like, you know, I would go to work and not see the kids all day and just see them in the evenings. But even when I ask her to babysit she

says she wasn't able to go out when she was in my position. I have to go by what my mum says otherwise there'd be an argument. She's good with the children but I'd have to argue with her to get her to agree to look after the kids while I worked.

Sylvia's mother's disapproval, and influence, even extended to the free respite care, by a childminder that Brighton social services had offered Sylvia for one night every month. This was in order to give her a break from her children and a chance to go out and socialise independently. Sylvia had initially taken up the offer but stopped after a few months, for:

My mum and the family didn't want me to do it. They said they'd rather help me out, which they have done. My mum said they go to complete strangers and come back little shits who play me up.

Thus, even though Sylvia would respond to a questionnaire by saying that she wanted paid work (like most British lone mothers – see Bradshaw and Millar 1991), if she actually pursued this course of action it would cause tremendous problems in her relationship with her mother, who is so important in her everyday life.[1] In effect, her mother sees the prospect of Sylvia taking up paid work as morally wrong. Sylvia herself, in balancing this view with her own desire for paid work, not only has to concur in order to avoid conflict with the most important adult in her daily life, but essentially agrees with her mother's moral view. For Sylvia, being a 'good' mother and being a worker are in conflict. This is despite the fact that becoming a worker would place her in a better financial position, and at the same time challenge what she sees as the unfair portrayal of lone mothers in the social threat discourse.

Fiona – a White 'Alternative' Lone Mother Living in Brixton, London

Fiona is 34 years old and has one child aged 6. For the past 14 years, she has lived in her owner-occupied flat on the edge of Brixton, in central Lambeth (see Figure 3.1). Fiona has had a female friend living with her as a lodger for the past six months, which she has found 'very helpful and supportive', but who is about to move out into her own flat. She likes Brixton for its 'sense of community', although she worries about her child's safety and will not let her play out in the street because of traffic and fear of child abduction. Fiona has a strong network of friends locally and has stayed in the area for this reason, but thinks that she might have to move in the future so as to be near a 'good' secondary school for her daughter. Fiona has no worries about being a lone mother, either for herself or her daughter, drawing on a mix of lifestyle and escaping patriarchy discourses to make sense of her situation:

> I've a great deal of pride in the fact that I'm coping, surviving and holding down a responsible job ... There is the possibility that I could get somebody, that I might live with another person, but I don't have to and I'm not willing to compromise ... Being a single parent isn't much different from being an ordinary parent. [My daughter] will grow up into an allright adult, but if she doesn't I don't think it would be cos I'm on my own.

Fiona and her husband separated just after the birth of their child: 'we both knew something had to happen even before she was born ... I made him leave, he didn't come up to my standards'. Her husband has moved away and she has little in the way of contact with him, and no support from him at all. For Fiona's daughter he largely exists as 'a sort of fantasy'.

Fiona is involved in a local voluntary organisation for parents and children. It is through this organisation that the network of friends who form the main source of her emotional and practical support was built. Her family lives far away in the north of the country. Most of Fiona's friends are 'professional women', like herself. Locally, Fiona feels lone motherhood is 'probably the norm, if not the norm it's probably around fifty per cent', and quite a few of her friends are also lone mothers:

> At first I felt very vulnerable and unusual, but once I'd been around for a while as a single mother – although each of them, in the beginning we were surprised to find each other. People seemed to think they were the only ones ... I know I tend to assume other people aren't single parents until I'm told.

It is through word of mouth amongst this network of friends that Fiona finds the childminders she has always used to enable her to work:

> I know I'm about to need a new childminder, I talk about it and – I don't think I've ever advertised for anybody yet, they've all been told to me. Somehow they've just come.

Fiona's current childminder, for example, is a friend of a friend's nanny. In this way, Fiona feels that she is able to find the right 'sort of person, the way they express their priorities'. She is, though, currently considering using an after school club, which the voluntary organisation she is involved in is trying to set up and run.

Fiona is a manager in the public sector and has never thought about not working: 'It was the natural order of things, it was what one does during the day. I've always thought people should work'. In contrast to Sylvia, Fiona's discussion of undertaking paid work is organised less around perceptions of her child's needs, other than for a good childminder, and more around her own need for independence:

I feel I'm much better off than living on benefits. Work gives me a structure to the day and I get a feeling of achievement from it. Yes, I enjoy the autonomy of working ... If I had the choice to work part-time? Not really. I mean I make sure that I take time off so that I can collect [my daughter] from school occasionally, and I always go to the school appointments and the school shows and all the rest of it. She never misses out.

Thus, Fiona's uptake of paid work is 'quite normal' in the context of her friendship network. Moreover, this network provides her with day care, not in a direct practical sense but in terms of information and introductions. For Fiona, being a 'good' mother is distinct from being a worker, and it is this separation of the two that allows her to feel that it is morally right and 'natural' to take up paid work, rather than the moral wrong it is for Sylvia.

Kim – a younger African-Caribbean Lone Mother Living in Brixton, Lambeth

Kim is 26 years old and has two children, aged 9 and just under one year. She has lived in inner-city Brixton for just over three years, having been rehoused by the local council from temporary homeless accommodation. She thinks that the large public housing estate she lives on 'is not too bad', especially with the tenants' association she is involved in, which is working 'to try to prevent crime and to try to make the estate a better place to live'. However, she feels there is a general lack of facilities for young children locally.

Kim's views on her lone motherhood were quoted in Chapter 2: she sees herself as supporting and taking care of her children, bringing them up in the best way she can, and believes that, if the parent's morals and discipline are good, one parent is just as good as two. For the most part, she enjoys being on her own with her children and doing what she wants 'without any hassles'. Kim's relationship with the father of her first child did not work out because 'we wanted to go different ways in life'. She feels bitter about his total lack of support. Her relationship with the father of her second child ran into difficulties just after the birth, and they parted, because 'he's not working so we argued about money, that he wasn't pulling his weight and providing what he should be providing'. Nevertheless, she maintains a good relationship with him and 'he does look out for his child'. Indeed, ironically and paradoxically, because he is unemployed he is able to provide Kim with the bulk of the child care she needs in order to work. Kim's family also help out with this. She has two sisters living just outside Brixton, and the sister she is particularly close to is married and has children, and is happy to provide child care outside her own part-time hours of work. This sister's eldest daughter also looks after Kim's children after she has finished school and during school holidays. Kim's other sister, also a lone mother, works full-time and so cannot help her out much in this particular way. Thus, the family core of Kim's social network support her uptake of paid work in a practical fashion. Neither they, nor her wider friendship networks (whom she does not turn to for child care), have ever said anything about her or other mothers working: 'I don't think they really mind what the next person wants to do'; and Kim reckons that most of the mothers she knows 'are out working, but some stay home with their children'.

Despite the child care support Kim receives from her ex-partner, niece and sister, she would prefer to use formal day care services. Her views on this were quoted in the previous chapter: she sees formal services as providing stability and social experiences for children. Her eldest child goes to an after school club three or four days a week, and Kim would prefer her youngest to be in a nursery. However, the weekly variation in the hours of her current hourly paid job, and hence in the pay she receives each week (even when supplemented by benefits) means that she cannot book a regular slot of hours in a nursery for her child or pay for a full-time place that she will not always need.

When her youngest child was three months old, after a short period of living on benefit, Kim took an hourly paid temporary job with an organisation that supports tenants' associations. On average, she

works about 20 hours a week, but this can go up or down depending
on her workload and her child care availability. Prior to her second
pregnancy, Kim was employed full-time in clerical and administrative
work, and she is now keeping an eye out for a more stable job again.
Kim is sure that she is better off working, financially and in other
ways, than living on benefits. Furthermore, and importantly, unlike
Sylvia and Fiona, she firmly links her employment to her responsibility
to bring her children up with the right attitudes:

> I work cos I couldn't live off benefits and I didn't just want to stay
> inside the house. I keep trying to push myself and better myself ... I
> can save more, I can buy more things, essential things for my house
> and children. It gets me by more than living on benefits ... I feel
> that, me personally, you go out and work if you want to better your-
> self and better your children and show them, you know what I
> mean, that it's not just to live off the government, you can go out
> and do something for yourself. And also that will show them why
> education is important ... I've got great dreams for myself and my
> children. By me working and trying to keep the household as stable
> as I can, I think my children may see a better life for themselves
> than I saw when I was growing up. I can't predict the future, but I
> hope it turns out okay.

In contrast with both Sylvia and Fiona, then, Kim's family and her
younger child's father support her uptake of paid work in the absence
of flexible and cheap formal day care provision. For Kim, being a
'good' mother encompasses being a worker; it is not only of benefit
financially, it is morally the right thing to do.

4.3   GENDERED MORAL RATIONALITIES

The cases of Sylvia, Fiona and Kim discussed above have revealed the
concrete ways in which lone mothers' support networks play a part,
subtly or more overtly, in their considerations about, and understandings of, the relationship between motherhood and paid work. Quite
different moral frameworks guide Sylvia's, Fiona's and Kim's conceptions of their responsibilities towards meeting the needs of their children. As became clear in Chapters 2 and 3, one of the most significant
concepts that symbolised their lone motherhood for the overwhelming
majority of the women interviewed for our study was their sense of

responsibility towards their children. This was expressed again and again in the lone mothers' descriptions of what it meant to live without a male partner and bring up children – no matter what their class or ethnic background, where they lived, or even whether or not they wanted to see themselves as a 'lone mother'. Rather, it was how this responsibility should be discharged that varied, including ideas about the compatibility of motherhood and paid work. This is a vital starting point for the analysis that follows, and the cases of Sylvia, Fiona and Kim are exemplars.

In contrast, conventional social policy analyses of lone mothers' uptake of paid work often work with an assumption of individual economic rationality, in which lone mothers' decisions about paid work are governed by a desire to maximise their financial income. We develop the critique of this assumption in Chapters 5 and 8. For now, however, it is worth briefly considering the contrast between this econ- omistic picture of lone mothers' behaviour in taking up paid work, and the socially negotiated rationalities about the compatibility or other- wise of motherhood and paid work as displayed by Sylvia, Fiona and Kim, and indeed more generally by the other interviewees, both in Britain and elsewhere.

Briefly, many studies of lone mothers and paid work place the emphasis on lone mothers as a set of individually specific attributes (age, qualifications, age of youngest child, receipt of maintenance, housing tenure, etc.) and, through the statistical analysis of large scale data sets, aim to measure how these predict lone mothers' propensity to participate in the labour market. Sometimes this model is more explicit, and is carried through in a more thoroughgoing quantitative way, as in the econometric literature, and sometimes is less explicit and less mathematically ambitious, as in the social policy tradition (see Chapter 8). In both variants, however, lone mothers' decision to participate in paid work is essentially determined by whether they are financially better off in employment or living off benefits. In turn, such economistic analyses, following the rather simple stimulus-response model we described in Chapter 1, are used to support social policy recommendations for improving lone mothers' participation rates (for example by altering benefits levels or day care costs). However, as we show in Chapter 8, this work reaches an explanatory cul-de-sac when the influence of 'cultural' and 'social' factors – which cannot be appre- ciated by this model – become apparent. The suspicion arises, there- fore, that the recommendations made may be inappropriate or even misleading.

What these pictures of economic rationality gloss over is the fact that lone mothers are indeed *mothers*, who socially negotiate particular understandings about what constitutes 'good' motherhood within particular cultural and neighbourhood settings. This negotiation and understanding proceeds in different ways to the process assumed in the model of individual economic rationality. This is not to say that economic calculations about benefit levels, wage rates, day care costs and so on, are not an important factor in lone mothers' decisions about entering the labour force or living on benefits. Rather this factor needs to be set within another model of rationality. It is socially negotiated, non-economic, understandings about what is morally right and socially acceptable which are primary factors in determining what is seen as rational behaviour – calculations about individual financial costs and benefits are secondary. Moreover, because these understandings are socially negotiated, the varying contexts in which they are negotiated is of substantial importance. The expression of this moral rationality will therefore be variable. These contexts include, at a more concrete level, the neighbourhoods, local labour markets and welfare state regimes in which the lone mothers live, but also at a more abstract level the basic gendering and class nature of current society in which they are situated. Both motherhood and participation in paid work, and the relationship between the two, are fundamentally gendered and for this reason these moral forms of rationality are also gendered.

Because these gendered moral rationalities are primary to lone mothers' uptake of paid work we address this issue, and establish its nature and generality, early on in this book in this chapter and the next. Consequent to this discussion we examine local labour market and welfare regime contexts (Chapters 6 and 7), prior to a broader discussion of concepts of rationality (Chapter 8).

Motherhood itself, quite apart from mothers' embeddedness and negotiations within social networks, is also a social relationship; for there to be mothers there must be children. As such the relationship is constituted in terms of children's needs, with such needs invoking a moral compulsion to be met. Needs are projected onto children in a number of ways. These include legislation at the level of the nation state, professional and expert practice at more local levels, as well as less formal assumptions operating within neighbourhood networks of mothers (see, for example, Bell and Ribbens 1994; Ribbens 1994). However, these needs are misleadingly assumed to derive from 'natural' inherent qualities of children themselves rather than being social phenomena formulated within particular cultural and historical contexts (Lewis 1986; Woodward 1990). The moral imperative to be responsible for, and meet, children's intrinsic needs is also vested primarily in mothers – 'good' mothering is meeting children's needs. This is not to say that notions of children's needs and the moral compulsion to meet them are simply imposed on mothers in a coercive sense, either through legislation, professional practice, or neighbourhood networks. As we have seen, such responsibilities formed part of the self-understandings of the lone mothers interviewed for our study. However, because these understandings are negotiated, sustained or modified in particular social contexts (as with the discourses around lone motherhood discussed in Chapter 2) different groups of lone mothers may view children's needs and the meeting of them in quite different ways. Moreover, as we will see, lone mothers do not necessarily understand children's needs in any unidimensional way, and different needs may indicate different courses of action in relation to the uptake of paid work.

We term the understandings the lone mothers held about their identity as mothers, and as lone mothers in particular, especially about their responsibilities towards their children, *gendered moral rationalities*. These rationalities, as illustrated by Sylvia, Fiona and Kim, are individually held but negotiated within social contexts. They provide answers to, or guidance on, questions such as 'Is it right that I, as a mother bringing up children by myself, should try for a full-time job?', 'What are my responsibilities; how will my behaviour affect my children?', 'What do others expect of me, what do they see as right, and how will they treat me in consequence?' These gendered moral rationalities thereby provide the lone mothers with particular orientations towards the uptake of paid work.

The combination of lone motherhood and paid work is not easily understood, therefore, through seeing individual economic rationality as the primary basis for human action. Fundamental are lone mothers' social and cultural understandings, and rationalisings, about what is best and morally right for themselves as mothers in relation to the uptake of paid work. These understandings and rationalisings are collectively created as well as individually held.

From the interviews with lone mothers themselves, we have identified three main 'ideal types' of this overall gendered moral rationality: primarily mother, mother/worker integral, and primarily worker, each containing a different orientation towards paid work.[2] While these three gendered moral rationalities correspond closely with the three different understandings and socially negotiated orientations towards motherhood and paid work demonstrated in the preceding individual cases of Sylvia, Fiona and Kim, not all the lone mothers in our study fell neatly into one ideal type, as we show later. Thus the three types of gendered moral rationality we have identified are essentially 'second order constructs' (Schutz 1979). These construct an abstract model of the key variations and features of the conceptual relationship between motherhood and paid work. They are intended to capture the key features of gendered moral rationalities without necessarily displaying all the particularities of individual cases.

Primarily Mother: In this form of gendered moral rationality, lone mothers give primacy to the moral benefits of physically caring for their children themselves over and above any financial benefits of undertaking paid work. The sorts of statements made by the lone mothers that fall within this ideal type include: 'If you have children you should be with them, not leave them with someone else', 'Bringing up children is a job in itself', and 'If you work you miss out on your children growing up'. A major children's need that mothers ought to meet within this ideal type is for care by their own mothers. Paid work (except perhaps for minimal hours) is not morally right.

Mother/Worker Integral: Within this ideal type, lone mothers see financial provision through employment as part of their moral responsibilities towards their children. The sorts of views expressed by the lone mothers in this gendered moral rationality include: 'You need to earn money to take care of your children', 'Working means that I can provide for my child and give her a better life', and 'Working sets a good example to my children, so they'll want to get on in life themselves'. In this gendered moral rationality, the children's needs that mothers ought to meet are for financial provision and employment role models. Long part-time or full-time paid work is morally right.

Primarily Worker: In this form of gendered moral rationality, lone mothers give primacy to paid work for themselves separate to their identity as mothers. In this ideal type, the lone mothers said things like: 'I think of myself as a career person rather than a mother', 'Staying at home and just looking after children feels like a trap', and 'Working gives me status and self-respect'. In this gendered moral rationality then, children may have needs but so too do mothers as separate people. Substantial part-time or full-time paid work is an autonomous moral right.

This three part ideal type model of the relationship between motherhood and paid work, abstracted from the views of the lone mothers interviewed for our study, is significant because it adds another dimension to the dominant polarised model implicit in many studies of, and attitudinal surveys regarding, mothers' employment generally (for example, Brannen and Moss 1991; Hochschild with Machung 1989; Scott and Brook 1997; Thomson 1996). This polarisation is also mirrored in 'mother or worker' discussions of policies towards lone mothers specifically (for example, Bradshaw 1989; Lewis 1989b). Much of this work assumes a polarised continuum in which, at the one end, (lone) mothers see themselves as mothers who care for their children full-time (often called 'traditional', but in our model characterised as 'primarily mother') or, at the other end, workers who are in employment (often characterised as 'progressive', but in our model called 'primarily worker'). In this way the two roles of mother and worker are only conceived of as separate; there is little sense that they may also be understood as integrated. This simple dichotomous conceptualisation may well be related to, firstly, the context for the authors, whereby debates over whether or not mothers should work outside the home are in the ascendant, and secondly, an ethnocentric perspective, based on White women's experiences. We can see this latter issue operating when we examine the position of the different social groups of lone mothers interviewed for our study within our gendered moral rationalities model.

Gendered Moral Rationalities by Social Group

The three forms of gendered moral rationality that we have identified can be conceived in a triangular relationship to each other.[3] (See Figure 4.1.) The 'primarily mother' and 'primarily worker' orientations, which each view motherhood and paid work as dichotomous or separate from each other, are positioned along the base of the triangle. The 'mother/worker integral' orientation, which combines the two, is positioned at the apex of the triangle.

As we have noted, in reality individual lone mothers may hold any combination of these different gendered moral rationalities, even if the components of their resulting orientation are internally contradictory in terms of combining 'primarily mother' with 'primarily worker' or 'mother/worker integral' ideal types. Furthermore, in terms of the social groups of lone mothers taking part in our research, not all lone mothers within one social group living in a particular area held the same combination of views. Nevertheless, Figure 4.1, which diagrammatically summarises our interview data about the lone mothers' views concerning motherhood and paid work for the seven British groups, shows that there were some general emphases.

Referring to the top triangle of Figure 4.1, we can see that the White working class lone mothers, living on the peripheral public housing estate in Brighton, were much more likely to give primacy to caring for their children themselves, over and above paid work – as exemplified by the case of Sylvia (and as Jordan and colleagues, 1992, also found for White working class mothers living on a similar deprived estate in Exeter). Only two expressed views that had strong elements of a perception of themselves as able to have a separate identity as a worker. Marilyn, for example, while feeling that her young daughter's needs were best met by full-time mothering in the first instance, and then later fitting in any paid work during school term hours, admitted to feeling bored at home. She hankered after a separate worker identity:

> Because once you've had a child you're a mum, you're nothing else. You're not a person in your own right, you're a mum. And when you've got kids there's not really much you can do, you can't go to work, you can't do a lot of things that you want to do ... I would work if I could, I enjoyed working. If I could get a well-paid job, a full-time one, I'd be better off cos I'd have more money and more self-respect, and I wouldn't just be another single parent on the dole. I think about it, like a little pipe dream in my mind, but I can't do anything till she starts school. I'll have to wait, I can go out to work part-time when she starts going to school full-time.

More of the White middle class lone mothers, living in a suburban area of Brighton, tended to combine a 'primarily mother' gendered moral rationality with elements of a separate identity as a worker. Given this, these lone mothers were subject to the same contradictory feelings as those expressed by Marilyn (above):

> Well, I mean I'm a career woman, or I was a career woman ... I wouldn't even consider [a job] now because I want to bring her up myself ... There's no question that, you know, mum can do a better job than anybody else, however loving and caring someone is. And I just wouldn't want it any other way ... Although I don't work, in my head I still see myself as someone who works. I still see myself as a person with a career.   (Jessie)

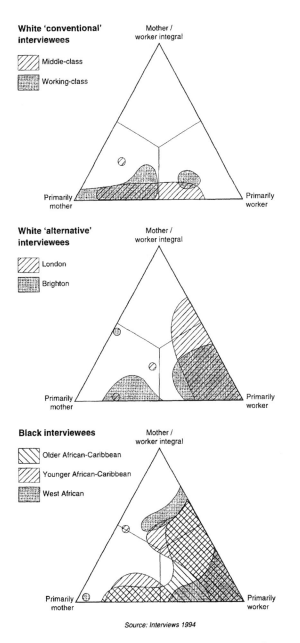

Source: Interviews 1994

Figure 4.1   Gendered moral rationalities by social and ethnic groups

Although the estate which housed the White working class lone
mothers and the suburban area in which the White middle class lone
mothers lived were not far from each other in geographical terms (see
Figure 3.1), there was a wide social gulf between the two groups.
Indeed, as we noted in earlier chapters, the Moulsecoomb area and its
lone mothers were sometimes used by the suburban lone mothers as
an example of the 'other' lone mothers who fuelled the social threat
discourse, and from whom they attempted to distance themselves.
Despite this social gulf, however, both groups tended to hold similar
views about the relationship between motherhood and paid work
(although there were no 'career women' amongst the White working
class lone mothers). Rather, the difference was that on the council
estate lone motherhood was largely seen as normal, and the lone
mothers were mostly embedded in relatively dense social networks of
family and friends in a similar position, while the suburban lone
mothers were either socially isolated or were located in social networks of married women, as friends and family, whose primarily
mother orientation was financially supported by their husbands:

> I would rather be at home for my child. I mean they grow up so
> quickly. When they're small they really need you ... My own friends,
> not many of them work, a very low percentage work. I mean they're
> all married with husbands ... I mean they're in a totally different
> position to me. I mean most of my friends have got nice houses,
> they've got a husband. Some of them perhaps don't need to work.
> You know, they're fairly okay for money. But I'm sure they would
> go along with what I say [that you stay at home for your children's
> sake, not just because financially you don't need to work].   (Lena)

In holding a 'primarily mother' gendered moral rationality, the
Brighton White working class and middle class lone mothers mirror
the dominant, conventional, orientation to motherhood and paid work
of British mothers as a whole. This is well documented in attitudinal
surveys (for example, Scott and Brook 1997; Thomson 1995). As we
argued in chapter three, lone mothers have become more subject to
such dominant understandings of mothers and their role since the
1970s. The remaining five groups of British lone mothers, however,
were less subject to these conventional understandings. They are, by
definition and proportion, exceptional in the population as a whole, in
that the two White 'alternative' groups often held views of gender
roles informed by feminism, while the three Black groups represented

ethnic groups that only form around 5 per cent of lone mothers as a whole.

The middle triangle of Figure 4.1 shows that both groups of White 'alternative' lone mothers, living across inner-city Lambeth and Southwark, and in a gentrified area of Brighton, were much more likely to have identities as workers for themselves, separate to motherhood – as exemplified in the case of Fiona. This 'primarily worker' gendered moral rationality was particularly evident across the London-based group of lone mothers, with several of this group combining it with some elements of a 'mother/worker integral' orientation. Linda, for example, felt that:

[Women] should have the freedom to decide if they want to work. Some women value more their time with their kids, but at the same time I think a lot of women find that, when it comes down to it, they get so incredibly bored with being a parent all the time. They're totally bored out of their brains most of the time.

Linda viewed paid work as providing 'fulfilment' and the chance to 'mix with people in a positive environment' – the negative environment being the boredom of home-based life and the surrounding public housing estate on which, as a middle class woman, she felt out of place. But she also saw employment as beneficial for her daughter, in that earning money would be a 'passport to a better life'. She and her school-age child would be able to move to an area nearer to her 'women Guardian reader' friends, where her daughter would be able to attend a 'good' school and 'grow up away from this absolutely horrendous place'.

In partial contrast to the London 'alternative' group, the Brighton-based group contained a few lone mothers with a mainly 'primarily mother' orientation. (With one other exception, who was unusual in combining a 'primarily mother' gendered moral rationality with a 'mother/worker integral' orientation – a position discussed in more detail below.) Tina, for example, spoke of 'satisfaction and fulfillment. I want work for myself, for development and enjoyment', but also felt it was 'very difficult to co-ordinate everything', and that 'you really have to kind of sort out your priorities', which to her meant being available for her son before and after school as well as doing things together during the school holidays. This obviously precluded full-time or long part-time work, or 'unsocial' short part-time jobs (see Chapter 6 for the labour market implications).

The tendency for the 'alternative' groups to hold 'primarily worker' gendered moral rationality, stressing an identity for themselves as workers separate to their identity as mothers, may be related to particular 'women's rights' or 'equal rights' strands of (White) feminist thinking about women's autonomy and personhood. These hold that, for women to achieve emancipation and citizenship, the 'ties' of motherhood must be loosened or transcended in favour of women's needs as individuals, so that they can then enter the public sphere on equal terms with men (see Bock and James 1992, and Everingham 1994, for critical discussions). Such a perspective, however, sidesteps any conceptualisation of children's needs. This then leaves a vacuum to be filled by more traditional notions of children's needs – that is, for care by their own mothers – however much these may conflict with individual autonomy. For Black lone mothers though, any vacuum concerning children's needs created by a 'primarily worker' gendered moral rationality could be filled by an alternative conception of what children need from their mothers that was not in conflict with this orientation.

The bottom triangle of Figure 4.1 shows the orientations of the Black groups of lone mothers. There is a greater tendency for them to include a 'mother/worker integral' orientation alongside a 'primarily worker' gendered moral rationality – as exemplified by Kim's case. The older and younger groups of African-Caribbean lone mothers, mainly living in large estates and smaller pockets of public housing in Brixton (Lambeth) and the south of Southwark respectively, contained women expressing views that gave primacy to motherhood, in terms of full-time care of children, but at the same time mostly demonstrated a separate identity as workers, and a conception of motherhood and paid work as synonymous. Vivienne, an older African-Caribbean lone mother, for example, initially said 'if I had enough money I think I would stay at home, ideally I would stay at home and do other things with the children', but then added:

> I think I could for a little while but not, I don't think, all day every day with the children, you know ... I like [working]. Work gives me some independence, and some stimulation ... It gets me out the house and I get a social life from it.

However, unlike most of her White counterparts, any tension that Vivienne might have felt between her contradictory 'primarily mother' and 'primarily worker' orientations was offset by her 'mother/worker integral' belief that her employment served as a model for her four children (two of school age and two toddlers): 'By working it'll give them an example that you have to work'. Indeed, Vivienne did not believe that she was financially better off in employment; she was working because she believed that it was the right thing to do for herself and her children.

One of the younger African-Caribbean lone mothers, like one of the Brighton 'alternative' group, was unusual among our interviewees in combining 'primarily mother' and 'mother/worker integral' orientations. Shirley, with one school age and one pre-school child, supposed that most mothers who worked felt:

It's not a matter of what they want to do, they have to do it. It's a need rather than something they want to do ... Obviously, it's better [to work] within school hours so you won't have to worry about, you know, child care, and the children can feel jealous [you are not spending time with them]. But full-time brings in more money!

However, Shirley was not driven just by economic motives. She also thought that full-time employment was not just the better option financially but was also a demonstration to her children, and other people, that you should 'try to better yourselves ... to give my children a good start in life'. Thus, within this position, children's needs are not unidimensional, straightforwardly leading towards one gendered moral rationality. Different aspects of children's needs can conflict. Children might need care by their mothers, but they also needed to be financially provided for and to learn from the example of their mother working.

The west African lone mothers, mainly living in public housing in the north of Southwark, also saw motherhood and paid work as integral. They demonstrated very little in the way of any 'primarily mother' gendered moral rationality, with only one lone mother in this group seeing herself in this way.

The Black lone mothers' stronger encompassing of orientations outside dominant either/or conceptualisations of motherhood and paid work may be explained by reference to Black feminist ideas. Many Black feminists argue that notions of gender roles and motherhood operate quite differently for Black women, as compared with White women, based on the historical interaction of racism with capitalism and patriarchy (for example, Anthias and Yuval-Davis 1983; Carby 1982; Phoenix 1987).

In summary then, the interviews with the seven social groups of British lone mothers show different combinations of emphases in terms of gendered moral rationality, most notably along the lines of race/ethnicity and 'alternative'/conventionality. For the groups of Brighton-based White 'estate' working class and White suburban lone mothers, marked social class differences were overshadowed by shared, and 'traditional', views about motherhood and paid work as incompatible. Here, children are seen as needing mothers who put their own care of their children above undertaking paid work. Consequently any middle class 'career women' were placed in a rather contradictory position. In partial contrast, the Brighton and London based 'alternative' groups of lone mothers, who held less traditional (feminist) views about gender roles were more likely to hold a sense of themselves as having an identity as an individual who can be a worker, separate from their identity as a mother. This view, however, still conforms to the dominant, dichotomous view of mothering and paid work as separate activities. However, it does mean that lone mothers who subscribe to such views can give priority to their worker identity – although some still feel 'torn' between the two. The views of the Black mothers, though, move away (to varying extents) from dominant conceptions of an either/or relationship between motherhood and paid work because these groups demonstrated an ability to hold notions of the two as combined rather than separate. From this perspective, lone (and other) mothers can meet their children's needs by providing for them through employment.

4.4   GENDERED MORAL RATIONALITIES: SOME COUNTER-ARGUMENTS

There are three important counter-arguments to our thesis that lone mothers' orientation to paid work is primarily determined by their varying gendered moral rationalities concerning motherhood and paid work. All start from the position of accepting the interview evidence that lone mothers do hold such moral views and that these can vary between different social groups. However, each counter-argument repositions these moral views as purely intermediary or secondary factors, and posits more traditional policy or economic factors as the 'real' cause of these rationalities and hence also of lone mothers' employment orientation. First, it could be argued that that gendered moral rationalities are determined by the different policy practices of welfare state regimes – in this sense lone mothers are just expressing verbally the options allowed to them by national policy. Secondly, it could be that lone mothers' expectations of repartnership determine orientations towards paid work (where in Britain the majority are repartnered within 10 years of becoming a lone mother). In this view, lone mothers would be expecting financial support or exchange with an employed man, and so would remain 'primarily mother' in their labour market orientation. In other words a purely economic rationale remains prime, albeit working through the gendered relations of partnership and marriage. Finally, it could also be argued that gendered moral rationalities merely provide *post hoc* justifications for lone mothers' current employment position. In this sense they would remain completely secondary to economic rationality. We deal with each of these issues in turn in this section, using the interview evidence.

Gendered Moral Rationalities and Welfare State Regimes

Is the systematic diversity of gendered moral rationalities we have observed among the British lone mothers merely a product of a particular welfare state regime? In Britain the policy rhetoric is that mothers have freedom of 'choice' in taking up paid work or not – but the lack of actual policy support for such a choice in practice means that the 'primarily mother' orientation will be dominant. Lone mothers, the argument would go, have little choice but to accept this rationality except perhaps in some exceptional cases, like the Black and 'alternative' groups. (Although the existence of these exceptions in themselves leaves the unanswered question of how they can escape these policy structures, while the majority cannot.) Hence, the argument might conclude, in welfare state regimes where mothers' uptake of paid work is actively supported then mothers, including lone mothers, would be more able to hold 'primarily worker', or even a 'mother/worker integral', gendered moral rationality. This counterargument would effectively bring the emphasis back to national state policy and, via this, to lone mothers' individual human capital attributes. We can assess this counter-argument by using the interview data on gendered moral rationalities from Germany, Sweden and the USA. Figure 4.2 presents this in summary form.

The welfare state regime in the USA is similar to that in Britain in so far as it maintains a similar 'hands off' approach to mothers' employment; on the other hand there is greater public support for mothers working as shown in attitude surveys (Scott and Brooke 1997). As Figure 4.2 shows, the young, mainly White working class lone mothers in the Near West Side of Cleveland did tend to hold a 'primarily mother' orientation. Joan is typical in stating that:

Well, I think it's better to stay home with my children and I feel that it's better for me to be home with them. Right now my priority is raising the children ... I'm just too busy with my kids, which is what's stopping me from working.

She quoted the views of a neighbour in support of her own:

There's a lady on the hall that stays home with her kids too and she couldn't imagine going out to work. She thinks that some of the parents that put their kids in day care are just doing the wrong thing.

However, this group also demonstrated quite a bit of diversity, with one lone mother holding a strong 'primarily worker' orientation and a

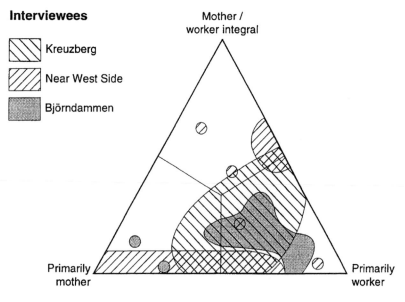

Figure 4.2   Gendered moral rationalities by welfare state regimes

few leaning far more towards a 'mother/worker integral' orientation. Interestingly, amongst the latter were the two Hispanic lone mothers. It may well be that the arguments made by Black feminists about the different operation of patriarchy for Black women apply also to Hispanic women. One of these Hispanic lone mothers, Yvonne, felt that paid work was best fitted around children and that working meant that mothers missed out on their children growing up, but also that earning money was important and paid work gave a sense of respect, both in her own and other people's eyes. Furthermore, she strongly believed that caring for your child also meant providing financially and that thereby she could provide a better start in life for her young son:

> I think it's important to stay home with the baby, but you just have to go out there ... I think people look up to you [if you work] ... You feel better about yourself. You're bringing home the food, you know, you're taking care of your baby, and I think that makes you feel better about yourself. The time that you don't spend with the baby, that's difficult. They're always doing new stuff and I don't want to miss anything. It's a beautiful experience ... But I need to make money so he'll go to a private school. No public schools for him!

Once again, Yvonne, demonstrates how responsibility for meeting children's needs is not straightforward for mothers who do not conceptualise those needs in a unidimensional way. Different aspects of children's needs mean different, even conflicting, courses of action.

The conservative welfare state regime in Germany, as well as public opinion, pushes mothers towards a domestic and caring role, although lone mothers with older children are more expected to be in paid work. However, the White 'alternative' lone mothers in Kreuzberg were similar to their British counterparts in holding a 'primarily worker' gendered moral rationality, with some elements of a 'primarily mother' orientation. Again, this may well be related to an 'equal rights' feminist perspective and its implicit silence concerning children's needs. Martina is typical in feeling some sense of conflict:

> Well, at least for me personally it wouldn't be enough for me just to bring up my son and not have anything else to do. Either I need my studies or my job as some sort of balance. But I also think it's important that every woman decide what's right for her. On the

other hand, there are some times when I think that the stress of working, studying and having a child is detrimental for my son. Maybe there are some deficits for him. On the other hand, I know I couldn't just take care of my child.

In Sweden, in contrast, both the welfare state regime, and public opinion more widely, strongly encourage and supports all mothers, as autonomous citizens, to take up paid work. The White, mainly middle class, group of lone mothers, living on a residualised estate in Partille, also largely adhered to a 'primarily worker' gendered moral rationality. Ulla summed up her own and, as she saw it, others' orientation:

> I don't think I've met anyone here [in the neighbourhood] who would like to stay at home and not go to work. I know there are lots of single mothers here, and I have the feeling that most of them go to work and they like it ... I decided to work full-time to cope [financially] on my own. It's fun to work too ... It's wonderful to get away, it's so nice to have two lives [as a worker and a mother].

The indications are that in Sweden lone mothers can more successfully reconcile the two identities of mother and worker precisely because of the support of both state and opinion, but that they do not necessarily move over to the mother/worker integral position.

Two exceptions to the largely 'primarily worker' orientation of the Swedish group are particularly effective in marking the dominance of this primarily worker rationality. These were the two working class women in this mainly middle class group, whose orientation was 'primarily mother' despite the expectations of both state and public opinion. One of these women, Britt, had two preschool age children and a teenage daughter. She knew that her own, and what she saw as her friends', orientation, with its lack of an autonomous sense of self and a desire for full-time motherhood, was not socially acceptable. (Nor was it easily understood by the Swedish researcher interviewing her on our behalf.) Indeed, Britt had social agency intervention in her life because of this:

> From an economic point of view I want to work full-time and then of course you can give the children a lot more, but that probably isn't what I want to give my children. Rather I would prefer to be with my children ... Many [of the mothers I know] have the same attitude as me. I say that I don't want to leave my children at the

nursery, I want to see them grow up. I say that I don't know how many times I've cried when I've gone to leave them at the nursery. But you can't show the children that, nor anyone else either, but you've got to go on in your loneliness and miss the children every day. And then [the agency] say that I've got to educate myself and think about myself more. And I seriously don't understand that. Perhaps it's me that's a little outside everything, for I think I do care about me and myself when I care for my children.

Interviewer: They mean perhaps that if you can't love yourself then you can't love someone else.

Yes, but I can!

Britt described the social stigma and pressure to conform that she felt from social agencies:

The social security office, you know, they want to press mums to the furthest limits ... Mums, my god, have not got to be at home with their children and there shouldn't be any breathing space anywhere. It's really hard to describe. It's like pressing the last drop of blood out of you ... I haven't worked since I had my younger children. I'm almost ashamed because I'm not in work ... That's how it is if you don't have a job and when you don't have work you're paid for. You're a little devalued in people's eyes. It's almost frightening actually.

Thus, in the Swedish context, our interview data give an indication that social class may be more significant for different orientations to motherhood and paid work than is the case in the British context – at least amongst White women. In Britain, excepting those from the 'alternative' groups, the White working and middle class British lone mothers tended towards the same, dominant, 'primarily mother' gendered moral rationality.

It appears that the counter-argument does not hold. The structural and institutional context for lone mothers' uptake of paid work, in the form of the rhetoric and practices of welfare state regimes, does not determine lone mothers' gendered moral rationalities in any straightforward way. This is not to deny the important enabling or constraining effect of these regimes, as we discuss in Chapter 7, and as the example of Britt shows all too well. Rather, as for the British lone mothers, these examples show that there are particular patternings of socially negotiated gendered moral rationalities, and that these are mediated by the key social structural features of ethnicity, class and conventionality.

Re/partnering

Do gendered moral rationalities in fact have an economic base
through expectations of re/partnering? This might explain some of the
variations observed in the interview data. Thus the 'alternative' lone
mothers, influenced by feminist views concerning autonomy, would be
more likely to expect, or want, to be a lone mother into the medium
and longer terms. Hence, because they did not envisage or desire
future financial support from a man, they would be more likely to see
having paid work as necessary. In turn, therefore, they would hold a
'primarily worker' gendered moral rationality. In contrast, the 'conventional' working class and middle class groups might see partnership, marriage or remarriage as more desirable and likely. Thus their
tendency to hold a 'primarily mother' gendered moral rationality
would be based on expectations of financial support from an
employed man.

Advocates of this counter-argument could point to our own cases of
Sylvia and Fiona (section 4.2) to support their argument. Like most of
the other lone mothers in the White working class group, living on a
peripheral public housing estate, Sylvia held to a 'primarily mother'
gendered moral rationality. She says the idea of parenting is to be at
home with your children and, in having no paid work, she carried this
out. She also largely finds lone motherhood a lonely experience and
says she would prefer to live with, or marry, a man than continue as a
lone mother. Indeed, Sylvia's response to a question about how she
saw the future for herself centred on the hope that she would be able
to find a new partner. Fiona, however, did not see repartnering as a
necessary part of her future life. Like many of the White 'alternative'
lone mothers, whether living in inner-city London or a gentrified part
of Brighton, Fiona held to a 'primarily worker' gendered moral rationality, enjoying the feeling of achievement and sense of autonomy that
being employed full-time gave her. She is proud of, and happy, being a
lone mother, and says she is not willing to accept any compromises
merely in order to repartner. Thus an argument could be made that
Sylvia and Fiona's rationalising is, at base, economic in its considerations, related to the likelihood of financial support being provided by a
man. Even so, this counter-argument would be unable to explain the
behaviour of the Black groups in these terms, especially as we know
that Black lone mothers tend to partner in middle age (Modood et al.
1997). This may be why the younger African-Carbbean interviewees
were more likely to say that they were not looking for a permament

relationship, while the older group were more likely to say that they would like to partner.

Furthermore, the interview evidence from the White groups is contradictory. While several of the White working class and White middle class suburban groups do express a wish for, or expectation of, repartnership, these cases are equally matched by others in these groups who – despite a strong 'primarily mother' gendered moral rationality – did not see repartnering as a route out of their lone motherhood. For example, Sasha, a White working class lone mother, believed that 'mothers ought to stay at home really' (doing this herself) but also felt, 'It's like a challenge to manage without a man – I don't want another relationship'. Similarly, Karen, a White middle class lone mother, put forward what she described as 'very strong views' about motherhood and paid work: 'Actually I fully believe if you have children you should look after them'. She had only minimal paid work, fitted in during school hours. Karen felt that 'to be a single parent isn't a nice thing', reflecting the locally prevalent social threat discourse. Nevertheless, repartnering did not figure in her future: 'I definitely wouldn't consider a new relationship for lots of reasons. I don't want to have to rely on anyone again.'

Similarly, many of the White 'alternative' lone mothers living in London and Brighton, who held a 'primarily worker' gendered moral rationality, nevertheless expressed a wish to re/partner. Doreen, for example, from the Brighton group, mixed minimal paid work with part-time study. She expressed a 'primarily worker' orientation to paid work, and saw this as continuing should she fulfil her desire to repartner in the future:

> I think to be a complete person you need to go out to work. Personally I couldn't sit and twiddle my thumbs. I mean if I was living with someone and I didn't have to work financially, I'd still want to go out and do something cos I feel I'd just vegetate.

The evidence in our intensive data for a link between repartnering expectations and gendered moral rationality is contradictory. However, even in the interview cases which might support this view, there is no necessary reason why it is economic, rather than moral, rationalising that inform expectations of re/partnering (see Chapter 8). For example, the interviewees sometimes considered that children needed a male role model or influence, as our discussion of lone mother's own discourses reveals (see Chapter 2). In other words re/partnership is often seen in wider moral and social terms; financial support remains a secondary issue.

Employment Orientation and Practice

Finally, are the gendered moral rationalities, and the associated orientations to paid work, that we identified in section 4.3 simply self-justifying rationalisations of whether or not the interviewees actually had paid work? There are two 'counter counter-arguments'. First, this does not account for the contradictory gendered moral rationalities, held by one person, that the interviews often displayed. Secondly, and decisively, notions of post-hoc rationalising are not borne by the interviewees' actual employment practices (see also Thomson 1996). Not all of those lone mothers whose form of gendered moral rationality encompassed paid work, whether as an integral part of their mothering or as a separate identity, were actually in employment. Similarly, not all of those lone mothers who held a 'primarily mother' gendered moral rationality were without substantial paid work.

Figures 4.3 and 4.4 chart the interviewees' orientations to paid work as against their actual practice in terms of current paid work. The figures have been created by taking the gendered moral rationality triangular model (as in Figures 4.1 and 4.2) and 'collapsing' the 'mother/worker integral' apex of the triangle down to the 'primarily worker' right hand base to form the horizontal axis of the graph. Although the moral rationality underlying each is quite different, their effect in relation to the uptake of paid work is the same – both encourage it. Hours of paid work per week are denoted along the vertical axis. This allows us to distinguish between no paid work, minimal paid work (under 15 hours), short part-time (16–21 hours), long part-time (22–30 hours), and full-time work (over 30 hours).

If the lone mothers' gendered moral rationalities were merely a justification of their actual practice in relation to their current uptake of paid work, then we would expect to see a correlation between the two. The lone mothers located towards the 'primarily worker' and 'mother/worker integral' end of the horizontal gendered moral rationality axis of the graph, would show long or full-time uptake of paid work (in other words, they would be located towards the upper right hand corner of the graph) and vice versa for the 'primarily mother' cases. There is some evidence for this for the lone mothers in Berlin, Cleveland and Göteborg (Figure 4.4), but very little for the Brighton and south London lone mothers in Figure 4.3.

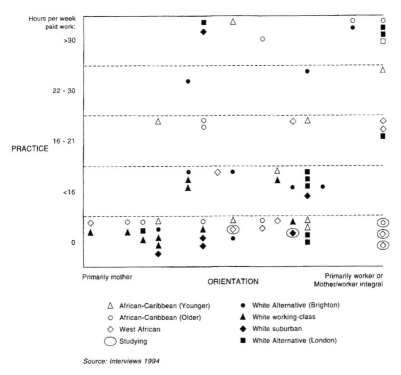

Figure 4.3 Lone mothers and paid work: orientation and practice – Brighton and South London

How can this relative lack of correlation between orientation and practices be explained?

Some of the exceptions can be easily explained – the lone mothers holding orientations to paid work, but who did not have paid work in practice, were studying full-time. This was so as to place them in a better position in the labour market. Thus their study can be equated to paid work. Tola, a west African British lone mother with one adult and three school-age children, was studying for a child care diploma:

Since I have been made redundant about two and a half years ago, I wasn't able to get any other job. There was no help from anywhere, nothing. That was what made me decide to go on the course ... I wanted to do a social work course but it was cancelled so I took this

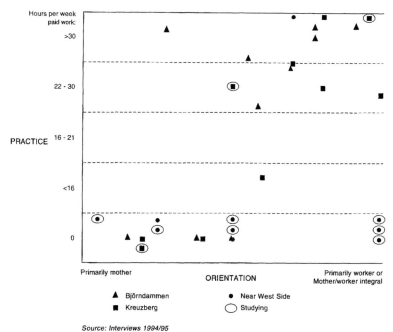

Figure 4.4   Lone mothers and paid work: orientation and practice –
Björndammen, Kreuzberg, Near West Side

course. I hope to get a job after it, and then the future will be bright.

Janice, a young White lone mother living in Cleveland with her preschool age son, was also studying, although she had originally felt coerced into this. Nevertheless, she wanted paid work and had ambitions:

> I was on welfare and they put me on leave, and I wasn't gonna go to school and they told me, well if you don't go to school we're gonna cut your cheque. They told me of the Centre and told me I had to call. But it's good ... I was looking into like the medical [as a career]. I don't know what yet. I don't have a high school diploma or CV, I need to get some kind of schooling before. You feel better about yourself when you work ... I would like to go to medical school with a vocational training.

These student examples could be employed to support the counter-argument that expressed attitudes merely reflected current practice. However, what of the cases of non-student lone mothers with a strong orientation towards taking paid work, but with no or minimal employment. There is clearly no obvious self-justification here, and indeed these interviewees were often searching for employment:

At the moment I work the odd day in my friend's shop, but I've just finished a PGCE course in Secondary Education and I've just applied for a teaching post ... I could move house if I got off benefits and try and get some peace and quiet. (Linda, a White 'alternative' London-based lone mother)

Alternatively, some were constrained from taking up paid work because they regarded it as economically irrational to follow their orientation:

They say they're having a trend towards re-employing mothers, getting mothers back in, but I think the jobs they're having are very unskilled, low paid jobs ... I don't want to be sitting around the house letting my brain die off ... If I could get a decently paid job I'd be better off working, but the average wage here is £150. After they've taxed that and I've paid the rent, paid for child care, I'd be worse off than I am on benefits. (Justine, a younger African-Caribbean lone mother)

We should also remember that the Black lone mothers, many of whom held gendered moral rationalities favouring full-time work, but in fact were not in employment (see Figure 4.3; Table 1.2) lived in the particularly polarised and, for those outside a few favoured professional and managerial sectors, declining labour market area of inner London. Indeed, this was the only area in Britain to have recorded a decline in female employment in the 1980s and early 1990s. The right kind of jobs that could fulfil a moral rationality emphasising household support by the lone mother's own jobs – that is a better paid full-time, or at least long-part-time, jobs may simply not have been available (see Chapter 6). Justine may regard the jobs available to her as not worth taking up because they are morally irrational in this sense, as well as financially marginal.

However, the major reason for this contrast between a strong orientation to employment, but minimal or no paid work in practice, was the contradiction embodied in those (mainly White) lone mothers who, although they had a strong 'primarily worker' identity, also had elements of a 'primarily mother' gendered moral rationality. As Susan, a White 'alternative' London-based lone mother, said: 'I have images of a stay at home mother and a strong independent woman with a job. It's hard to fit both together'. As was the case for Jessie, the White 'suburban' middle class lone mother quoted earlier (p. 122) and who still thought of herself as a 'career woman', the 'primarily mother' orientation exerted the stronger moral pull.

Even more intriguing are the few lone mothers with a stronger 'primarily mother' than 'primarily worker' or 'mother/worker integral' orientation, but who nevertheless had full-time paid work (located in the top left hand corners of Figures 4.3 and 4.4). Hannah, a White British 'alternative' lone mother living in London, was one of these. Hannah strongly felt that mothers 'should stay at home, it's nicer for the child in that they have the security'. Nevertheless:

> I've just gone back to work, about six weeks ago. I'm a nursery nurse, an NNEB. I qualified about 14 years ago, and gave up work when I had my daughter and intentionally stayed off work. I wanted to stay home, I wanted to have the main influence on her. I could have returned to work, but then I just thought I'd made the decision to have the baby, I wanted to be there ... I hadn't thought about going back to work but the opportunity arose, somebody actually approached me and offered me a job, so it's sort of – I couldn't turn it down ... I'm working in a private – it's nannying actually. I've worked for the family before actually ... It fits in perfectly, [my daughter] comes with me.

Thus Hannah was in the happy position of being able to both follow her 'primarily mother' gendered moral rationality and still be in full-time employment, by taking her young daughter to work with her. Similarly, Patsy, a White 'suburban' middle class lone mother with a strong 'primarily mother' orientation, was able to work full-time as a teacher because her son attended a school close to the one she worked in. He came to work with her and walked the short distance to and from his school, waiting in the classroom with her after school teaching hours while she finished any administrative work.

Agnetta, one of the two White working class Swedish lone mothers, was also working full-time even though she believed 'you should stay at home'. Like Britt, the other working class Swedish interviewee (who was a friend of hers), Agnetta felt that she had no option but to place her young daughter in day care, against her better judgment. Unlike Britt, however, she had a job:

> They put kids in nurseries when they are one and a half years and it's awful. They can't feed themselves, they can't do anything then, no. I don't agree with it, but of course people need the money. You really are compelled to put them in whether you want to or not. I think that most people I speak to in any case think that children shouldn't go in when they're only one and a half ... I had to [work], you get nothing otherwise. [I work] at the pizzeria. I got that through the labour exchange, it's a job experience for six months.

Agnetta, perhaps, is expressing here the power of particular welfare and gendered cultures to force people to behave in ways they believe is morally wrong.

Thus the relationship between the lone mothers' orientations towards paid work and their actual practice in taking up paid work is mediated by several factors. On the one hand lone mothers with a 'primarily mother' gendered moral rationality could either be pushed into taking up paid work by the practices of the welfare regime, or have jobs that encompassed their commitment towards meeting their children's needs, as they saw them, for care by their own mothers. On the other hand, lone mothers with a 'primarily worker' or 'mother/worker integral' gendered moral rationality could be constrained in taking up paid work either by low wages, high day care costs, and the lack of jobs that could fulfil their expectations or, for those with a 'primarily worker' orientation, by their own (contradictory) acceptance of children's needs as constructed within the 'primarily mother' gendered moral rationality.

4.5 CONCLUSION

The lesson to be drawn from this chapter is that whether or not lone mothers decide to try for paid work is a social and moral choice, which reflects socially negotiated and socially patterned gendered moral rationalities about mothering roles and children's needs. The decisions the interviewed lone mothers made about paid work were not simply determined by instrumental and individual financial considerations, but through their beliefs about what constituted 'good' mothering. Furthermore, we showed that children's needs were not construed in any uniform or unidimensional way by the lone mothers, but that different aspects of these needs were regarded as requiring different, even conflicting, actions *vis-à-vis* the uptake of paid work. The three 'ideal types' of gendered moral rationality identified each contained different orientations towards the uptake of paid work: the 'primarily mother' position sees anything more than minimal paid work as not morally right for mothers, the 'mother/worker integral' position views long part-time or full-time paid work as morally right for mothers, and the 'primarily worker' view regards long part-time or full-time paid work as an autonomous moral right separate from motherhood. These gendered moral rationalities were not constructed and held either in isolation, or in some random or serendipitous collective fashion; they were patterned around key social factors of class, ethnicity and conventionality.

We argued that this gendered moral rationalities model transcends the dominant polarised 'mother or worker' conceptualisation of the relationship between motherhood and paid work underlying much mainstream research and debate on lone and other mothers' employment. We also assessed the strength of possible counter-arguments, which would see gendered moral rationalities as expressed by the interviewees as merely reflecting the imperatives of welfare state regimes, the relative expectation of re/partnering, or the justification of current employment practice. None of these arguments was strongly supported by the interview evidence. Thus, while gendered moral rationalities are a product of human – collective – agency, rather than being a property of social structure over which individuals have no control, there is also a sense in which they become structural features. As socially patterned moral guidelines, they both constrain and facilitate certain courses of action for particular social groups of lone mothers.

A criticism of our argument in this chapter could be that it is based on a small total sample, with even smaller numbers for the different groups. How typical and generalisable are such findings? In one sense this criticism is misplaced, in that the validity of intensive research in general, and of case study data in particular, depends on its discovery of process. The attribution of causation does not then depend upon statistical representativeness. This is only necessary for extensive research, which usually does not access process directly and attempts to infer cause (often inappropriately and sometimes misleadingly) on the basis of correlation (Mitchell 1983, Sayer 1994). None the less, we can still ask how typical these process results are. The next chapter goes on to evaluate this using extensive research based on the British census.

NOTES

1. This also raises questions about the use of questionnaires to elicit information about values and understandings.

2. The gendered moral rationalities were identified by taking from the interview transcripts all statements about motherhood and paid work, and children's needs, made by the lone mothers, including contradictory statements within one account. Statements that were similar were then grouped together. In this way the three ideal types of the relationship between motherhood and paid work were abstracted.

3. The triangular model of of gendered moral rationalities was constructed out of the ideal types abstracted from the interview accounts. The position of each lone mother was then plotted as appropriate for each group, and drawing clusters for each group by eye. Figures 4.1 and 4.2 are thus concerned with the lone mothers' expressed orientations rather than their actual practices. Orientations and practices are combined in Figures 4.3 and 4.4.

5 Lone Mothers and Paid Work: Human Capital or Gendered Moral Rationalities?

5.1 INTRODUCTION

The previous chapter showed that whether or not the interviewed lone mothers decided to try for paid work was, for them, first and foremost a social and moral choice. This choice, in turn, reflected socially negotiated and socially patterned 'gendered moral rationalities' about what constituted 'good' mothering and how this might be combined with paid work. Calculations about individual utility maximisation, and in particular perceived economic costs and benefits, were only important once these understandings were established. The task of this chapter is to assess the typicality of these process findings, and it does this by using extensive research based on the British census. Section 5.2 undertakes this task with reference to how different social groups of lone mothers combine motherhood and paid work, using the 1991 Household Sample of Annonymised Records (SARs), and section 5.3 examines how these combinations may change over time using the Longitudinal Study (LS) for 1981–91.

The more conventional view of lone mothers' participation in the labour market, underlain by ideas of rational economic man, focuses research on the individual characteristics of lone mothers. In this view levels of human capital (education, training, experience) determine a lone mother's potential income through employment. At the same time competition from the 'reservation wage' available from benefits will set the level around which it becomes rational to take up a job. The higher a lone mother's human capital, therefore, the higher the difference between potential labour market wage and benefit income, and therefore the more likely she is to participate in the labour marlet. This equation is subject, however, to constraints on using this capital. For example a lone mother with a young child, or several children, may only be able to take up short part-time work or even be effectively barred from the labour market completely given the paucity of day care provision in Britain, even if she possesses a high level of human capital. In contrast the notion of 'gendered moral rationalities', developed from the interview evidence in Chapter 4, focusses attention onto lone mothers' social understandings about motherhood and how these are collectively produced in social networks in neighbourhoods and local labour markets. Thus, as we saw in Chapter 4, some lone mothers may have high levels of human capital but also hold views, supported and reinforced by the social context in which they live, that see paid work as contradicting good motherhood. The views expressed by Jessie, one of the 'suburban' group of White middle-class lone mothers in Brighton, are an example (p. 122). Jessie saw herself as a career women and indeed, before the birth of her child, had considerable experience working full-time in a high-powered and high-paid job in the music industry. But in her view the responsibilities of motherhood meant that now she would, at the most, take up short part-time work and even then only once her daughter went to school. Currently, she had no paid work at all. Other lone mothers, sometimes with low levels of human capital, see paid work as an essential contribution to good motherhood, and again live in social contexts which support this. For example Kim, a Black lone mother living in Brixton (pp. 114–16), had held a full-time job after the birth of her child – even though her formal qualifications were low and she had become a mother at the age of seventeen. Consequently, this job was in relatively low paying clerical work. The birth of her second child had indeed forced her to give up this job, but after only three months she took a long part-time job of around 20 hours per week, and planned to get another full-time job as soon as she could.

In a more formal sense, then, the gendered moral rationalities approach sees social relations and understandings as the primary factors in explaining lone mothers' uptake of paid work. This does not mean that levels of human capital and constraints are seen as having no effect. Clearly, these will be important to the ability of lone mothers to take up paid work, as ample research has shown. So too, although this has more often been neglected, will the availability of jobs in different local labour markets (see Chapter 6). Different national policies will also affect both the level of constraints, like the availability of day care, and the reservation wage provided by social transfers (Chapter 7). Rather the gendered moral rationalities approach positions these factors, however important they can be, as contingent and secondary factors. It is lone mothers' motivations, as informed by their understandings of what motherhood means, that come first in explaining their decisions about paid work. The combination of 'intensive' and 'extensive' empirical research designs we have used for this study (see Chapter 1) allows us to better evaluate the relative efficacy of these two views of lone mothers' economic decision-making. On one hand we are able to assess the generality of the qualitative interview information about lone mothers' social relations and understandings by using representative quantitative information from the British census as a check. Conversely, the interviews provide process explanations for the descriptive data on lone mothers' socio-economic positions found in the census. This allows to better link evidence on social process and cause (on how and why things happen) with evidence about social patterns (on what has happened). As we also mentioned in chapter one, extensive research and quantitative methods have been, incorrectly, accorded a privileged place in much of social science research. This is unfortunate not only because this sort of research is weak in explanatory terms (its strengths lie elsewhere) but also because the type of information normally produced by extensive research is not very useful in telling us much about social relations and understandings. The human capital approach then seems self-evident for research on lone mothers' uptake of paid work, not only because rational economic man is assumed, a priori, but also because that is all the data can represent. Empirical evidence on lone mothers' actual beliefs, understandings and motivations becomes peripheral on both counts. In contrast, this sort of evidence forms one important strand in the analysis of lone mothers' uptake of paid work presented in this book.

5.2 EMPLOYMENT POSITION AND GENDERED MORAL RATIONALITIES

Employment Position by Gender and Parent Type

Figure 5.1 uses the SARs to map employment position by gender and parent type. We have taken total employment rate (per cent in paid work) as an indicator of the overall level of employment (the horizontal axis on the graph). The nature of this employment can vary substantially however, in particular the hours employed are crucial for the income generated and, in addition, are important for the status accorded to paid work both by the individual employed as well as more generally. In Britain, women's earnings from part-time employment are rarely enough to release married women from financial dependence on a male breadwinner to support a household (see

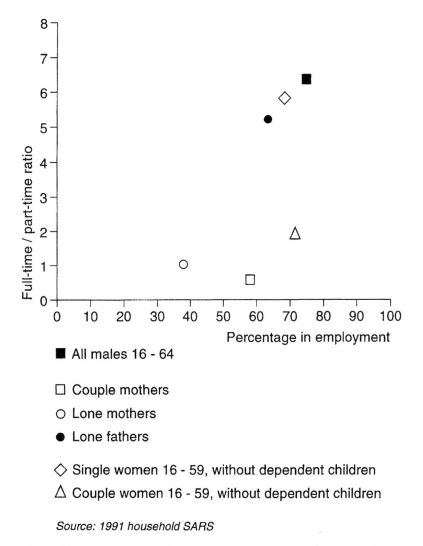

■ All males 16 - 64

□ Couple mothers
○ Lone mothers
● Lone fathers

◇ Single women 16 - 59, without dependent children
△ Couple women 16 - 59, without dependent children

Source: 1991 household SARS

Figure 5.1   Employment position: gender and parent type, Britain 1991

Chapter 5). Furthermore, in Britain women's part-time work is often organised around unpaid domestic and caring work, where the latter is given priority both in terms of time and duty, and where it is full-time work that best accords the status of 'worker' as opposed to 'homemaker' (see Morris 1990; Dale and Joshi 1992; Joshi et al. 1995; Hakim 1996). We have therefore taken the the ratio of the percentages of full to part-time employment as an index of relative orientation to the labour market as opposed to domestic and caring work.

Returning to Figure 5.1, it is striking that employment position in 1991 did not primarily reflect parent type, in other words it did not simply reflect individual constraints in terms of caring responsibilities. Thus lone fathers were close to the 'standard' male norm of majority full-time employment, while couple mothers were closer to the lone mother average of minority employment with substantial part-time work.[2] Although couple mothers had higher overall rates of employment, they are even more oriented to part-time work than lone mothers. This is despite the fact that couple mothers experience lower constraints in terms of child care than lone mothers, as they have greater access to partners and partners' relatives for babysitting, as well as possessing higher household incomes with which to purchase day care. The evidence is that this income is not used to buy day care (Popay and Jones 1990, Marsh and McKay 1993). It may be economically rational to increase household income even further by purchasing day care and selling mothers' labour in the labour market. However, given gendered moral rationalities about what mothers should do, and what they feel about their responsibilities to their children (see Chapter 4), this becomes morally irrational.

Figure 5.2 on age participation rates, and 5.3 on hours of work for those with employment, allow us to examine these contrasts by gender and parent type in more detail. Young lone fathers (the majority, especially for those with young children) do indeed show lower rates of economic activity than the male average (Figure 5.2a). This, presumably, reflects the constraints of child care. However, they still show consistently higher participation rates than both couple and lone mothers, and fall into the higher 'male' part of the graph rather than the lower 'mother' part. This contrast is even more marked for full-time work (Figure 5.2b). The hours actually worked by those with jobs makes this all the plainer (Figure 5.3). Employed lone fathers are virtually indistinguishable from employed men as a whole, with an overwhelming majority working between 32 and 42 hours per week. Returning to Figure 5.2, it would appear that for lone fathers full-time

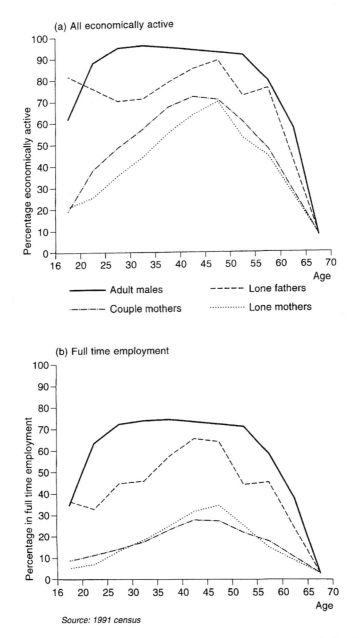

(a) All economically active

Adult males
Lone fathers
Couple mothers
Lone mothers

(b) Full time employment

Source: 1991 census

Figure 5.2   Age participation rates by gender and parent type: Britain 1991

work is substantially the only option. It may be economically rational to take up part-time work, either long part-time of over 20 hours per week or, conversely, short-time below 16 hours per week to keep within benefit eligibility criteria, but very few lone fathers take either option. For both couple and lone mothers in work the opposite is the case. A majority, especially of couple mothers, take up part-time work.

Figures 5.1 to 5.3 reflect a striking gender division of labour, rather than a parental division. The constraints of child care experienced by lone fathers, the lessening of these constraints for couple mothers, or their absence for couple women without dependent children, do little to change a gendered orientation to the labour market. The contrasting employment positions of single women and couple women without dependent children in Figure 5.1 suggest that this gendered division of labour is based on marriage/partnership, that it is living with a man and with having children (or the expectation of having children), rather than around sex *per se*. Thus single women without dependent

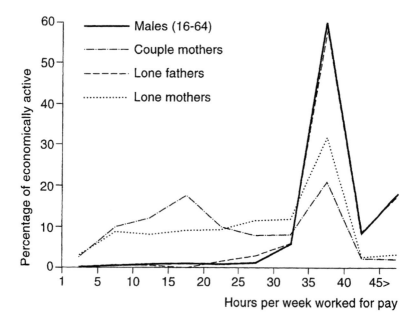

Figure 5.3   Hours worked by gender and parent type, Britain 1991

children have an employment position near the 'male norm', but couple women also without dependent children are firmly positioned within the 'mother' part of the graph. Figure 5.4, showing the employment position for these women in different age groups, allows us to take this argument further. It is older couple women (aged 40–59) without dependent children who are located in the 'motherhood' part of the graph. In fact most will have been mothers with dependent children previously in their lives. In contrast, the youngest couple women (16–24) without children show very high full-time rates (above the 'male norm'), presumably in advance of childbirth. Finally, single women without children in this youngest age group have very low full-time rates (similar to the older couple women without dependent children) – presumably because of education and training.

These figures are not surprising given research on both actual and expected divisions of labour within the conventional British gendered moral rationalities about marriage/partnership and motherhood (Joshi 1989; Morris 1990; Dale and Joshi 1992; Hakim 1996). For women in couples, labour is allocated to full-time work before childbirth, even at the expense of education and training. We may suspect that the social and household negotiation of gendered moral rationalities determines that the acquisition of 'human capital' by these future mothers is not a priority. This is despite the fact that young women in Britain are now, on average, better educated than young men (Weiner et al. 1997). When children are born, the labour of what family economists might call 'female partners' (but in fact now socially defined as 'married mothers') is chiefly reallocated to an unpaid caring role, with some part-time work. The position of couple mothers in Figures 5.1 to 5.3 reflects this allocation. As is well documented (for example Joshi 1996), this further reduces mothers' acquisition of 'human capital' and leaves them in a weak labour market position when their children become independent. Experience in caring is not counted as human capital and the growth of mothers' involvement in part-time work, as we discuss in Chapter 6, usually means little training, few promotion prospects, and low wages. At this stage women are often 'redrafted' into unpaid care for the elderly, and it is those without full-time paid work who are especially likely to take on this role (Finch and Mason 1993). The combination of these two factors is reflected in the employment position of women in this age group as shown in Figure 5.4.

In other words gendered moral rationalities about marriage include expectations about reproductive and caring responsibilities, as well as domestic work more generally. Heather Joshi (1985) has estimated

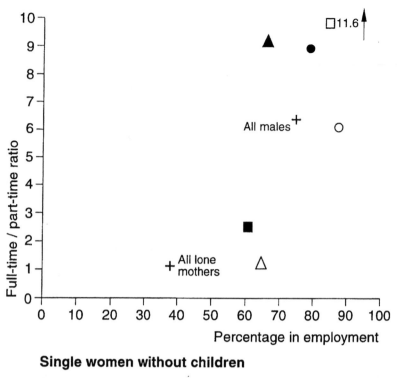

Single women without children

■ 16 - 24
● 25 - 39
▲ 40 - 59

Couple women without children

□ 16 - 24
○ 25 - 39
△ 40 - 59

Source: 1991 household SARS

Figure 5.4   Employment position: single women and couple women without dependent children by age, 1991

that in Britain the individual cost of this arrangement is equivalent to 12–14 years of women's life-time earnings. These gendered divisions of labour, as mediated by marriage/partnership, are of course well-known from previous research – not to mention our experience of everyday life. What is important for our purposes here, however, is to relate this information to our critique of the human capital theory of mothers' economic decision-making. Gender, a collective and social relationship, is primarily determinant in accounting for differential labour market behaviour. Potential levels of individual constraint and human capital have a relatively minor effect. This is why couple mothers do not participate in the labour market in the same way as men, and why lone fathers do not behave like lone mothers. We say 'potential' because what seems to happen is that caring and domestic duties, and indeed the acquisition of human capital – are differentially assumed by men and women in line with gendered expectations.

Ethnicity, Human Capital and Lone Mothers' Employment Position

This evidence so far on employment position by gender and parent type could still, however, be incorporated into a hunan capital approach. Granted, the argument might go, the acquisition of human capital and work roles is highly gendered, reflecting a patriarchal society. Nevertheless, within this 'given' cultural context mothers – including lone mothers – would still act as rational economic men in choosing paid work in accordance with the human capital they have got (however unequally acquired). In this view it would be the exogenous environment that is subject to gendered moral rationality, not individual economic decision-making. We can examine this argument further by comparing the employment position of different social groups with similar levels of human capital and constraints.

Figure 5.5 begins with the employment positions of couple and lone mothers for different ethnic groups.[3] (Note that this and subsequent graphs also show the average male and the lone mother employment positions as reference points.[4]) While the difference between lone and couple mothers referred to earlier is replicated (the latter have higher overall employment rates but are more oriented to part-time work), the major difference is that between ethnic groups. Both African-Caribbean/Black and African lone mothers show higher employment rates and in particular much higher orientations towards full-time work than White lone mothers. Indian and Pakistani lone mothers have the lowest overall employment rates but, even so, a fairly high orientation to full-time work for those in employment. (Low employment rates for this group may be partly a function of hidden homeworking or unpaid work in family businesses; see Modood et al. 1994.) Lone mothers in different ethnic groups behave differently in employ-

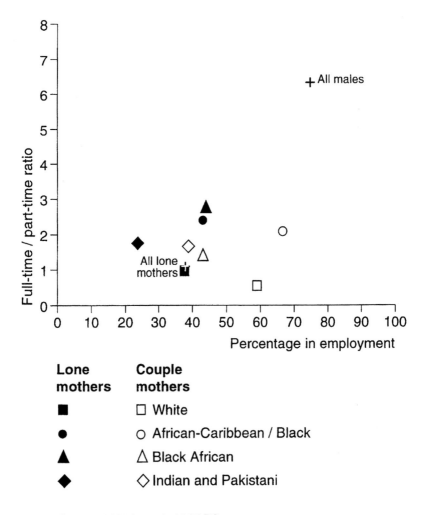

Source: 1991 household SARS

Figure 5.5   Employment position: lone mothers and couple mothers by ethnicity, 1991

ment terms, therefore. The same pattern of differential employment behaviour by ethnic group extends to couple mothers. This confirms research by Clare Holdsworth and Angela Dale (1997) showing that the 'British' pattern of women's employment, where becoming a mother means leaving the labour market either completely or partially, is in fact a White British pattern. Not only are there marked differences in economic activity between ethnic groups, but it is only White women who take on high levels of part-time working (see also Bhavani 1994). In other words, if motherhood is a constraint to labour market participation, it is ethnically variable, both for couples and lone mothers.

We can measure the effect of this 'motherhood' constraint more precisely by examining the employment positions of different ethnic groups of lone mothers by the age and number of their children. These two factors have repeatedly been shown to be associated with the employment rates of lone mothers, as well as their relative propensity to take up full or part-time work (for example Ford et al. 1995). Child care is both more difficult to arrange, and perceived as less suitable, when children are younger (it often thought unnecessary for teenage children). In addition, the more children a lone mother has then the more difficult and costly child care becomes. Figures 5.6 and 5.7 measure levels of child care constraints in this way and, as expected, these clearly influence employment position. However, the effect of these constraints is much less pronounced for Black lone mothers. In addition, and most striking in the figures, for any level of child care constraint Black lone mothers have higher full-time rates and, usually, higher overall employment rates. This is especially the case for the most constrained Black lone mothers.

Do ethnic differences in employment position persist for lone mothers with the same level of human capital? Figure 5.8 takes lone mothers' age and housing tenure as indicators. Housing tenure is highly correlated with educational level, socio-economic group and class both for the population at large and for lone mothers. For example, the 1991 Policy Studies Institute survey found that only 25 per cent of owner-occupying lone mothers depended on income support as their sole source of income, compared with 73 per cent of public housing tenants (McKay and Marsh 1994; see also Moore 1996). Age also correlates with educational level and employment experience, especially for lone mothers (Burghes and Brown 1995). On average, therefore, older lone mothers who are also owner-occupiers will possess higher levels of human capital, while young lone

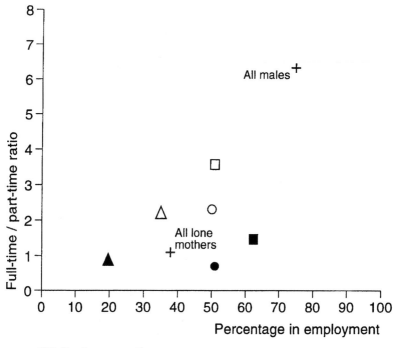

White lone mothers

■ youngest child aged 13+

● 5 - 12

▲ 0 - 4

African-Caribbean / Black lone mothers

□ youngest child aged 13+

○ 5 - 12

△ 0 - 4

Source: 1991 household SARS

Figure 5.6 Employment position: lone mothers by ethnicity and age of youngest child, 1991

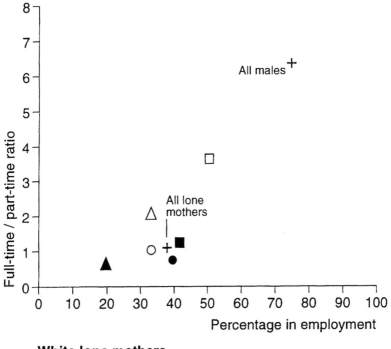

White lone mothers
■ with one child
● two children
▲ three children

African-Caribbean / Black lone mothers
□ with one child
○ two children
△ three children

Source: 1991 household SARS

Figure 5.7   Employment position: lone mothers by ethnicity and number of children, 1991

mothers who live in publicly rented housing will possess lower levels. In addition, the younger lone mothers are also more likely to have young children. As we would expect, therefore, Figure 5.8 shows that older, owner-occuping, lone mothers have both higher employment rates and full-time ratios. But again it is ethnic differences which are most apparent. For example, the full-time rate for the least advantaged Black lone mothers (aged 16–29 in public renting) is above that for even the most advantaged White group (aged 30+ and owner-occupying). Even the overall employment rates for these two groups are similar. At the other end of the spectrum the most advantaged Black lone mothers hold an employment position near the 'male norm'. These (relatively few) Black lone mothers with the highest levels of human capital have moved out of the 'motherhood' part of the graph altogether. Similarly advantaged White lone mothers remain well within it.

This contrasting employment position of Black and White lone (and couple) mothers has nevertheless been explained in human capital terms: Black mothers in Britain have higher average educational levels than White mothers. A significantly higher proportion of White women, across all age groups, have no qualifications, while a markedly higher proportion of Black women have GCSE or A-levels. This is becoming more marked over time, with the greatest differences in the 16–24 age group. For this group even the proportion of Black women with degree level qualification is now approaching White levels (Modood et al. 1997). Indeed, this is the explanation used in the econometric literature for Black lone mothers' greater propensity for employment, especially full-time, and clearly this argument appeals to a rational economic man view of behaviour. (This explanation is rather astounding for underclass theorists, however, especially for those with a predilection for seeing Black people as possessing genetically lower intelligence, such as Hernstein and Murray 1996.) This could explain, for instance, why the employment position of Black lone mothers outstrip Whites for the same level of child care constraint (Figures. 5.6 and 5.7), and similarly why young Black lone mothers are more likely to have a job and to work full-time than their White counterparts (Figure 5.8).

This educational capital explanation is to some extent a chicken and egg argument. If Black women hold gendered moral rationalities which value the combination of motherhood with paid work (as we saw in Chapter 4), then they are more likely to invest in education so that they can put this into effect – and to support their daughters,

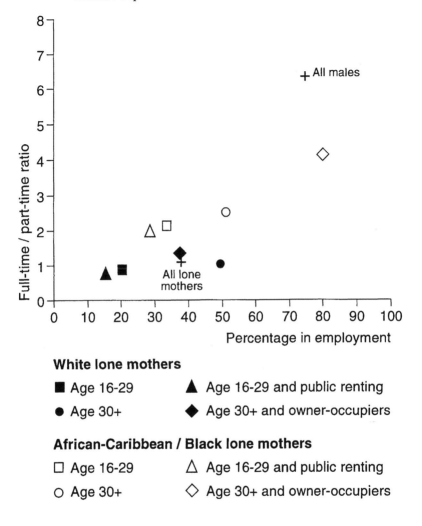

Figure 5.8 Employment position: lone mothers by ethnicity, age and tenure, 1991.

relatives and friends in doing the same. Conversely, those White lone mothers (the majority) who see motherhood and paid work as incompatable are less likely to invest in education, and also less likely to support others in this role. The relative importance of the chicken and the egg can however be assessed further by examining ethnic differences in employment position for lone mothers with equivalent educational levels. Figure 5.9 shows that, as we would expect, a higher education level (this includes nursing and teaching qualifications as well as degree level and above) means higher employment levels and more full-time work. Those mothers with higher education will mostly have better access to higher paying, career professional jobs and will normally be able to afford day care. Yet again, however, the ethnic contrasts are striking. White lone mothers with higher education have a full:part-time ratio which is not much higher than that for all lone mothers, while the Black groups move towards the male 'norm' with little part-time work.[5] The same relative differences apply to the remaining SAR sample without such qualifications.[6] The higher the educational level, the greater the access to the labour market, but this does not seem to alter the contrasting labour market orientations of Black and White lone mothers. These hold just as much for those who have most choice in the labour market as those who have least.

What about the nature of the jobs held by these different groups of lone mothers? This could be one reason for their relatively greater orientation to paid work, especially full-time. If Black lone mothers hold better jobs, offering more pay, more training, easier promotion prospects and greater job security then they will be more likely to stay in the labour market. This argument does seem to be borne out by the evidence. (Again, this will be startling for underclass theorists.) The 1994 Fourth National Survey of Ethnic Minorities found that while 'Caribbean' women were grossly under-represented in the top-jobs category of managers and professional workers, and suffered a higher rate of unemployment, they were more strongly represented than White women in intermediate and junior non-manual work. In particular, as many as 61 per cent of full-time working Caribbean women were in the public sector, compared with just 38 per cent of full-time working White women. In this sector proportionally more Caribbean women were in higher grades (except the top grades). Despite the privatisations and cuts of the last decade, these jobs are likely to have better and less discriminatory career structures, security and pay. White women were more likely to be in unskilled and semi-skilled work. Caribbean women also showed higher upward occupational mobility rates between 1982 and 1994 (except into top jobs). Overall, this meant that Caribbean women on average earned significantly more than White women, even when the latter's greater propensity for part-time work was discounted (Modood et al. 1997).

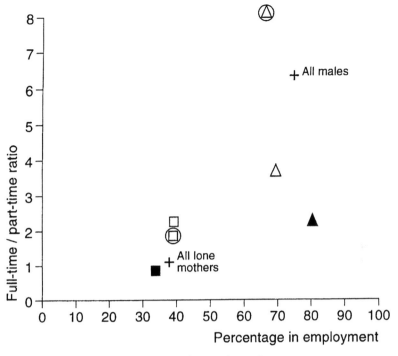

Lone mothers with higher education

▲ White

△ African-Caribbean / Black

⊿Ⓐ African

Lone mothers without higher education

■ White

□ African-Caribbean / Black

▣ African

Source: 1991 household SARS

Figure 5.9   Employment position: lone mothers by ethnicity and qualification level, 1991

Table 5.1 shows that African-Caribbean/Black lone mothers seem to do even better, compared with their White counterparts, than the 1994 Survey's category of Caribbean women as a whole. The differential for top jobs was less, and Black lone mothers had over twice the White employment rate in professional, secretarial and clerical work. Black lone mothers were more likely to hold public sector professional jobs, while White lone mothers were more likely to be employed in personal services and shopwork (notorious for low pay, security and promotion), and in manufacturing. Overall, we can assume that the rewards of staying in employment are greater for Black lone mothers.

There is, however, a problem with the census evidence used in Table 5.1; it refers to occupations held by women over the previous 10 years who were lone mothers on census day in 1991. We do not know how long they held this job and, crucially, whether the 'last occupation' reported in the census was held before or after a child was

Table 5.1   Lone mothers by occupation and ethnicity, Britain 1991

Occupational group	*White lone mothers* %	*Black lone mothers* %
1. Top managers and owners	5.1	3.7
2. Professionals in business, engineering, science, and higher sales employees	1.4	2.5
3. Teaching and health professionals	8.0	12.0
4. Clerical and secretarial	13.8	21.1
5. Personal services and lower sales	29.3	21.7
6. Industrial, distribution and primary	11.1	5.0
7. Others and armed forces	0.4	0.5
8. No occupation in last 10 years / not stated	30.9	33.4
TOTAL	100	100
of which:		
public sector professionals	*7.4*	*11.7*

Source: 1991 household SAR.

born. Because of this limitation it is best to see the data in Table 5.1 as another measure of human capital, but this time focussing on job experience rather than formal qualifications. In these terms, Black lone mothers are likely to hold more human capital than White lone mothers. (Although note that around a third of both ethnic groups recorded no employment at all in the previous 10 years; these lone mothers would therefore hold little or no human capital at all in terms of job experience.) This returns us to a human capital explanation, therefore – on average Black lone mothers have more and are therefore more likely to be employed.

But this line of reasoning also returns us to the same chicken and egg objections as with explanations stressing Black mothers' higher educational levels. If Black lone mothers hold gendered moral rationalities which value the combination of paid work with motherhood, then they are more likely to invest in the labour market, and to find social support in doing so. The converse will hold for those groups of White lone mothers who see motherhood and paid work as contradictory. Hence it would not be surprising that on average Black lone mothers possessed better job experience. Fortunately, we can again use the SARs to assess the relative importance of chicken and egg. Figure 5.10 shows the employment positions of African-Caribbean/ Black and White lone mothers for different socio-economic groups. (Socio-economic groups are based on occupational categories; the third of lone mothers with no job over the previous 10 years are excluded, therefore.) In effect, this horizontal axis of Figure 5.10 shows the drop-out rate from employment, either 'voluntary' or involuntary – for all these lone mothers will have been employed at some date in the previous 10 years. Again, as we would expect, the higher the socio-economic group, the greater proportion still in employment and the higher the full-time ratio. Thus around 80 per cent of lone mothers with professional and managerial work experience were still in employment, mostly full-time, in 1991, while most in semi-skilled and unskilled employment experience had either left work or worked part-time. As before, however, the ethnic contrasts are marked. First, Black lone mothers were more likely to work full-time whatever their socio-economic group (the higher service group which includes nursing and teaching is a partial exception). Secondly, and particularly striking, is the position of Black mothers with the lowest human capital in these terms, those with semi-skilled and unskilled jobs. These were among the least likely to leave the labour market and a majority stayed in full-time work, in stark contrast to White lone

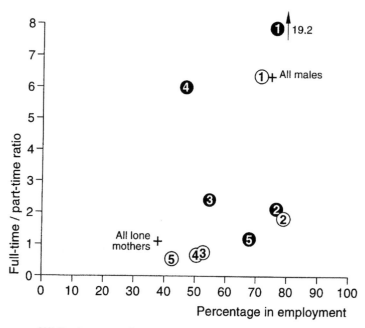

White lone mothers

① Professional and managerial SEGs
② Higher service SEGs
③ Lower service SEGs
④ Skilled manual SEGs
⑤ Semi and unskilled manual SEGs

African-Caribbean / Black lone mothers in

❶ Professional and managerial SEGs
❷ Higher service SEGs
❸ Lower service SEGs
❹ Skilled manual SEGs
❺ Semi and unskilled manual SEGs

Source: 1991 household SARS

Figure 5.10   Employment position: lone mothers by socio-economic group and ethnicity, 1991

mothers in this group. In other words, Black and White lone mothers tend to behave differently in labour market terms even when occupation is held constant.

This sort of conclusion becomes even more emphatic when we remember that there are important differences in the labour market context for different groups of lone mothers, as we discuss in Chapter 6. Black lone mothers are predominantly located in unfavourable inner-city labour market areas where the decline in lone mothers' employment rate as a whole was particularly marked in the 1980s. Indeed inner London, where around 40 per cent of African-Caribbeans and west Africans live, was the only area in Britain where the number of female jobs actually declined over the 1980s. In contrast, more White lone mothers live in those smaller towns and outer metropolitan areas where the expansion of women's employment has been more marked. It is even more remarkable that Black lone mothers with low levels of human capital, and/or high constraint levels, who usually live in unfavourable labour market areas, show employment rates near those of better resourced White lone mothers who in addition mostly live in more favourable labour market areas.

In summary, for any level of human capital or individual constraint, as measured by census variables, Black lone mothers in Britain showed a higher orientation to full-time work, and usually had higher rates of employment, than their White counterparts. Often the less resourced and most constrained Black lone mothers occupied an employment position similar to the least constrained and most resourced White lone mothers, while the most resourced Black lone mothers approached the 'male norm' of majority full-time work. As a result Black lone mothers in Britain are likely to have higher incomes than their White counterparts and their children are much less likely to be deprived (Moore 1996). They even smoke far less and prepare more nutritious meals (even controlling for income, Dowler and Calvert 1995).

How can we explain these ethnic differences in lone mothers' employment positions, which persist even when levels of constraint and human capital are held constant? For this we need to refer back to our discussion of the interview evidence in Chapter 4, and in particular to Figure 4.1 which summarises this information. White lone mothers largely saw motherhood and employment as dichotomous, incompatible or separate activities demanding different identities. Both the working class White mothers living on a peripheral public housing estate, and middle class White lone mothers living in nearby 'suburban' owner-occupied housing, shared a moral view of their responsibilities as mothers that placed staying at home with their children as central. The accounts of Sylvia and Lena (pp. 110–12 and 124) give examples from each. These 'conventional' views of motherhood and employment were shared despite the wide social gulf between the two groups (see Chapter 3). While 'alternative' White lone mothers were more likely to see themselves as primarily workers rather than mothers, these two identities were still seen as dichotomous. (See the views of Fiona and Linda, p. 125). These lone mothers are also likely to remain in the minority, where attitudinal surveys show that the majority of mothers in Britain hold a conventional 'primarily mother' view (see Thomson 1995). In contrast African-Caribbean and west African lone mothers were more able to integrate the two identities of mother and worker and, for some, to be a good mother meant being in full-time work. In Chapter 4 we used Kim's views as an exemplar. This also fits in with what attitudinal data exists for different ethnic groups in Britain; thus Geoff Dench (1996) shows that African-Caribbeans born in England showed the strongest attachment to family arrangements with non-traditional gender divisions.

In other words the interview evidence shows systematic differences between social groups in gendered moral rationalities about the relationship between motherhood and paid work. These differences are reflected in the representative census evidence for different ethnic groups of lone mothers we have presented in this chapter. (The census does not give a measure of 'alternativeness'.) Whatever the level of constraint and human capital, Black lone mothers, largely with gendered moral rationalities where paid work was less contradictory to being a good mother, were normally more likely to be in paid work, especially full-time. In comparison White lone mothers, largely with gendered moral rationalities stressing the primacy of looking after children at home, were more likely to be outside the labour market or working part-time.

5.3   GENDERED MORAL RATIONALITIES AND EMPLOYMENT POSITION OVER TIME

So far we have been examining a static 'snapshot' picture for the early 1990s, where the census evidence is from 1991 and the interviews were carried out in 1994. However, lone mothers' views about whether to take up paid work or not will have a time dimension. For example, as we have seen the age of children affects views about the morality about taking up a job, and child care can be easier to arrange for older children. Lone mothers will obviously expect their children to grow older over time, and hence their views and practices about combining paid work and motherhood may change. Similarly, some lone mothers may think it is quite likely that they will repartner and, if they subscribe to conventional views of gender roles, these mothers would be more likely to downplay investing in jobs – especially if their children are young. Others may see themselves as remaining lone mothers in the medium or long term and, especially for those with alternative views of gender roles, investing in the labour market becomes more rational in an economic sense as well as a moral sense.

Our interview data does give some indications about why lone mothers may change their employment practices over time. Heather, one of the White lone mothers living in the peripheral public housing estate in Brighton, provides a compelling example. Heather had two children, aged four and eight in 1994. She had previously lived with her partner, in owner-occupied housing, in Lambeth in Inner London. She worked full-time as a local government officer from when her older child was a baby, who was placed with a childminder, and she was in her words 'career-minded'. Subsequently the family moved to Brighton, where she had another child, gave up work, and split from her partner in violent circumstances. This resulted in rehousing in Moulscoomb. By 1994 Heather said that she would no longer want to leave her children to be looked after by someone else – 'I want to be there for my children'. Reflecting on her career-minded days she says: 'I decided I would go back to work with a view of bettering myself, so I left [my son] with a minder. But I regret that now. Not being with him, I think I missed out on a lot'. Downward social mobility, accompanied by a shift in both geographical location and her social networks (from mainly friendship to mainly family) was accompanied by a shift from primarily worker to primarily mother gendered moral rationality, and from full-time work to being full-time at home.

How can we disentangle the effects of a change in economic circumstances, which Heather had experienced so abruptly, from a change in socially negotiated moral circumstances – and which comes first in explaining changes in employment? The example of Ella, an African-Caribbean lone mother aged 38 in 1994 and with two children aged 11 and 17, helps us do this. Ella had been a lone mother for the previous nine years following cohabitation breakdown, living on a small local authority estate in East Dulwich, Southwark (see

Figure 3.1). Located in the very south of the Borough, in a predominantly middle-class (and White) area with much owner-occupied housing, and even with a prestigious private school, this area moves out of the 'inner-city' category. None the less, it is within easy access to central London, where Ella worked full-time in both catering and clerical work until after the birth of her second child. But then her views about motherhood and paid work began to change. In her words:

> Well, I think mothers should work if they want to, but if they're in a position not to work and still be alright financially then I'd stay at home with the child. I didn't used to think that, but I've changed my views. When I had [my youngest child], by the time she was five months old I went back out to work for two years, then I stopped. I tried it again when she was about five, when she started school, and then I stopped again after a while. And I've been at home with her ever since.

Ella plans to go back into catering work in a year or so when her youngest child is settled into secondary school, but now – in line with her changed views – only part-time as she wants to be at home for her daughter when she returns from school. In terms of the categories we developed in Chapter 4, a primarily worker or perhaps a mother/ worker integral gendered moral rationality has been replaced by a primarily mother rationality.

This is a particularly interesting case, because the change in Ella's employment practices has apparently run counter to economic rationality. She dropped full-time work despite the fact that child care constraints lessened as her children became older, and despite substantial job experience. (Although her first exit from employment was coincident with becoming a lone mother.) Her friends, most of whom live further into the 'inner-city', also think she should be in full-time work. Rather, perhaps because of the length of time Ella has lived in a relatively affluent middle-class area (15 years in all), she has reconceptualised what constitutes 'good mothering'. Her gendered moral rationality changed towards a primarily mother view, and a change from full-time employment to staying at home with her children accompanied this; the economic possibilities, costs and benefits of employment remained secondary factors.

The example of Beata, living in Björndammen, tends towards the same conclusion – although here employment practice went in the opposite direction. Beata preferred to be a full-time employed lone mother in Sweden rather than being an unemployed housewife, married to a high-earning husband, in England. Similarly, she preferred to live on a 'problem estate' in Sweden than in high status owner-occupation in Britain. However, in Beata's case it seems that her gendered moral rationality had not changed. Rather, she had migrated back to Sweden where this could be more easily fulfilled (and of course where she had first developed her relatively egalitarian beliefs about gender roles, motherhood and paid work). It was easier to be a lone mother in Sweden rather than a lone mother in Britain – and much less likely to lead to poverty, but in terms of a purely economic rationality it would have been best to remain married to a high earner in Britain. Again, moral rationality seems primary in explaining a change in employment position.

It is possible to use census data to evaluate the interview evidence in a more representative way, where the Longitudinal Survey (LS) follows a 1 per cent sample over census dates. Table 5.2 shows the 1991 and 1998 employment positions for all lone mothers in the 1981 sample.[7] As in the previous section we focus on the different employment behaviour of Black and White lone mothers. ('Black' refers to the census categories of African-Caribbean, Black Other and Black African.)

Table 5.2 presents aggregate figures, simply giving the total 'snapshot' picture for the whole sample at the two dates, without distinguishing actual 'flows' of people between particular employment categories. This form is useful as a starting point, however, in confirming that the 1991 snapshot census evidence presented in the last section is stable over time. We would expect greater labour market participation over time, as some mothers leave lone parenthood, either through repartnering or as their children become independent, and as remaining children became older. (Lone mothers are relatively unlikely to bear more children.) We would also expect an overall improvement in human capital over time through education and job experience, especially for the youngest lone mothers. However, it is only White lone mothers who show any substantial increase in full-time work over the decade, with reductions in both part-time work and joblessness. Black lone mothers already, in 1981, had full-time rates at around double the figure for White lone mothers. In this light, the increase in full-time work for the White group seems relatively small, with 1991 rates still well below the Black figure. Similarly, Black lone mothers were much less likely to take up 'short' part-time of less than 22 hours per week. This confirms the

Table 5.2   Lone mothers' employment position by ethnicity, 1981–91 (%)

White lone mothers in 1981
(n = 6146)

	Full-time	Part-time	Student	No job	TOTAL
1981 employment	23.4	23.3	0.6	52.6	100
1991 employment	32.7	19.7	0.3	45.9	100
		of which:			
		long short			
		6.1 13.6			

Change 1981–91	+9.3	–3.6	–0.3	–8.7	

Black lone mothers in 1981
(n = 350)

	Full-time	Part-time	Student	No job	
TOTAL					
1981 employment	44.6	10.3	0.5	44.6	100
1991 employment	46.9	9.1	0.6	43.7	100
		of which:			
		long short			
		4.0 5.3			

Change 1981–91	+2.3	–1.2	+0.1	–0.9	

'Long' part time defined as 22+ hours per week.
Source: 1981–91 LS.

analysis in section 5.3 showing that similar constraints and human capital levels are differentially experienced by the two groups, because of differences in gendered moral rationalities about combining motherhood and paid work.

Table 5.3 provides similar aggregate 'snapshot' information for changes in family status over the decade. It confirms that lone motherhood is substantially a transitional status over a 10 year period, although this is less the case for Black women where almost 40 per cent, double the figure for White women, were still lone mothers in 1991. The table also shows how leaving lone parenthood is not primarily a matter of repartnering, as is so often assumed. Rather, for both groups over 40 per cent became single person households as children left home. Even half of those repartnered by 1991 did so in

Table 5.3   Household type in 1991 for 1981 lone mothers by ethnicity (%)

Household type	White lone mothers in 1981	Black lone mothers in 1981	Ethnic difference
Lone mother	18.8	38.6	+19.8
Single person	40.1	40.9	+0.8
Couple mother	20.2	10.3	–9.9
Couple (no children) and other	20.7	9.7	–11.0
TOTAL	100	100	

Source: 1981–91 LS.

conjunction with becoming a childless household. However, repart-nering for Black lone mothers ran at only about half the rate for White lone mothers. Again, this tends to support evidence suggesting that Black women hold different views of gender roles and respons-ibilities, and on whether or not this necessarily implies the conven-tional family.

For the small minority of the 1981 sample of White women who remained lone mothers ten years later there was very little change in employment position, except for a small movement from part-time into joblessness, as Table 5.4 shows. The larger proportion of Black women remaining lone mothers, on the other hand, show more move-ment over the decade. At first sight this seems unexpected, in that this is a movement from full-time work into part-time and joblessness. We may speculate that this might reflect the high 1981 rate for full-time work for Black lone mothers, in line with gendered moral rationalities stressing a combination of motherhood with paid work, but that this desired position could not always be sustained. As we know (see Chapter 6) the areas where Black lone mothers tend to live have been the more unfavourable in terms of job supply, while their relative con-centration in the public sector may have led to job loss in a decade of cuts and privatisation. Maybe also the constraints of finding, organis-ing and paying for child care became too much for some Black lone mothers, especially if the economic gains of working were small. Perhaps, like Ella (pp. 167–8) gendered moral rationalities changed. Certainly this erosion implies an important policy point which we will

Table 5.4   Staying a lone mother and employment by ethnicity, 1981–91 (%)

Employment	1981	1991	White change	1981	Black 1991	change
Full-time	23.4	24.2	+0.8	44.6	35.0	–9.6
Part-time	23.9	20.5	–3.4	10.8	16.1	+5.3
Jobless	52.6	55.2	+2.6	44.6	48.9	+4.3
TOTAL	100	100		100	100	
% 1981 sample	100	18.8		100	38.6	

Source: 1981–91 LS.

take up in Chapter 9. Even so, for Black women who were lone mothers at both census dates, the 1991 full-time rate remains substantially above the rate for their White counterparts.

What effect does repartnering have on employment position? As discussed in section 5.2, in terms of economic rationality we would expect greater labour market participation for lone mothers who repartnered; both family labour and income would be greater, child care would be less of a problem, and mothers could then better dispose of their human capital in the marketplace (Except for the probably small number who 'pick up' extra young children through repartnering.) As Figures 5.1 and 5.4 showed, however, such economic rationality appears to be overridden by gendered ideas of 'proper' divisions of labour, such that couple mothers and even married women without dependent children do not take on more full-time work. (See also the theoretical discussion in Chapter 8, pp. 259–63.) Table 5.5 assess this conclusion over time, now using disaggregated data on actual flows of 1981 lone mothers to couple motherhood (that is repartnered with dependent children). It confirms that there is little repartnering affect for White lone mothers in terms of increased uptake of paid work. Granted, about half the 1981 jobless had moved into part-time and full-time work consequent to repartnering, and about a third of 1981 part-timers had become full-timers, but at the same time about half of 1981 full-timers had moved in the other direction into part-time work or joblessness, and a third of part-timers had also become jobless. Repartnering is neutral for White lone mothers in employment terms; the proportion becoming more integrated in the labour market was balanced by a similar proportion becoming less integrated. (Although in arithmetical terms, because the 1981 jobless group was so large, this does mean an increase in the numbers in paid work.) For Black lone mothers, on the other hand, the repartnering affect is more marked (note that this group is a small minority of Black lone mothers and that the sample becomes very small). Again, this tends to support the conclusion reached in the last section that the two ethnic groups behave differently in combining motherhood and paid work: Black lone mothers tend to hold gendered moral rationalities stressing full-time work, and repartnering better allows them to achieve this. White lone mothers tend to hold gendered moral rationalities stressing staying at home with children, and apparently repartnering is often a means of doing so.

Table 5.5 showed that Black and White lone mothers behaved differently in response to changing constraint levels over time. What about levels of human capital? Table 5.6, again showing actual flows,

Table 5.5   The 'repartnering effect' by ethnicity, 1981–91 (%)

1981 White lone mothers who had become couple mothers by 1991
(n= 1239)

| | | 1991 employment destination | | |
		Full-time	Part-time	No job	Total
1981 employment origin					
	Full-time	54.2	24.0	21.8	100
	Part-time	31.6	37.0	31.3	100
	No job	21.6	25.0	53.1	100

1981 Black lone mothers had become couple mothers by 1991
(n= 36)

| | | 1991 employment destination | | |
		Full-time	Part-time	No job	Total
Total 1981 employment origin					
	Full-time	69.2	15.4	15.4	100
	Part-time	100	0	0	100
	No job	36.4	9.0	54.5	100

(Students counted as part-time)
Source: 1981–91 LS.

uses 1981 employment as a proxy indicator of job experience. Just over 60 per cent of those who were in full-time work in 1981 remained so in 1991, with particularly high drop-out rates into joblessness (although as Figure 5.10 shows this erosion is experienced differently by Black and White lone mothers). Similarly, an almost identical proportion of the jobless remained in this group 10 years later. Here,

Table 5.6   The 'paid work' effect by ethnicity, 1981–91 (%)

Lone mothers who worked full-time in 1981

1991 employment	White lone mothers (n =1442)	Black lone mothers (n =156)	Ethnic difference
Full-time	63.2	62.8	–0.4
Part-time	11.9	8.9	–2.0
of which: long	4.8	5.1	+0.3
short	7.1	3.8	–3.3
No job	25.0	28.2	+3.2
TOTAL	100	100	

Lone mothers who worked part-time in 1981

1991 employment	White lone mothers (n =1432)	Black lone mothers (n = 36)	Ethnic difference
Full-time	37.2	55.6	+18.4
Part-time	32.7	27.8	–4.9
of which: long	11.5	13.9	+2.4
short	21.0	13.9	–7.1
No job	30.1	16.6	–13.5
TOTAL	100	100	

Lone mothers with no job in 1981

1991 employment	White lone mothers (n = 3233)	Black lone mothers (n =156)	Ethnic difference
Full-time	19.5	26.9	+7.4
Part-time	17.9	10.3	–7.6
of which: long	4.5	5.8	+1.3
short	13.4	4.5	–8.9
No job	62.6	62.8	+0.2
TOTAL	100	100	

(Students counted as long part-time)
Source: 1981–91 LS.

however, there are greater ethnic differentials with more Black lone mothers moving into full-time and long part-time work, whereas the White lone mothers are more likely to take short part-time jobs. These contrasts are even stronger for those who worked part-time in 1981. Black lone mothers (although again this is a very small sample) were most likely to use this as a bridge to full-time work, whereas White lone mothers were more likely to slip into joblessness or short part-time. Finally, over 60 per cent of those of both ethnic groups who were jobless in 1981 remained unemployed in 1991. However, of the remainder, Black lone mothers were the most likely to enter full-time work, while White lone mothers were more likely to enter part-time work. Overall, and as expected, existing employment status has an important effect on future job status for lone mothers. However, Black lone mothers were most likely to move towards full-time and long part-time, while their White counterparts were more likely to move towards short part-time and joblessness.

Our analysis of the employment and household destinations of a one per cent sample of lone mothers from the Longitudinal Survey, from 1981 to 1991, shows that the ethnic differentials in labour market behaviour displayed in the 1991 SAR snapshot (section 5.2) are broadly confirmed. For any change over time in levels of constraint and human capital, Black lone mothers will be more likely to take on full-time and long part-time work, while White lone mothers are more likely to become jobless or take up short part-time work.

5.4 CONCLUSION

In summary, for any level of human capital or individual constraint, as measured by census variables, Black lone mothers in Britain showed a higher rate of full-time work, and usually had higher rates of employment overall, than their White counterparts. Often the less resourced and most constrained Black lone mothers occupied an employment position similar to the least constrained and most resourced White lone mothers, while the most resourced Black lone mothers approached the 'male norm' of majority full-time work.

These results support the explanation for these differences advanced through the interview evidence (Chapter 4). Black lone mothers possess gendered moral rationalities which favour a combination of paid work, especially full-time, with motherhood, and were more able to integrate the two identities where, for some, to be a good mother meant being in full-time work. In contrast White lone mothers mostly possess gendered moral rationalities which see paid work and 'good' motherhood as dichotomous, incompatible or separate activities demanding different identities. In turn this supports our claim that it is gendered moral rationalities which take prime position in accounting for lone mothers' economic decision-making; economic rationality is morally evaluated.

These results also suggest that the 'new right' response to lone motherhood is misplaced. It is those lone mothers who subscribe to traditional views about motherhood and employment that are least likely to be in paid work. Those Black lone mothers with less conventional views, mostly living in spatially concentrated areas in inner-cities, often in public housing and with high rates of single (never-married) lone motherhood – all supposed traits of the 'underclass – are in fact more likely to take up paid work, especially full-time. That the new right 'underclass' theorists neglects this sort of information reinforces the criticism that they are more interested in policing moral behaviour than they are in increasing social opportunity.

However, as every mother knows, 'want doesn't mean get'. Even if lone mothers do see getting paid work ar the proper course of action for them, either because they see it as part of good mothering itself as in the mother/worker integral gendered moral rationality, or because they see themselves as workers as well as mothers, the sort of jobs they require may simply not be available. Jobs are provided by employers in the context of local, national and world economies that are largely outside the capacity of lone mothers to influence directly. This problem becomes especially acute when we remember that lone mothers live in particular local labour markets with specific employment characteristics and traditions. The next chapter turns to the labour market context for lone mothers' uptake of paid work.

NOTES

1. We have included self-employed with employees in full-time employment, and self employed without employees in part-time employment, reflecting both status and earnings. Both categories are small for lone mothers (see Curran and Burrows 1989).
2. 'Fathers' and 'mothers' defined as those with co-residing dependent children. The term 'couple mothers' refers to those cohabiting with a male partner, both married and unmarried.

3.   Ethnicity is as self-defined in the 1991 Census. There are small cell counts for the west African group in the household SAR, hence further disaggregations were not generally used.
4.   The employment position of particular class and ethnic groups will deviate from this average male position. In particular, men in ethnic minority groups have lower employment rates, for example 31 per cent of African-Caribbean men and as many as 38 per cent of Pakistanis and 42 per cent of Bangladeshis were unemployed in the 1994 Fourth National Survey of Ethnic Minorities (Modood et al. 1997). None the less, as the authors of this report make clear, most men of all ethnic groups were in full-time work with very few in part-time work, and that while different groups experience different levels of constraint in achieving lifelong full-time work, this is still seen as the male norm. This was one reason why average educational levels for ethnic minority men were significantly higher than for white men.
5.   There are small cell counts for the Black groups, with large sample errors.
6.   Unfortunately the census does not disaggregate for educational qualifications below higher educational level.
7.   None of the 1981 lone mothers disappeared from the sample through death, international migration or other reasons. We also assumed, given the age distribution of lone mothers, that very few would have moved into retirement age between 1981 and 1991. Significant numbers of long-term sick will be included in the 'no job' category.

6 Lone Mothers in Labour Markets: Employment Availability and Geography

6.1 INTRODUCTION

Chapter 4 shows how different social groups of lone mothers hold different ideas about the compatibility of motherhood and paid work, and Chapter 5 goes on to link these ideas with employment position as recorded in the British census. However, even if lone mothers do consider that substantial paid work is compatible with being a good mother, and even when they receive support for this through their social networks, appropriate jobs have to be available to put these ideas into practice. And these jobs are provided by employers in the context of local, national and world economies that are largely outside the capacity of lone mothers to influence directly.

Put this way, this seems an obvious point. However, the discourses about lone motherhood we discussed in Chapter 2 all focus on the capacities of lone mothers themselves (even though they posit these in widely different ways) and implicitly assume that adequate jobs are simply available. In the social threat discourse for example, lone mothers willingly remove themselves from the labour market where jobs are assumed to be available, while at the other side of the coin the escaping patriarchy discourse can implicitly see lone mothers as having superior access to jobs than their erstwhile, less socially functional, male partners. In some ways this is a general consequence of the tendency, as discussed in Chapter 1, to focus research on lone mothers isolated from their social contexts. This is perhaps why it is the social problem discourse, with its close links to traditional social policy research, that most clearly shows the problems of assuming that jobs are simply available in the labour market. It is also this discourse which sees most lone mothers as wanting paid work so that they can support themselves and their children without relying on benefits, but where they are prevented from doing so because of the failings of the welfare state. In this view improving the accessibility of paid work through providing day care, and removing the poverty trap imposed by the benefit structure, possibly buttressed by further education and job training, is seen as decisive. Lone mothers would then be able to enter the labour market and support themselves and their children at acceptable levels. But what if jobs are not available or, if they are, that they are the sort of jobs that do not provide a household income? No amount of motivation, day care provision and training facilities can create income if the right sort of jobs are simply not there. And, even if the newly trained and resourced lone mothers do find employment, does this not imply that other people will lose jobs and become worse off?

In this chapter we discuss the constraints for lone mothers set up by the variable supply of jobs in relation to the reform scenarios put forward in the social problem discourse. Section 6.2 examines these purely in the largely spaceless terms of 'the national economy'. Not only are there more or fewer jobs available at different points in the economic cycle, but both gendered occupational segregation, and economic restructuring over the longer term, will affect the types of job available. Jobs of the right sort, or even any sort, may simply not be there for lone mothers to take. Section 6.3 turns to a further limitation to the 'social problem reform scenario'. Both the type and number of jobs are differentially distributed through local labour markets, and these different local labour market characteristics, giving lone mothers better or worse employment opportunities, interact with local cultural understandings of what social role women are expected to hold. Where lone mothers live, as section 6.4 shows, has therefore considerable implications for their employment prospects. Our analysis in this chapter concentrates on Britain. However, as we indicate at various points, the same arguments will apply in other national contexts (see also Duncan and Edwards 1997).

6.2 THE SUPPLY OF JOBS AND NATIONAL ECONOMIES

The social problem discourse sees the provision of daycare and training, combined with reform of the benefit structure, as the key to getting lone mothers 'back' into employment. In Britain lone mothers have lower employment rates than other mothers and are much more likely to be in poverty, with 60 per cent with incomes below half the national average, compared to just 24 per cent of married parents.

Lone mothers in Britain also have greater difficulty, compared to married mothers, in finding day care (where public provision is among the lowest in the EU), on average possess lower educational levels and are particularly affected by the poverty trap, where many face marginal tax deduction rates of 70 per cent and over. Hence the initial persuasiveness of this line of thought (as in Burghes 1993). Some studies imply that as many as 70 per cent of lone mothers would be employed if adequate child care was available (Bradshaw and Millar 1991, Holtermann 1993), a conclusion buttressed by comparisons with other countries with both higher lone mother employment rates and day care provision (Bradshaw et al. 1996). Other studies, while admitting child care constraints as a barrier for lone mothers getting into employment at all, see increased education and training as offering the best prospects for lone mothers to get better jobs and hence increase their income (for example Bryson 1997).

What, however, about the supply of jobs for this newly-trained and newly-available labour force? Put simply, without jobs being available, these reforms will just not work. Even if jobs are available, such reforms will have only a limited and partial effect if these do not offer secure wages which can support a household. All that may be achieved is that lone mothers swap low, but relatively secure, benefit income for nearly as low, and more insecure, wage income.

Implicitly, therefore, the social problem reform scenario assumes growth in the number of jobs, and hence economic growth, and also the maintenance – and even the improvement – of job quality and conditions. These assumptions are not necessarily likely to apply. For instance in economic downturns, or even more in recessions, lone mothers will share higher levels of unemployment. There was a noticeable fall in the proportion of lone mothers employed in the early 1980s recession, for example, especially for those working full-time (Haskey 1997). Indeed, relatively deregulated national economies such as Britain's are likely to show deeper recessions and hence more volatile employment. Proponents of the social problem reform scenario might however reply that, at least, if these reforms were implemented, lone mothers could compete on equal terms in the labour market; they would not be hindered by extra child care constraints for instance. Given lone mothers' low employment rates and their high poverty rates, then this would still be a gain of sorts.

This response would beg further questions, however. For without job growth, these gains to lone mothers will be at the expense of other workers, including partnered mothers and fathers, who would become unemployed in the face of this new competition. In addition Family Credit – the benefit available to low paid parents working over 16 hours per week – allows lone mothers to accept lower wages and hence undercut many of their competitors (Bryson 1997). All that would happen is that poverty would be spread around more, rather than reduced. The viability of the social problem reform scenario then depends on the argument (which does not seem to have been made explicitly) that lone mothers are in some way more 'deserving' than other parents, and that jobs should be redistributed towards them.[1] Whether this remains implicit or is politically articulated, the effect will be to sharpen the antagonism of the 'middle third' of the income range who, in general, are already the most hostile to social policy solutions (Donnison and Bryson 1996).

The likely performance of national economies, and the effects of this on job quantity and quality, is therefore crucial both for lone mothers' job prospects and for the viability of the social problem reform scenario. In western Europe as a whole, and for Britain in particular, job growth overall has been sluggish since the 1970s. This is partly because of slower growth rates, with marked recessions in the early 1980s and again in the early 1990s, but also because of an increasing trend towards 'jobless growth' – output (and profits) may increase, but the number of workers still declines. This has been a consequence of rationalisation and productivity increase, and has affected both the private and public sectors alike (especially with privatisation in the latter). There has also been a widening of inequalities not least in Britain, where there are now more low paid (and insecurely employed) people – many earning even less than they did ten to fifteen years ago in real terms (Hills 1996). The fact that the British labour market is biased towards low-paid jobs with low educational content is a particular problem for those who emphasise training and education as a solution to lone mother poverty and dependency. As Peter Robinson (1997) has shown, fully two-thirds of employment in Britain is concentrated among the six lower occupational groups, usually with lower pay and often with poor security and prospects. Only 13 per cent of these jobs require reading skills above grade C GCSE (that is the standard level for 16-year-olds) and just 3 per cent need numeracy skills at grade D (a minimum level of ability) and above. Furthermore, according to Robinson, while 37 per cent of all jobs require literacy at grade C and above, 50 per cent of pupils currently attain this level, and this rate is rising. The same relationship between qualifications required and those attained exist at other educational levels. In other words there is already an overproduction of education in terms of what the British labour market offers. Improving the educational levels of lone mothers will only increase this surplus, therefore.

However, this economic restructuring in both the number and type of jobs has also been a gendered process – there have been marked difference in the employment fortunes of men and women. This factor potentially lets the social problem reform scenario off the economic hook. For while male activity rates have slowly declined in the EU, and more precipitously in some countries such as Britain, female activity rates have increased. In Britain, for example, women made up 45 per cent of the labour force in 1995, compared with 36 per cent in 1971. In absolute numbers this equates with a gain of 2.6 million jobs for women, and a loss of 1.3 million for men. This is partly a direct result of economic restructuring, where job decline has been most marked in those sectors (such as heavy manufacturing) and occupations (especially for skilled manual workers) dominated by men, while growth has occurred in the service sector where women are mostly employed. What is more, because of the drop in activity rates for both young and elderly people (due to increased education and earlier retirement, although some of this is induced by economic restructuring), this increase in female activity rates has been especially marked for women between 25 and 49 years old – exactly that age group when most women have dependent children. Given remarkably persistent and prevalent occupational sex segregation (of which more below) we might conclude therefore that the social problem reform scenario remains possible. Although this scenario mistakenly treats the economy as an unchanging and unproblematic 'given', because the economy is actually changing so as to deliver more jobs to mothers then this error does not matter too much (cf. Finlayson and Marsh 1997). More job competitive lone mothers will not push partnered mothers into unemployment, because more women's jobs are being created. Similarly, while men are losing jobs, by and large these are jobs where women are not direct competitors. The conclusion might then be that the social problem reform scenario can still work, despite itself.

Unfortunately, there are two severe qualifications to this argument. The first concerns the quality and nature of women's employment, and the second concerns the location of the jobs. Many of the jobs held by women do not provide a secure household income, and would not therefore take lone mothers out of poverty. While partnered mothers may welcome such jobs as a supplement to a partner's income, this option is not available to lone mothers. In addition. lone mothers are concentrated in the large urban areas where female job growth has been weak. We turn to the first of these two factors below, and deal with the second factor in section 6.3.

Remarkably persistent horizontal and vertical occupational sex segregation, whereby women are concentrated in particular occupations and at lower status levels, means that the jobs available to women are generally the least well-paid and secure (Ruberry and Fagan 1993, OECD 1994). In Britain there are few occupational differences between lone mothers, partnered mothers and other women. In other words most women share a disadvantaged position in the labour market because of their gender; it is employment rate – not occupation – that diverges according to women's marital and civil status (Bartholomew et al. 1992, Glover and Arber 1995). It is not that lone mothers earn less than partnered women (although some exceptional groups, such as young and poorly educated groups, do earn less, see Burghes and Brown 1995). Rather, lone mothers share the employment situation of mothers as a whole, but do not have recourse to a compensating male income which is likely to be both higher and more secure.

Although women's average pay rose sharply compared to men's in the 1970s, partly because of equal pay legislation, the rate of advance stagnated and even declined in the 1980s and 1990s. This is particularly the case in deregulated economies such as Britain's (Perrons 1994). Indeed, the gender wage gap in Britain seems to be especially large. Even for full-time workers, women earn only about 65 per cent of the average weekly male wage; this is lower than in any other EU country except Ireland (CSO 1995, Duncan 1996).[2] For part-time work, still quintessentially women's work across the EU but especially in Britain (Meulders et al. 1997), wages are even lower – average hourly rates are only around half the male full-time rate and, what is more, this relative share is actually declining (Land 1994, Hills 1996). In 1995 82 per cent of all part-time workers in Britain were women, and these accounted for 44 per cent of the female labour force. (Only 8 per cent of male workers were part-time, and these were generally new entrants, students, or those over retirement age.) Minimum wage legislation introduced in 1998 may halt this downward drift, and should increase the wages of the very worst paid (mostly women part-timers), but set at the low level of £3.60 per hour for the over-21s until 2001, is unlikely to make much difference to this gender gap. Hours worked are of course also less in part-time work, sometimes considerably so where the average part-timer worked only 16 hours per week in 1995; nearly half worked less than this and as many as 10 per cent worked below 8 hours. Consequently, take home pay for most female part-timers is even smaller compared with the wage received by full-time male workers – almost a third do not even earn enough to pay national insurance contributions (Hakim 1996). By 1994 women part-timers constituted the largest single group – over 40 per cent – of the low paid in Britain (Webb et al. 1996).

The viability of the social problem reform scenario begins to falter in this light, therefore. True enough, plenty of women's jobs have been created in the British economy since 1971. However, over 70 per cent of these extra jobs have been part-time with the greatest rate of growth for short part-time jobs of less than 16 hours a week (Dickens 1995). As Catherine Hakim (1996) shows, for all the much vaunted 'feminisation' of the British workforce since the war, the total hours worked by women has hardly increased. The vast number of women part-timers (over 5 million) account for little more than 10 per cent of paid hours worked – indeed those women who are are employed are now much more likely to be in part-time jobs than women in the 1960s or even the 1930s. Most of these jobs do not offer a household income. This means that getting a job is a much less effective way of escaping poverty in the 1990s than it was in the past. In fact the most common route out of poverty is to have a spouse whose earnings lift the combined household income over the poverty line (Webb et al. 1996). Lone mothers with part-time work, unable to benefit from a spouse's income, will therefore normally remain dependent on benefits (or possibly maintenance) – and in addition risk the greater insecurity that part-time work often brings. This does not look like a solution to lone mothers' poverty and dependency.

At this point the argument is often made that part-time work is what women, especially mothers, prefer. As we should not (presumably) force people to take jobs they do not want, the social problem reform scenario may still stand, therefore. The changes would at least allow lone mothers to take the sort of jobs they prefer, even if these are likely to be part-time. But how, we might ask, are preferences formed in the first place? This presumably takes place with some reference to what is possible and feasible. For employers, at least, the advantages of part-time work are fairly obvious: remuneration is usually lower and, for short-time paid work in particular, social security or other overheads can often be legally avoided in most European countries. In 1996 as many as 60 per cent of part-timers in Britain did not receive the same contractual rights as full-timers, such as paid holidays and sick leave, and few have access to occupational pensions (although this may change by the end of the century with implementation of the Social Chapter, *The Guardian* 4.6.97). Certainly the Conservative British governments from 1979–97 were assiduous in blocking or exempting themselves from EU reforms that might give this largely female workforce greater rights and pay. In the terms of the EU Social Chapter (from which Britain was exempted), this allows 'social dumping' by employers – that is unfair competition through low wage rates – and it is largely women part-timers who are being 'dumped' (Duncan 1997). If part-time work is also flexitime employment, then employers can also synthesise the advantages of numerical and wage flexibility (Meulders et al. 1997). A part-time 'labour reserve' allows easy adjustment of employment to the volume of work (numerical flexibility) and in addition avoids the need for expensive overtime (wage flexibility). Employers, therefore, often have considerable interests in creating part-time employment, and to this extent employees – especially those with less human capital or greater constraints, and mothers are disproportionally affected by both factors – will have to 'choose' what is offered.

At the same time, however, surveys suggest that the majority of part-time workers – especially women – express satisfaction with their working arrangements. In Britain, for example, only 10.5 per cent of women working part-time were doing so 'involuntary', in that they could not find a full-time job, according to a 1993 Labour Force Survey (ibid.). Over 60 per cent (the highest rate in the EU) expressly did not want full-time work. The greater possibility of reconciling family and paid work is often given as the major advantage of part-time work, where working hours can be adjusted to the socially defined need for women – especially mothers – to be at home at certain prescribed times to care for other family members. Looking at Britain, Catherine Hakim (1996) interprets women's satisfaction with part-time employment as showing that most women see homemaking as their principal role. Far from being forced into secondary, part-time work by employers, Hakim argues that it is women, especially mothers, who prefer this. Janneke Platenga (1995), drawing on the situation in the Netherlands, also emphasises the positive employment aspects of part-time work where careers can continue through motherhood. This is especially so when most women – and increasingly men – do not subscribe to the traditional model of the 'pure' worker devoid of any domestic duties.

We must remember, however, that people make choices within the
constraints of what already exists. In this case most women, in particular mothers with dependent children, have to adjust to both persisting
gender divisions of labour, where they take the chief responsibility for
caring and domestic work, and to trends in the supply of jobs emphasising flexibility. We should also note that many part-time jobs staffed
by women, as in personal services, catering or transport, actually
demand hours corresponding to peak periods which are particularly
inconvenient for family life. Indeed, a majority of mothers, including
lone mothers, working part-time were working 'unsocial' or 'very
unsocial' hours in 1992, especially those with young children and with
manual jobs (Glover and Arber 1995; see also Ford et al. 1995).
Certainly, whatever the preference for work times, the associated
'choice' in many part-time jobs of low hourly earnings, less job security, fewer employment rights and benefits, little training or skill acquisition, few promotion prospects and sometimes poor working
conditions (Ruberry et al. 1994, Dickens 1995) can hardly be seen as a
free choice. And it is mothers working part-time who are especially
exposed to these disadvantages. Surveys indeed show that once in
work women – not surprisingly – do value good wages, employment
rights and job security (Martin and Roberts 1984, Ford et al. 1995).
The evidence suggests that while some mothers in the professional
and managerial groups, with higher levels of human capital, could use
part-time work to minimise the impact of motherhood on their career
patterns (as Platenga suggests), the majority were likely to experience
penalties through part-time working (Glover and Arber 1995).

These arguments can be put into perspective by comparison with
Denmark and Sweden, where 'women-friendly' welfare states emphasise public support for parenting and women's participation in the
labour force (see Chapter 7). Nearly all mothers, including lone
mothers, are in employment. Although over 40 per cent of employed
women, including lone mothers, work part-time the great majority are
in 'long part-time' – between 20 and 35 hours per week. (In fact, in
Britain, many of these jobs would be defined as full-time – over
30 hours per week.) Rights, status and pay rates are usually comparable with full-timers; in Sweden many are mothers with young children
exercising their right to a six-hour day in the same job which they held
before childbirth. Here only 4 per cent of mothers with dependent
children worked fewer than 20 hours. This is one reason why the
gender wage gaps in Denmark and Sweden are the lowest in the EU,
where on average women earn 75–90 per cent of the male average

wage. In the terms that Catherine Hakim might use, women in Denmark and Sweden. including lone mothers, are 'choosing' a superior part-time package than in Britain, one that in addition gives them the opportunity of economic independence – but we should add that this choice can be made effective in the different environment of 'women-friendly' welfare states.

In contrast, women's earnings from part-time employment in Britain are rarely enough to support a household. It may be the case that most partnered women themselves 'prefer' this work as supplementary to the male breadwinner wage and secondary to their own unpaid domestic and caring work, as Hakim (1996) argues, despite its disadvantages in other ways. However, such preferences are quite different for lone mothers simply because they are the major household earner, where the material well-being of their children largely depends on their income alone. As Stephen McKay and Alan Marsh put it, based on a 1991 survey of almost 1,000 lone parents, what lone mothers 'wanted was a better paid job they could rely on' (1994, p. 19). Although respondents looking for work had a low 'reservation wage' (they were pessimistic about their likely earning power and would accept even less) they also had a 'reservation security'. Most would be willing to accept such jobs only if they were 'secure as long as I wanted it' (ibid.). McKay and Marsh go on:

Life on Income Support is not fun but it is predictable. Getting into work, paying set-up and travel costs … rebudgeting to cope with a differently structured income, all present difficulties and uncertainties. The likelihood of making such an adjustment only to be flung back on Income Support after a few weeks is a threat, especially if it involves the surrender of long term benefits such as full payment of mortgage interest. It is a threat people know about. (ibid. p. 19)

In addition, despite their low 'reservation' wage, lone mothers appeared to have a different attitude to part-time work to that of partnered mothers, simply because fewer hours usually means lower take-home pay. (Indeed, as Ford et al. 1995 show, lone mothers' average pay is declining, in real terms, just as more do take on part-time work.) Partnered mothers can take a part-time job for supplementary income, and gradually increase hours as their children get older; often they will stop short of full-time work. But lone mothers intending to support themselves and their children through employment – that is by obtaining a primary household wage – go straight into full-time work. If they do work part-time, they generally work only a few hours, sticking close to the Income Support threshold of disregarded earned income (£15 a week at the time of these studies), and only if this could be achieved easily and without paying for day care.

Our own sample of lone mothers expressed similar attitudes. In Lambeth and Southwark in Inner London, nearly all the lone mothers from all groups thought it was hard to get a job within the local area, especially one that was well paid, although some added this was less likely to be the case if applicants had experience or qualifications. They thought most of the jobs available were low skilled, part-time and low paid, mostly mentioning work in shops and restaurants. A few also felt that employers were prejudiced against lone mothers.

> Well there isn't anything much really. I mean apart from if you want to work in a shop, be a shop assistant, or do sort of catering or work in a sandwich bar or in a pub. That's the only really local thing that is available, which doesn't really pay much money. Any job that doesn't really pay much money is what's available. And they're always part-time mostly. (Kim, a younger African-Caribbean lone mother, working long part-time)

In Brighton, although only a few lone mothers thought that it was hard to get a job within the local area, most were dissatisfied with the quality of the jobs that they thought were available to them. Shop work, restaurant and bar work, and cleaning were mentioned as the sort of low skilled, part-time and low paid jobs they thought they would be able to get. The white working class mothers in Moulsecoomb were most likely to think it was hard to get a job, and also thought that employers were prejudiced against people from their neighbourhood (the neighbourhood's poor reputation was a source of ambivalence to the lone mothers living there, as we saw in Chapter 3). The 'alternative' lone mothers in particular often thought that it was difficult to get a job that matched their qualifications or experience:

> I wouldn't think there was any jobs available for people like me. My lodger's been looking for work, and she's just finished her degree so she's very highly qualified. I've never known anyone look so hard for a job. I could maybe get a job in a pub and there's shops ... I mean it would be dire if I lost my job, I can't imagine actually being able to get another one.

The dilemma of the supply of jobs remains for the social problem reform scenario therefore. Yes, the supply of jobs to women, especially mothers, has increased in Britain, and training, public day care and restructuring of the benefit system would make these jobs much more accessible to lone mothers. But most of these jobs are part-time; many are low-quality, insecure and/or short part-time, and they do not offer lone mothers a secure household income. Furthermore, lone mothers, perceiving these disadvantages, by and large do not see these jobs as offering them a real alternative to living on benefits. To be successful the social problem reform scenario must square up to the issue of job quality in general and equality between men and women in the labour market in particular. This, in turn, implies 'women-friendly' reforms on the Scandinavian model (see Chapter 6). Freiderike Maier (1991, quoted in Land 1994), puts this very well in concluding her international comparison of part-time work:

> instead of being taken for granted as a norm, full-time work needs to be treated as problematic: a more general process of overall working time reductions would provide a mechanism for breaking down the distinction between full-time and part-time work which is so overlaid with gender and the domestic division of labour. Working time, social and employment policies that do not consider the gender specific labour market situation will otherwise be in danger of keeping women in a position described as 'living on half rations' (p. 10)

Most partnered mothers do not have to 'live on half rations' because they have access to a male wage, which is generally higher and more secure. But for lone mothers, without this option, 'half rations' will hardly resolve problems of poverty and dependency – with the added disadvantage of decreased time for parenting. The implicit assumption that lone mothers will behave similarly to partnered mothers, in taking on part-time work, reveals the continuing gender bias of the social problem reform scenario and indeed the social problem discourse that informs it. Women, including (paradoxically) lone mothers, are essentially seen as secondary workers dependent on a male income. Not only will this leave most lone mothers in dependency and poverty, but their position will be worsened even more when, as in the USA and Britain, governments begin to withdraw from the replacement 'male provider' role.

6.3   THE SUPPLY OF JOBS IN LOCAL LABOUR MARKETS

The Geography of Jobs versus the Geography of Lone Mothers

Section 6.2 has pointed to a substantial limitation in the 'social problem reform scenario': providing lone mothers with day care and training, and removing the poverty trap, does nothing to provide the sort of jobs they need in order to attain financial security for themselves and their children. There is also another substantial limitation to this scenario. The location of new jobs that have been provided in the British economy does not match up very well with the location of lone mothers.

Most workers do not of course have daily access to all jobs in an economy, but only to those within daily commuting distance. Furthermore, women – and mothers especially – have more limited commuting and job search areas; the shortest commuting areas of all are for those with part-time jobs (Flowerdew and Green, 1993; Atkins et al. 1996). This is because women's time is constrained by domestic responsibilities, transport difficulties (where women disproportionately depend on public transport) and sexual harassment (Pickup 1988), while the trade off between travel time/costs and wage received will often mean that long distance travel for low paid jobs is simply unrealistic. It is, of course, just this sort of job which has accounted for the bulk of job growth in the British economy over the last two decades, as section 6.2 has shown. These constraints are likely to be even more severe for lone mothers. In our interviews with lone mothers in Lambeth, Southwark and Brighton virtually all of those who had jobs worked within the same local authority area in which they lived. Only some of the 'alternative' lone mothers, interestingly just those who are more likely to hold a 'primarily worker' separation between motherhood and paid work (see Chapter 4), would seriously consider a job outside these areas. For many even travel to work outside the immediate neighbourhood area would be a problem. The reason most gave for working, or wanting to work, in or near their neighbourhood was primarily that of care and responsibility for their children, buttressed in some cases by an appreciation of the inadequacy of the jobs on offer that made them hardly worth travelling to in any case. As Phyllis, a White working class lone mother in Brighton, working minimal part-time hours, put it

Usually they're low paid jobs, cleaning, bar work. They're miles away really, in the centre of town. Or you can go for auxiliary work, but that's all they way up Hove [ie. about 3 miles away], if you want to work with old people ... You try to better yourself but you get nowhere.

Bonnie, living in Lambeth, and working part-time and claiming Family Credit (an in-work benefit) focused more directly on time with her children:

> I'd like to be able to afford to live without benefits on a part-time job. I could do it if I was prepared to travel more, say into London [i.e. across the river Thames to the City or West End] ... I don't want to spend the time travelling when I could spend it with my children. I'm actually applying for a job now, but I'm a bit dubious about even wanting to travel like another ten minutes out of my way.

These travel constraints are all the more telling where most lone mothers do not possess a car. Nor can lone mothers very easily move to areas where jobs may be better provided. This is not only because of financial constraints, where most British lone mothers have few, if any, savings, they do not often have a house to sell (and it is difficult to swop council houses) and a great number are in debt (Marsh and McKay 1993, Ford et al. 1995). Also, as Chapter 3 has indicated, lone mothers may be more constrained than other households from moving to another area just because of their dependence on informal neighbourhood networks.

So where do British lone mothers live? Crudely, they are concentrated in Inner London, the inner parts of other large cities, and in the older industrial towns of the north of England, Scotland and Wales (N. Bradshaw et al. 1996, Dorling 1995, Forest and Gordon 1993). Put together, these areas accounted for more than 60 per cent of lone mothers in 1991. As Figure 6.1 shows, there is also a relative concentration of lone mothers, as a proportion of all families with children, in coastal resorts.

The reasons for this concentration are complex. In part this reflects housing market factors, where lone mothers are disproportionally concentrated in cheaper private rented and older public rented housing which is most available in large urban areas (Crow and Hardey 1991, Winchester 1990). Coastal resorts also have more private renting, as well as the temporary accommodation (including 'bed and breakfast hotels') where up to a sixth of lone mothers have to

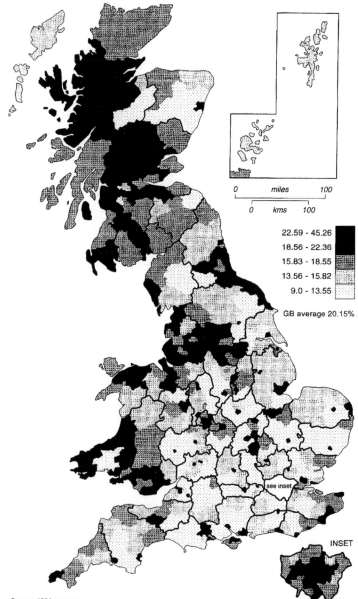

Figure 6.1   Lone parent families: percentage of all families with dependent children 1991

live at some time. These housing market factors are more relevant to the 'fine grain' of geographical location, however. (This explains why lone mothers are concentrated in Ipswich and Aberdeen, for example, and not in the surrounding rural areas and small towns of Suffolk and Grampian.) Why lone mothers are concentrated in particular types of area – the large cities and older industrial towns – is better explained by other social and cultural factors.

In some areas, lone motherhood is more linked to births to single mothers who do not live with a partner, and this may in turn be may be connected to economic and social deprivation – Figure 6.2 shows strikingly high rates for this category of birth in economically depressed areas in South Wales, the North-East, Merseyside and Greater Manchester (data was not available for Scotland). Inner London also shows high rates of single motherhood. In other areas, as Figure 6.3 shows, births to unmarried cohabitees are more common. These unions experience greater rates of separation than married parents and – nationally – account for the greatest proportion of 'single' lone mothers as statistically defined by the fact that they were unmarried (see Chapter 1). Higher rates of these births are found in London (including suburban areas in Outer London where single motherhood is less common), the larger cities, attractive university towns like Lancaster, and many coastal areas especially in south-west England. Some of these areas may function as 'alternative' spaces for 'counter-cultural' lifestyles which may attract or support like-minded people (similar to the alternative neighbourhoods described in Chapter 3). Brighton,with one of the highest rates of cohabitee births, combines several of these elements. Areas where women are more likely to be in full-time work (see section 6.4) such as the Lancashire and Yorkshire 'textile towns' also show higher rates of cohabitee births. (Again, some of the more picturesque Pennine towns are also experiencing an 'alternative/refuge' revival). The 'traditional family' of married parents is most prevalent in English rural areas and small towns, and also in relatively high status commuting areas. Here, rates of lone motherhood are both lower (Figure 6.1) and mostly accounted for by marital breakdown. In contrast African-Caribbeans and other Blacks (including west Africans and the self-defined census group of 'Black British') have high rates of lone motherhood and are concentrated in larger cities in the South and Midlands. Inner London alone contains over half of all African-Caribbeans in Britain and nearly all Africans. This distribution is itself a result of a complex amalgam of factors, the most important being the demand for immigrant labour in

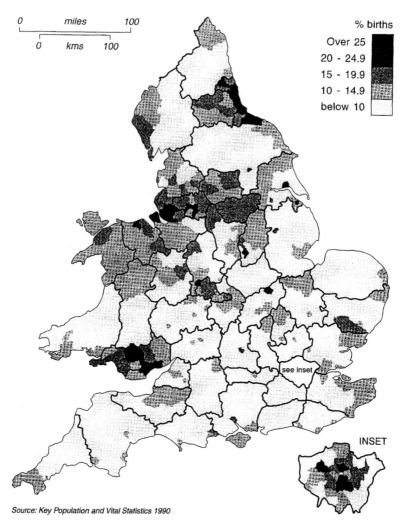

Source: Key Population and Vital Statistics 1990

Figure 6.2   Births to lone mothers (includes two parents at different addresses), 1992

the 1950s and 1960s combined with the links of particular groups, as directed through their social networks, with particular areas and industries (Peach 1994). Thus Pakistanis (with low rates of lone motherhood) show a concentration in the old textile towns of

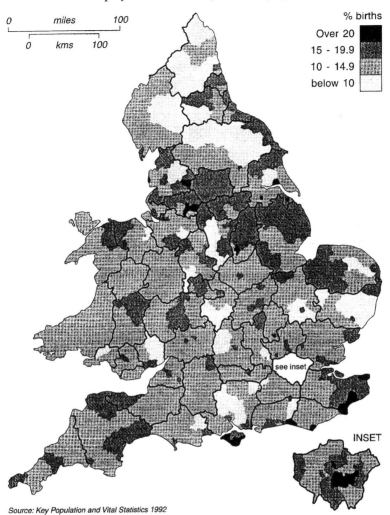

Source: Key Population and Vital Statistics 1992

Figure 6.3   Births to unmarried cohabitees (parents at same address), 1992

Lancashire and Yorkshire where African-Caribbeans are relatively less common. A number of these factors combined mean that overall rates of lone motherhood are particularly high in much of inner London and north-west England (Figure 6.1).

Whatever the reasons for this geographical distribution of lone mothers, it almost precisely reflects the geography of job growth – although unfortunately in a negative sense. Indeed, N. Bradshaw (1996) and his collaborators found that the best geographical predictor of the prevalence of lone motherhood in an area was the level of unemployment (see also Turok and Webster 1998). The strongest employment growth in Britain since 1981 took place in new towns, rural areas and small towns; nearly all the cities lost jobs, with the largest cities and their inner areas losing most (Aberdeen, Edinburgh, Bristol and Leeds were exceptions). Inner London lost almost 10 per cent of jobs from 1984–91. While women's employment was more buoyant (male employment contracted in all areas except the new towns and 'remoter rural districts'), relative rates of growth follow this same urban-rural gradient, with Inner London the only area to experience a fall in women's employment (Townsend 1993, Atkins et al. 1996, Green and Owen 1998). In terms of average hours worked (rather than just participation rates) women's employment fell in all the conurbations, but increased most in the small towns outside urban Britain. The areas where men's employment fell least, therefore, were also those where women's employment grew most (and vice versa). In other words the gendering of job change, far from compensating for the division between relatively job-rich and job-poor areas, in fact exacerbated this divide. As Daniel Dorling (1995) shows, the distribution of families headed by lone parents (where over 90 per cent are lone mothers), and their relative increase over time, is almost an exact inverse match of this employment gradient.

Much of the impetus to the social problem reform scenario has arisen from the situation where lone mothers' employment, in Britain, is steadily decreasing over time. By 1994 only 38 per cent of lone mothers had paid jobs, with just 16 per cent in full-time work. In 1980 these figures were 49 per cent and 25 per cent respectively (Haskey 1997). However, this decline is differentially distributed – the decrease in lone mothers' employment was particularly marked in the conurbations; elsewhere, lone mothers employment was more stable, fluctuating with the economic cycle (Bartholomew et al. 1992). As we have seen, this also implies that single mothers and lone mothers from ethnic minorities, who are most concentrated in the areas of low job growth, will be particularly constrained in taking up a job (whatever their gendered moral rationality about the desirability of doing so). Traditionally, in the social policy literature, the 'weaker' employment status of single mothers, compared to other lone mothers, has been explained by their relative lack of human capital in terms of education (sometimes simply equated with their younger average age). But this weak employment position may in large part simply result from where they live.

The 'social problem reform scenario' is not only economically blind, and possibly 'gender blind' (as we showed in section 6.2) – it also suffers from a strong dose of what can be called 'spatial amnesia' (Duncan 1989a, 1995). The reform scenario assumes we live in a spaceless world, or at least one with uniform space. But because empirical analysis cannot be divorced from geographical differences, simply because social phenomena are so unevenly developed over space, the result is to aggregate to the national level. This follows where the nation state is the most obvious spatial container. Note that 'obvious' does not necessarily mean 'most important', it is just that modern social and political discourse is heavily infused by national assumptions (cf. Williams, 1995). And this infusion is particularly strong in social policy, with its Fabian origins. In particular, the state is enthroned as dominant social actor. The effects of geographical variations at sub-national levels, in regions, labour markets and neighbourhoods, are simply missed, therefore. As this chapter (and Chapters 3 and 4) show, the analytical implications can be serious. The 'social problem reform scenario' not only forgets that many of the jobs available to lone mothers are inadequate for their needs, it is misses the fact that many are simply in the wrong place.

Spatial Divisions of Labour and the Geography of Women's Work

Where lone mothers live has substantial implications for their employment possibilities, therefore. What social processes produce these geographical variations in employment? This is an important issue if we are going to intervene, successfully, in 'getting lone mothers back to work'. For this we need to know why it is that jobs are distributed in particular ways to different local labour markets, and why women are more or less involved in paid work in these different local areas.

There has in fact been substantial work, in the political economy of space tradition, which has addressed these issues over the last twenty years (Massey 1995; Peck 1996 for review and retrospect). To use Doreen Massey's (1984) memorable and now classic title, the division of labour in capitalism is also a 'spatial division of labour'. Particular jobs are differentially distributed to different labour markets – and hence job opportunities, economic and social infrastructure, the development of human capital and income levels will also vary widely on the local level. The pattern and nature of these spatial divisions of labour are formed and reformed not only in line with changes in the international division of labour, but also as these interact with local conditions and attributes. In this way, as Peck puts it, 'all labour markets are locally constituted' (1996, p. 95). The employment profile of any labour market area can then be understood in terms of a 'geological metaphor' – the current economic and social landscape will preserve relics of past spatial divisions of labour, overlain and reformed by newer ones. This local economic and infrastructural differentiation will interact, if in a complex way, with social, political and cultural differences, as amply documented by the British 'localities projects' of the 1980s (Cooke 1989, Harloe et al. 1990, Bagguley et al. 1990, see Duncan and Savage 1991 for review). Quite often these local labour markets specialise and interact within regional economies focused around a particular product range, so that this local labour market geography is appreciated at the regional scale. So if in the past the cotton towns of north-east Lancashire presented a particular social and economic geography (with a continuing importance, despite the near disappearance of the cotton industry itself), the 1980s were associated with the emergence, for example, of the 'M4' corridor between Heathrow Airport and south Wales, specialising in high-tech, research and electronic products (Hall et al. 1987; Townsend 1993). Both economic and social opportunities will be structured by spatial divisions of labour operating at the scale of local and regional labour markets.

An important conclusion of this research tradition, for our discussion here, is that spatial divisions of labour are heavily gendered. The jobs which are distributed to different labour markets are also normally gendered as women's or men's jobs. Once jobs are gendered these divisions seem remarkably rigid and enduring, only relatively rarely do jobs change 'gender' (Walby 1986). Again, this gendering of spatial divisions of labour is not simply a top-down economic process, but is also a locally constituted social process conditioned by historical conditions and mediated by cultural understandings and negotiations. The upshot of all this is that the economic and social geographies created through spatial divisions of labour are also gender geographies (Duncan 1991a, b). Women's roles, possibilities and expectations vary at the level of local labour markets and lone mothers are part of this gendered geography.

Figure 6.4 maps aggregate patterns of dominant work roles, at the local labour market scale, for women between 16 and 60 in Britain. It uses information from the 1991 census to construct a typology of 'homemaker', 'dual role' and 'mixed' areas at the District Council level.[3] Homemaker areas were defined as those with over 35 per cent of women in what the census terms 'economic inactivity' (but where nearly all were in fact working unpaid as carers and 'housewives' see Duncan 1991a) combined with high levels of female part-time paid work (as measured by the full:part-time ratio). Although the social position and status of women's part-time work varies (as discussed in section 6.3) in Britain it is most commonly defined as supplementary, and secondary, to the domestic/caring role and this is how we have treated it here. Dual role areas were defined as those where over 40 per cent of women between 16 and 60 were in full-time work, with low levels of economic inactivity and a low part-time:full-time ratio. We have called these areas 'dual role' because the evidence shows that women in full-time paid work do not usually shed their domestic and caring role, and that the sharing of such work by male partners does not normally significantly increase for this group. Indicitavely, it appears that women with part-time work carry out even more domestic work! (ibid.). The mixed areas were those that did not fall into either end of this continuum, and as can be seen are geographically, as well as statistically, intermediate. These categories refer to gender roles in terms of women's paid and unpaid work, as recorded in the census. In terms of the discussion in Chapter 4, however, the categories will encompass women who hold various gendered moral rationalities about the relationship between motherhood and paid work. The two elements of the 'dual role' for example, may be understood as separate or integrated.

A first impression to emerge from Figure 6.4 is the salience of broad regional divisions, rather than finer scale urban–rural differences. Sometimes urban areas can be distinguished from their more rural hinterlands, for example Hull and Exeter stand out as 'mixed' within extensive 'homemaker' regions. But overall there is little correspondence between urban status and women's work role. Many large urban areas are in the mixed, or even homemaker categories, such as the commuter area east and south of London, Bristol, Merseyside, Southampton, South Wales, east London, Tyneside and South Yorkshire. Conversely, some small towns and rural areas, such as parts of Lancashire, the Scottish borders and the East Midlands, fit into the dual role category. Nor does the map show a plethora of detailed distinctions between different local labour markets, although some exceptional local areas do stand out (such as Taff-Ely, a small

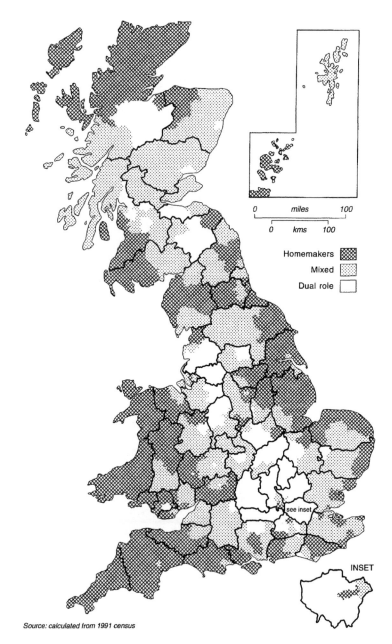

Homemakers
Mixed
Dual role

Source: calculated from 1991 census

INSET

Figure 6.4   Dominant work roles for women in Britain, 1991

'dual role' area within South Wales). Rather, it is broad regional associations which dominate.

As Figure 6.4 shows, dual role areas encompass most of London (except east London), parts of the so-called 'western crescent' and 'M4 corridor' of relative economic growth to the north and west of London, parts of the East Midlands especially around Northampton and Leicester, industrial Lancashire and Greater Manchester, Stoke and north Staffordshire, Leeds, all the major Scottish urban areas as well as parts of the Borders and the Highlands. Within this group it is industrial Lancashire, Greater Manchester and west Inner London which achieve the highest scores. It is interesting that only a few Scottish areas are categorised as 'homemaker' areas; the new towns around Glasgow have some of the highest rates for women's full-time work, regional cities like Dundee and Aberdeen stand out as dual role areas compared with English and Welsh counterparts like Newcastle, Southampton or Cardiff – even some of the old coal-mining areas in Scotland come into the mixed category. Homemaker areas account for most of Wales and the south-west of England and (if some contiguous mixed areas are included) much of East Anglia, Kent and Sussex, together with Fenland, and much of eastern and northern England apart from Lancashire and West Yorkshire.[4] This regional pattern is replicated in similar work. For example Helen Jarvis (1997) measures the regional distribution of 'traditional' and 'dual-earner/career' households (rather than women's role alone as here). 'Traditional' households (men in full-time work, women working as full-time housewives) are most common in the south-east of England, especially in commuting areas while Lancashire, together with greater Manchester, have the lowest proportion of traditional households and the highest rates of 'dual-earner/career' households. London combines high levels of both categories. Similarly, these patterns seem enduring. In Britain, the 1981 map of women's work roles is basically the same as in 1991 (Duncan 1991a). For Germany, Rosemarie Sackmann and Hartmut Häussermann (1994) have compared the relative propensity of women to take up paid work, by region, for 1890 and 1990. Despite fundamental shifts in regional economies over the last 100 years (with the south replacing the north as economic leader), two world wars, the depression and the rise and fall of Nazism, and all those other changes over the century in which Germany was often the fulcrum, the pattern of women's labour force participation remained the same. It is the regional pattern which dominates in the geography of gender divisions of labour.

This regional pattern is a relatively unfamiliar one, however. The more familiar regional map of Britain, as well as in popular consciousness, is that of the 'North-South divide'. While this standard map has many variations depending on the particular topic being mapped, its general form is based upon economic indicators of growth and prosperity, and on social indicators of class and well-being (see for example the national atlases produced by Dorling 1995 and Champion et al. 1996). As we have seen, the other more familiar British socioeconomic map of the 'urban – rural divide, also based on economic and social class indicators, does not apply to the gender geography of Figure 6.4 either. Thus in terms of the gender division of labour London is rather like Lancashire and central Scotland, Bristol and Southampton resemble Merseyside and Tyneside, while the outer commuting belt in Sussex and and Kent is more like Fenland or mid-Wales. Researchers are sometimes surprised that 'economic buoyancy' has little direct association with women's work role (for example Pinch and Storey 1992 on Southampton). The geography of women's work roles does not simply correspond with the geography of economic growth or prosperity.

The explanation for this apparent paradox between the more familiar geography of economic growth and class, and the less familiar, but rather different, geography of women's work roles is complex, and is beyond the scope of this book. One important conclusion of the debate so far, however, is that it is not just spatial divisions of labour that define women's roles, it is also people's own gendered expectations, negotiations and demands about what being a women or a man is, and what they should do in consequence. These understandings are not only informed by economic conditions in local labour markets, but also by other social relations in households, neighbourhoods and community networks. In a general sense, capitalism is combined with patriarchy in positioning women within society.

This discussion leaves us with an important point. Local labour markets provide a crucial context for lone mothers' abilities to take up paid work or not. First, gendered spatial divisions of labour determine what jobs are available. Secondly, social expectations within local labour markets, about whether women (and in particular mothers) are seen primarily as paid workers or homemakers, will influence how lone mothers see their role in combining motherhood with paid work. As we have discussed earlier in this book, lone mothers do of course face particular difficulties in taking up paid work, such as a relative lack of access to child care. However, their relative propensity to take paid work – whatever additional obstacles they may face as lone mothers – will be related to gendered divisions of labour at the local labour market level. In the next section we go on to examine this more fully.

6.4 LONE MOTHERS IN LOCAL LABOUR MARKETS

Section 6.2 showed how it was full-time work that best offers lone mothers economic support and security. Indeed, the evidence is that many prefer to avoid part-time employment unless it is so part-time that it can be taken on at little cost. Concomitantly, such short part-time jobs give little chance of economic support or security. However, in section 6.3 we went on to show how women's employment is differentially distributed between different types of local labour market. In Britain women's jobs have grown most in rural areas and small towns – although most of these jobs are part-time and in any case these are the areas where there are fewest lone mothers. Areas where most lone mothers live, in the inner cities and older industrial towns, have shown lower growth rates and sometimes stagnation or even decline as in Inner London. Furthermore, the relative propensity for women to take on a 'worker', rather than a 'homemaker' role also varies between different regions and local labour markets , and this cultural and economic context provided a further 'filter' to the likelihood of lone mothers taking on full-time or long part-time jobs.

Figure 6.5 summarises the outcome of all these spatial filters to lone mothers' employment. The graph positions the 474 British District Councils (DCs)[5] by the proportion of lone mothers in employment (the x-axis) and, within this, the proportion in full-time work (the y-axis, as measured by the full:part-time ratio). We have then distinguished between four DC categories by reference to average rates of employment and the full:part-time ratio for lone mothers in Britain as a whole. In *'low full-time, low employment'* DCs, lone mothers have least chance of achieving economic independence and security through paid work; Knowsley, a DC largely composed of outer metropolitan council estates fringing Liverpool, is the extreme outlier in this category. In *'low full-time, higher employment'* areas lone mothers have a better chance of finding employment. (We have used the term 'higher' rather than 'high' because of course Britain is everywhere a 'low' employment area for lone mothers compared with most other European countries, see Chapter 7.) However, as much of this work is

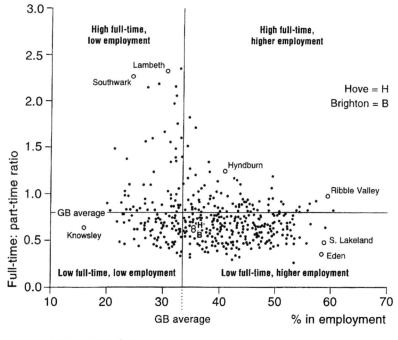

Source: 1991 Census

Figure 6.5   Dominant employment regimes for lone mothers: GB district councils 1991

part-time, economic support and security through employment will still be difficult. South Lakeland and the contiguous area of Eden, centred around the small, rather 'nice' towns of Appleby, Kendal and Penrith, and set in beautiful countryside edging into the Lake District national park, are extreme outliers in this category. Turning to *'high full-time, low employment'* DCs, here most lone mothers have not been able to access economic independence and security through paid work, but for the minority who have done so most have full-time jobs which do offer better prospects. The Inner London boroughs of Southwark and Lambeth (two of our case study areas with a high proportion of Black lone mothers, see Chapter 3) are the extreme outliers. Finally, in the *'high full-time, higher employment'* areas lone mothers have the best chance of all in gaining economic independence and security through paid work. Hyndburn and the Ribble Valley, contiguous DCs in Lancashire centred around the old cotton towns of Accrington, Clitheroe, Nelson and Colne are extreme outliers of this category. There are also of course a large number of intermediate DCs, and some average on all four categories. Brighton and Hove, our two other case study areas in Britain, come within this intermediate group although tending towards the 'low full-time, higher employment' category – the category that contains almost half the DCs in Britain.

Figure 6.6 maps the four categories. In view of the descriptions of the outliers in the preceding paragraph, and the discussion in section 6.3, the geographical locations of each category comes as no surprise. 'Low full-time, low employment' DCs are mostly situated in areas where there has been both economic decline and little tradition of women as paid workers; Tyneside and Wearside, South Yorkshire, Merseyside, West Cumbria, South Wales, and parts of Kent are major examples. Most of the remaining smaller areas in this category, like the Wrexham area in north-east Wales, Anglesey and Caernarvon in north-west Wales, Plymouth or Grimsby, pinpoint the same conditions. These are also areas where there are substantial numbers of lone mothers, especially single mothers (see Figures 6.1, 6.2). In contrast 'low full-time, higher employment' areas cover most of rural and small-town Britain. These are the areas that have seen rapid growth in women's employment, but most is part-time and few of these DCs have much tradition of women as workers (compare with Figure 6.4). There are also fewer lone mothers in these areas, and a larger proportion of those that are will be divorced.

The 'low employment, higher full-time' DCs are predominantly located in those metropolitan, especially inner-city, areas with a 'dual role' tradition of women's full-time work (see Figure 6.4). Women, including lone mothers, often expect full-time work but these areas have shown least growth, or even a reduction, in women's employment during the 1980s and so preferred jobs are often unavailable. Inner London and the Scottish cities are the major examples with the West Midlands a transitional area in respect to both traditions of women working and lone mothers' employment. Most of the African-Caribbean population of Britain, with both high rates of lone motherhood and gendered moral rationalities emphasising mothers with full-time work (see Chapter 4), live in these areas. Finally, the 'high full-time, higher employment' DCs are located in those areas with a tradition of women in full-time jobs, but usually with somewhat brighter employment prospects than the large cities. Examples are the

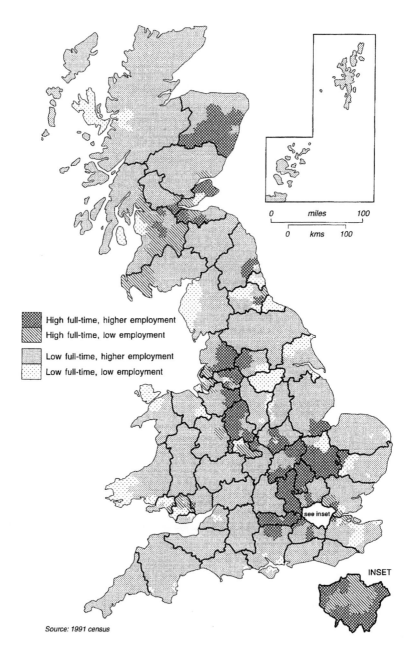

High full-time, higher employment
High full-time, low employment

Low full-time, higher employment
Low full-time, low employment

see inset

INSET

Source: 1991 census

Figure 6.6   Dominant work regimes: lone mothers Britain 1991

old Pennine textile towns in Lancashire, Yorkshire, and Cheshire, the Staffordshire 'potteries' and some east midland areas including Northampton and Leicester. These areas also contain relatively large numbers of lone mothers. The 'dual role' parts of the 'western crescent' with most job growth also join this category, although relatively few lone mothers live in this area (see Figure 6.1). Some smaller 'outer metropolitan' zones in areas of relative job growth in or near dual role areas are also included, especially in Scotland.

The geography of lone mothers' employment is therefore rather like that for women as a whole. Some further statistical evidence of this association was revealed by census analysis at the DC level. First, there is almost no correlation between the full-time and part-time employment rates for lone mothers. This suggests that it was not lone motherhood, and its disadvantages as perceived by employers or lone mothers themselves, which was a determinant in lone mothers' varying employment rate (otherwise these variables should be highly correlated). Rather, this suggests that it is the type of labour market and the number and type of jobs offered within them which is important. Second, and conversely, there are higher correlations between the employment rates for lone mothers and couple mothers at the DC level, both for part-time and full-time work.[6] It is the gendered effect of labour markets which is influential for the employment of both lone and couple mothers. Indicatively, high negative residuals from the regression equation for this second correlation (that is areas where less lone mothers than expected were in employment) were predominantly located in those areas of economic decline and high rates of single motherhood such as South Wales, Merseyside and Clydeside. High positive residuals, with more lone mothers employed than expected, were concentrated in 'western crescent' type DCs with the highest job growth and a larger proportion (although fewer numbers) of divorced lone mothers.[7]

The association between lone mother employment and female employment as a whole reflects the combination of occupational gendering, spatial divisions of labour and cultural definitions of motherhood which affect both categories of women. There appear to be similar geographical differences in lone mothers' employment in Germany, Sweden and the USA, as well as in other European countries, if varying around different national averages (see Duncan and Edwards 1997). This lends weight to our overall theme (see Chapter 1) that too much research and political attention is given to lone mothers as a 'closed box' categorical or taxonomic group. On the one hand, lone mothers are not that different to mothers as a whole when it comes to employment; on the other hand there are substantial differences between lone mothers according to where they live.

6.5 CONCLUSIONS

We began this chapter by querying the assumptions of what we called the 'social problem reform scenario'. This is the assumption that in providing lone mothers with affordable child care, education and training, and by removing the 'poverty trap' produced by an inappropriate benefit structure, then the problem of lone mother poverty and dependency will be greatly reduced. The chapter found that this scenario is seriously deficient in a number of respects. First, as we discussed in section 6.2, it is largely economically blind; severe and persistent gender segregation, combined with dominant labour market trends, means that many of the jobs available to lone mothers will not provide them with a secure household income. In a paradoxical way (given its emphasis on lone mothers) this scenario is in some ways 'gender blind' in that it implicitly accepts current gender divisions of labour in Britain which position most women in a disadvantaged position. While the living standards of partnered women are usually (but not always) taken above poverty levels through dependency on a male income, this option is not available to lone mothers unless they repartner. Of course, whether this continuing dependence on marriage and partnership is acceptable is a moot point, particularly when partnership breakdown is increasingly common. Secondly (section 6.3), the social problem reform scenario is spatially naive. Not only are many new jobs located in those local labour markets with the fewest lone mothers, but the operation of gendered spatial divisions of labour deliver a differentiated mix of jobs to local labour markets – the scale at which jobs are actually available to lone mothers. Whatever lone mothers' levels of training and education, or indeed whatever their moral rationalities about the desirability of paid work, these will have little impact on poverty and dependency levels if adequate jobs are not available. These limitations in the scenario are exacerbated by a substantial dose of 'state fetishism' – the implicit assumption that the state is the only effective actor, and that the national scale is the only scale on which socially effective processes operate. This results in a sort of explanatory blinkering so that the changing nature of labour markets, and their spatial divisions, cannot be properly recognised. In the memorable words of Freiderike Maier (see page 189) the danger is that implementing the 'social problem reform scenario' would simply leave lone mothers continuing to live 'on half rations'. We saw in Chapter 4 that lone mothers have very well defined ideas about 'good mothering', although this definition will vary between groups. The evidence discussed in this chapter shows that they also have quite defined ideas about 'good work'. This is work that is secure, compatible with their caring responsibilities and commensurate with their qualifications. Full-time and long part-time work should be available, and short part-time should not mean work with poor conditions, insecurity and low pay. This concept of 'good work' implies 'women-friendly' reforms on the Scandinavian model. Enabling lone mothers to share the disadvantaged position of women in general in Britain will be of little help, rather it is the social and economic position of all women, especially mothers, that needs to be improved. The next chapter turns to national state contexts for lone mothers and paid work.

NOTES

1. This unexamined argument can sometimes transcend into the position that lone mothers are so 'deserving' that they should be forced into jobs 'for their own good', for example by the withdrawal of benefits. (The withdrawal of lone parent benefit in Britain in 1997, a top-up to universal child benefit, may owe something to this). As we saw in Chapter 4, many lone mothers feel paid work to be incompatible with their responsibilities as mothers.
2. These figures refer to gross monthly earnings, and therefore include overtime. For 1971–94 men in the manual sector worked an average of six hours overtime per week, compared with just three hours for women. For the non-manual sector corresponding figures were one and below half an hour. Hourly rates, which exclude overtime, are a better measure of perceived worth, and hence gender inequality, within the labour market, and are used for this purpose by Hakim (1996). Even so, women's average rates were only 68 per cent of men's in the non-manual sector in 1995, and 73 per cent in the manual sector. In this discussion we are concerned with the relative size of men's and women's pay packets, as an indicator of the resources available, and the effect of this on inequality outside the labour market; hence measures of monthly or weekly earnings are more appropriate.
3. District Councils (DCs) are used to represent local labour markets for women where the conventionally designated Travel To Work Areas (TTWAs), defined as areas where 75 per cent of work trips begin and end within the area, in fact simply average out different TTWAs for

different groups. For women TTWAs are smaller and more numerous, approximating DC scale (Flowerdew and Green 1993).

4. Women's part-time work is included within the 'homemaker' axis in creating the topologies mapped in Figure 6.4. However, apart from some specialised labour markets (e.g. Grimsby), the highest rates of female part-time work is to be found in the outer South East, especially in the 'western crescent' (Duncan 1991a; Townsend 1986). Taking part-time work separately would if anything reinforce, rather than disrupt, the geography of work roles constructed in Figure 6.4.

5. The City of London and the Scilly Isles, with very small populations, were excluded.

6. Correlations are still not high in the statistical sense, although this is to be expected where there is a high level of geographical aggregation. Research disaggregating by labour market type would be useful.

7. The whole question of the relationship between different types of lone mother and the type of area in which they live is one requiring further research.

7 Lone Mothers and Genderfare: Positioning Lone Mothers in Welfare States

7.1 INTRODUCTION

In this chapter we examine how different sorts of welfare state position women, and how this positioning in turn presents a differentiated set of opportunities and constraints for lone mothers. While we refer to particular policies as appropriate, our concern is therefore not to provide a comprehensive account of different policies affecting lone mothers in different countries (for which see Bradshaw et al. 1996, Millar 1996). Rather, we wish to provide an analytical account of how lone mothers are differentially positioned by social policies in different countries. We have also been at pains to point out, in earlier chapters, that national state policy is only one of several social contexts in which lone mothers negotiate their lives. Nor should we see state policy as in some way autonomous from these contexts (see especially Chapter 2 on discourses). Nevertheless, in that national policies continue to provide or restrict access to resources, based on a concentration of collective social authority within the state, then the national context will remain particularly important in forming constraints and opportunities for lone mothers.

Section 7.2 begins where the last chapter left off – with an account of lone mothers' relative poverty and employment rates in different welfare states. The dramatic differences between countries revealed immediately posits the question of why, and by what means, these have arisen. Section 7.3 begins by examining the concept of welfare state regimes, which attempts to encapsulate this variation within a theorised typology of how states intervene in markets, in contrast to alternative models which place gender in a more central position. We end the section by proposing an alternative 'genderfare' model which recognises the combination of two dual structures – welfare state regimes (derived from the capital –

labour relation) and gender contracts (derived from the gender relation).

Section 7.4 follows by using this combined genderfare model to examine the economic position of lone mothers in welfare state regimes, focussing in turn on the three major available income sources – benefits, maintenance and employment. We end this section with brief pen pictures of the positioning of lone mothers in our four case study countries – Britain, Germany, Sweden and the USA. Finally, we return in section 7.5 to lone mothers themselves, recognising that they are not prisoners of either welfare states or prevailing gender contracts. The example of Beata, who prefers life as a lone mother in Sweden, rather than married motherhood in Britain, is revealing. We conclude, in section 7.6, that lone mothers are not simply positioned by welfare state regimes or gender contracts, they also position themselves. This sets up the core issue of rational choice for Chapter 8 which follows.

7.2. LONE MOTHERS' EMPLOYMENT AND POVERTY RATES IN WELFARE STATES

Figure 7.1 presents comparative poverty rates (where poverty is defined as an income below 50 per cent of the national average) for lone mothers by employment status for a range of welfare states for which data are available. The contrasts are dramatic. Four groups of countries can be distinguished (ignoring for the moment their 'welfare state regime'). First, in Sweden, Finland, Denmark and Norway, most lone mothers are in paid work (graph 1 in Figure 7.1). Of these, very few – always less than 8 per cent and in Sweden just 2 per cent – were in poverty in the early 1990s. However, even for the minority without paid work (graph 2 in Figure 7.1), it was still the case that few of these lone mothers were in poverty – always below 17 per cent and just 10 per cent in Sweden. By some means the labour market and social transfer systems in these countries has largely removed the problem of lone mother poverty.

Secondly, in France and Belgium most lone mothers have paid work, as in the Scandinavian countries, and these lone mothers were also unlikely to experience poverty. However, the minority of lone mothers without jobs have higher poverty rates of around 25 per cent. The social policy regime, through transfers such as benefits, child allowances or maintenance, is clearly less adequate for unemployed

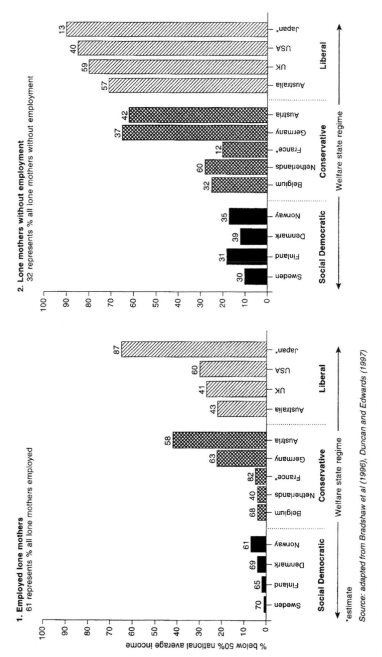

Figure 7.1 Lone mothers with incomes below 50% national average: developed countries early 1990s

lone mothers than in Scandinavia. The Netherlands is similar to this group except that fewer than half of lone mothers have paid work so the proportion at risk of poverty is correspondingly higher. Third, in Australia and the United Kingdom, only around 40 per cent of lone mothers were employed in the early 1990s, and these lone mothers also showed relatively high rates of poverty (almost a third of employed lone mothers were in poverty in Britain, for example). Most startlingly, however, were the very high poverty rates for lone mothers without jobs in these countries – around 70 to 80 per cent. In these countries we can imagine that not only is the labour market relatively inefficient at removing lone mothers from poverty (as we discussed in Chapter 6 for Britain), but also that the social transfer system is almost completely ineffectual in this respect. Ireland seems to show a variant of this situation, with even fewer lone mothers with jobs, but only a medium rate of poverty for those without (McLaughlin and Rodgers 1997). Lastly, are a group of countries – Austria, Germany and the USA, with Japan as an extreme – which seem to represent the worst of both labour market and social policy worlds as far as lone mothers are concerned. Most lone mothers are in paid work – as high a proportion, or even higher, as in the Scandinavian countries – but even so substantial proportions of these working lone mothers (in Japan probably the majority) live in poverty. For the minority without paid work poverty rates are very high indeed. While comparable data is unfortunately not available for the southern European countries, what evidence we have indicates that they would swell the ranks of this group (Roll 1992, Bradshaw et al. 1996).

This information is particularly interesting because of the light it sheds on the relationship between poverty and paid work, where 'getting lone mothers back to work' is so often seen as the solution to lone mother poverty, as we discussed in Chapter 6. True enough, as Figure 7.1 shows, more lone mothers are in paid work in Scandinavia, France and Belgium, and poverty rates are lower. For example, in Sweden 70 per cent were in paid work and only 2 per cent of these had incomes below half the national average. In contrast, in Britain, 60 per cent of lone mothers did not have paid work and fully 80 per cent of this majority were in poverty. All this supports the 'getting them back to work' thesis. But a closer look at Figure 7.1 shows that this thesis does not hold. In Sweden, even for the minority without employment, the vast majority (90 per cent) escape poverty. Clearly, in Sweden income transfers from the state, or from fathers, must usually be high enough to prevent poverty even for those lone mothers without paid work. In contrast in the USA 60 per cent of lone mothers had jobs, but fully 30 per cent of these were in poverty – as well as 85 per cent of those without work. In Japan an even higher proportion of lone mothers with jobs remained in poverty (although this figure is a rough estimate). Mitchell (1992) illustrates the same point rather nicely for Australian lone mothers, showing that if the same people lived in Sweden, more would be in paid work and poverty rates would fall substantially. However, if they lived in the USA, again many more would be employed but poverty rates would increase substantially. Having a job is no necessary protection against poverty.

It is of course the nature of employment, its rate of pay and hours of work, that is crucial to income (see Chapter 6). In addition the level of income transfer through the welfare system, or enabled by it (as in the case of maintenance), will also be important for the incomes of those with jobs, as well as for those without. We suggested in Chapter 6 that all that may be accomplished by moving lone mothers into the labour market, without adequate support from the welfare state or access to higher paid jobs, is a partial transfer to another income source which can be just as low and quite possibly less secure. This conclusion is supported by the comparative international evidence we show here.

The policy implications are twofold. First it is the nature of the jobs supplied, and the distribution of work between men and women (including unpaid domestic work) which needs to be changed if lone mothers are to improve their situation by taking up paid work. This is most achieved in the Scandinavian countries (although still only partially), where most women – including lone mothers – hold full-time or 'long' part-time jobs (20–34 hours per week), with normal job security and, on average, wage levels not far below male rates. There is also some evidence of a shift in domestic and caring work from women to men, although this is in part compelled by women's absence from the home in their paid work (Nilsson 1994). Secondly, an approach based on employment alone is inadequate. Partly this is because participation in the labour market, particularly for the full-time jobs that are most likely to provide a household income, is better supported by universalistic, high standard welfare systems typical of the Scandinavian countries. Pervasive and publicly funded daycare, long parental leave, the provision of paid leave to be with sick children, and the right of parents with young children to a shorter working day, all make it more possible to combine motherhood with paid work and career. In addition, and crucially, social transfers such as state advanced maintenance or housing allowances are vital to lone mothers' living conditions, both those with and without jobs, as the data in Figure 7.1 suggests. Again, these features are most achieved in the Scandinavian countries. The second policy implication, therefore, is that social transfers to compensate for the cost of parenting (which Joshi 1995 calculates as equivalent to 14 years' paid work for the average woman in Britain) should be an essential part of any reform package.

A question raised by Figure 7.1, and the discussion accompanying it, is why, and by what means, these startling differences between countries have arisen. Section 7.3 examines competing explanations for this in terms of welfare state regimes, differentiated patriarchy and gender contracts, and concludes by suggesting a combined model of 'genderfare'.

7.3 WELFARE STATE REGIMES AND GENDER CULTURES: POSITIONING LONE MOTHERS

Gendering *The Three Worlds of Welfare Capitalism*

We start with the work of Gøsta Esping-Andersen, especially his *The Three Worlds of Welfare Capitalism* (1990). Esping-Andersen provides a systematic classification of three basic welfare state regimes into which different advanced capitalist states fall. Crucially, this classification is not merely ad hoc and descriptive, but is based on analytical distinctions about what the welfare state does, how this can differ and, hence, why we would expect different outcomes in terms of social policy. Hence any particular policy, and comparisons between them, could be related to an explanatory account of the structure of the welfare state. Policies towards lone motherhood should be no exception. Esping-Andersen's theory of welfare state regimes should therefore give us a key for understanding the patterns of lone mother poverty and employment presented in Figure 7.1. Indeed, this is why we have grouped countries according to his regime categorisation in the figure.

Esping-Andersen's starting point was to ask how far different welfare states erode the commodity status of labour in a capitalist system (how far people are independent from selling their labour) and, as a consequence, how far welfare states intervene in the class system. Empirically, relative levels of this 'decommodification' were measured with reference to the level and nature of income transfers for sickness, unemployment and old age, and this resulted in the identification of the three worlds of welfare capitalism.

In *Liberal Welfare Regimes* social policy is used to uphold the market and traditional work-ethic norms, with modest and means tested benefits aimed at a residualised and stigmatised group of welfare recipients. While no one country presents a pure case of any regime, and countries may straddle or move between them, the USA is a type case – with Britain moving in this direction. In *Social Democratic Welfare Regimes* social policy reforms based on decommodification are extended to all classes, with equality at the highest standards rather than minimal needs. Typically, the labour movement has high levels of access to state power. The market is de-emphasised but the high taxation necessary to finance universal welfare means that the emphasis is on avoiding problems in the first place, where every adult should be able to participate in the labour market. Sweden is archetypical. In *Conservative Welfare Regimes* states also intervene in a highly regulatory way, but this intervention is essentially concerned with the preservation of status differences. Social rights are connected to status and class, guided by the Catholic inspired principal of subsidiarity where states should only support – not replace – existing social institutions such as families or firms in providing welfare. The 'social market' is therefore presented as a third way between the excesses of both liberalism and socialism. West Germany is the type case. Finally, we should add (as does Leibfried 1993) the *Rudimentary Welfare State Regimes* of southern Europe to this scheme. Here, there is little right to welfare or any history of full employment, and a recent history of authoritarian politics has prevented their development. While residualism and forced entry to the labour market remind us of the liberal model, the state can rely on surviving elements of the household subsistence economy, a large informal sector, and church inspired charities to both provide welfare and top-up employment. More recently, there have been attempts to develop this last category in terms of a '*Southern Model*' of welfare (e.g. Ferrera 1996), paying particular attention to political forms such as clientilism where some restricted but favoured groups (for example civil servants) may receive high levels of benefit. It may be possible to extend these categorisations further, where there may be 'non-western' welfare regimes, such as the authoritarian populism emerging in parts of Eastern Europe or the 'East Asian' model (Deacon 1992). Similarly, Ito Peng (1997) shows how a concept of the 'Japanese style welfare state', stressing the

work ethic within traditional norms, has been promoted in overt opposition to both liberal and social democratic regime types.

These different welfare regimes have different implications for
women and men, and hence for the level and nature of gender
inequality. As Barbara Hobson puts it 'Both women and men are
more and less poor in certain welfare states because of the fact that
welfare regimes are systems of stratification'. Within these systems,
lone mothers are the 'residuum' in this gendering of policy, so that
they can be taken as 'a litmus test, or indicator, of gendered social
rights in different welfare regimes' (1994, pp. 175, 171; see also Millar
1995). We can therefore expect that the welfare and income of lone
mothers will be highest in countries with a social democratic welfare
regime where they are supported as worker-citizens, just like partnered mothers. In the liberal regime they will be stigmatised as
'mothers on welfare', and will be worst off. In the conservative regime
lone mothers will be peripheralised as mothers without men, but may
nevertheless gain as mothers, while in the southern regime they will be
both few in number and largely unsupported. This proposition does
indeed show a rough correspondence with the information provided in
Figure 7.1. Both lone mothers in employment, and those without
employment, are much less likely to be in poverty in the social democratic regime. Conversely, both groups of lone mothers are more likely
to be in poverty in the conservative and especially the liberal regime.
Hobson comes to a similar conclusion using data from the
Luxembourg Income Study on income sources and poverty rates for
five countries – Germany, the Netherlands, Sweden, the UK and the
USA.

The problem is, however, that this rough correspondence remains
just that – rough. It is not only that there are exceptions and transitional case (something to be expected in in any categorisation), there
are complete category splits. Thus France, Belgium and The
Netherlands – ostensibly within a conservative welfare state regime –
are more like the Scandinavian countries within the social democratiic
regime. Austria and Germany, on the other hand, are nearer to Japan
and the USA in the liberal regime group. At the same time the liberal
group is split where Australia, Britain and Ireland form a group of
their own. There is more going on than a division by decommodification
as understood by Esping-Andersen's model.

The source of this problem is that the Esping-Andersen model is
largely gender blind. Women disappear from the analysis as soon as
they disappear from the labour market. Even in terms of the original

model, this has major implications. Thus, Esping-Andersen sees the social democratic countries as the most decommodifying welfare state regime but it is here that women are in fact most commodified. They predominantly sell their labour – and it is the development of the social-democratic welfare state that facilitates this. Similarly, women are perhaps least commodified in the conservative regime, again not surprisingly as it is here that the housewife role is most supported institutionally (cf. Borschorst 1994). Esping-Andersen also neglects the fundamental role played by unpaid domestic and caring work, and by families as institutions, in mediating individual levels of commodification. These omissions are, of course, heavily gendered. As Mary Langan and Ilona Ostner (1991) point out, women are different 'gendered commodities' from the outset, they already have different positions vis ... vis markets and welfare states because of their gender (see also Bussemaker and Kersbergen 1994; Daly 1994).

Some followers of Esping-Andersen have therefore paid more attention to the gender specific outcomes of welfare state regimes. Indeed, Stephan Leibfried (1993) sees gender as central to the concept of social citizenship established in the conservative regime (renamed 'Bismarckian institutional welfare states') where public policy is used to consolidate traditional male citizenship. This is opposed to the gender-neutral citizenship of 'Scandinavian modern welfare states'. (In 'Anglo-Saxon' residual welfare states social citizenship is being progressively reduced while on the 'Latin rim' of rudimentary welfare states social citizenship remains weakly developed.) Langan and Ostner (1991) go furthest in using Leibfried's variant to place the socio-economic position of women at the centre of the classification. Figure 7.2a represents this cartographically.[1] Alan Siaroff (1994) has produced another 'gender sensitive' reworking of Esping-Andersen's typologies. Siaroff uses indices of family welfare orientation, which parent is in receipt of benefits, and female work desirability. Relative rankings on these indices produce country groups not unlike the four groups produced by Esping-Andersen and Leibfried. The only major difference is that Switzerland and Ireland join a 'Late female mobilisation welfare state' cluster that otherwise includes the 'Latin Rim' countries. Perhaps Ann Orloff (1993) goes furthest in gendering the basic Esping-Andersen model, and repositions his class based power-resources model to concentrate on gendered outcomes, where decommodification is supplemented by a gendered notion of citizenship. However, as far as we know this scheme has not been used empirically.

Adding in the socio-economic position of women in these ways improves the descriptive value of the welfare state regime model as far as gender is concerned, even though the grouping of countries remains virtually unchanged. However, this 'gendering' of the worlds of welfare capitalism does not help us very much in extending the understanding the relative positions of lone mothers as depicted in Figure 7.1. However gendered, the categories are the same as in the original and therefore just as inaccurate. Indeed, the whole exercise of gendering welfare state regimes has been criticised as not going far enough (Sainsbury 1994; Duncan 1994a, 1995). This is for two major reasons. First, in terms of content, the model does not say enough about unpaid work, largely carried out by women and fundamental to gendered public–private divides, nor about the consequent salience of service provision in enabling or constraining women. Similarly, the role of familial and gender ideologies is in structuring welfare policies is underplayed. The second criticism focusses more on the explanatory dynamic where gender remains an optional add-on. The theoretical core of Esping-Andersen derived models is firmly rooted in capital–labour divisions in a capitalist system, based around the relationship of (male, standard) workers to markets as modified by the welfare state. This is how the welfare state typologies are differentiated and where they come from. The explanatory dynamic remains gender blind however much gender description is added on. This is why, in downplaying the original theoretical core – but in not providing an alternative – gender welfare models become descriptive (and rather inaccurate at that) rather than analytical. As Jane Lewis puts it, the categorisation 'breaks down as soon as gender is given serious consideration' (1992b, p. 112). We now go on, therefore, to discuss alternative ways of understanding how welfare states position women, based on other theoretical traditions which place gender in a central position.

The Three Worlds of Gender Culture

Welfare state regime models overemphasise paid work. In arguing against this Jane Lewis (1992b) shifts attention to unpaid work and family relations and develops a categorisation of 'strong', 'modified' and 'weak' 'breadwinner' states – Ireland, France and Sweden are type cases of each category (see also Ostner 1994). Again, this model is represented cartographically in Figure 7.2b. This neatly solves the problem of the split in Esping-Andersen's conservative welfare regime

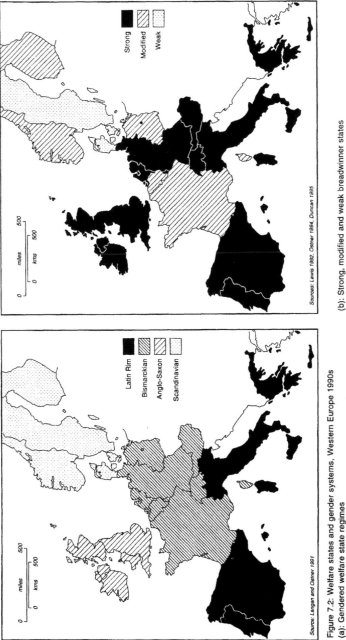

Figure 7.2: Welfare states and gender systems, Western Europe 1990s
(a): Gendered welfare state regimes

(b): Strong, modified and weak breadwinner states

Figure 7.2 Welfare states and gender systems, western Europe 1990s

as far as lone mothers are concerned – for France and Belgium (although The Netherlands appears to be misallocated) move off into the 'modified breadwinner' category. Indeed, it is in this group that poverty rates for employed lone mothers are as low as those in the Scandinavian (weak breadwinner) countries, while poverty rates for those remaining unemployed are higher – although still much lower than in strong breadwinner countries like west Germany or the UK (see Figure 7.1).

The weakness of this solution is that it remains a descriptive model (Sainsbury 1994; Duncan 1995). How and why are these breadwinner states strong, modified or weak? Similarly, 'weak' and 'modified' are both characterised in terms of what they are not. This is partly why new classification problems arise. Most countries fall into the 'strong' group, where cases like Britain, Germany and Greece are quite different both in terms of the position of women in general and lone mothers in particular. In recognising these limitations Eithne McLaughlin and Caroline Glendinning ask for the development of 'notions of process ... which relate to the terms and conditions under which people engage in non-market caring relations'. These would 'both intertwine with the individual-state-market commodification-decommodification processes and have their own historical trajectory'. Using a direct analogy with Esping-Andersen's use of decommodification, they propose to label these processes 'familisation' and 'de-familisation', where these relate to 'the terms and conditions under which people engage in families, and the extent to which they can uphold an acceptable standard of living independently of (patriarchal) 'family' (1994, p. 65). What they do not say how this development should proceed. However, we can use a body of work developed in feminist political history and cultural sociology, particularly in Germany and Sweden, to provide this 'missing link'.

We start with Scandinavian ideas of the 'gender contract'. These developed in a situation where welfare states had an expressed commitment to gender equality, with explicit sex equality programmes and substantial 'women-friendly' reforms, such as comprehensive public day care. Thus women can be both mothers and full-time workers (cf. Hernes 1987). The meaning of motherhood also changes, becoming less of a defining division of labour and more of a private social role (cf. Björnberg 1994). As discussed in Chapter 4, there are different social conceptions of what being a mother is but state policy can variously support or oppose these conceptions. Figure 7.1 shows the positive effects for Scandinavian lone mothers, in terms of employment rates and poverty levels, of state support for a 'primarily worker' conception. However, the overall effect of these changes was to alter women's lives rather than men's. Women could act in a male role, although inevitably less efficiently than men could. Activities, tasks and objects all remained resolutely gendered; the gender coding of society and its equipment had not been removed – it was merely that women's space was enlarged (see Acker 1992, Holter 1992, Forsberg 1994).

Theories of the 'gender contract' developed in this context of both substantial change in women's roles and the maintenance of gender divisions. According to Yvonne Hirdmann (1988, 1990a, b) the gender system (*genussystemet*) arranges people according to two overall rules: (1) virtually all areas of life are divided into male and female categories and (2) this distinction is hierarchical, the male is the norm, the female is ascribed lower value. However, it is the 'gender contract' (*genuskontrakt*) which operationalises the gender system in specific circumstances. Each society , at any time, develops a contract between the genders, which sets up any particular gender coding – what people of different genders should do, think and be.

Note that the notion of a contract does not imply equality, men and women are not equals and so the contract is an unequal one. Rather, the notion was developed in ironic analogy with the idea of the social-democratic contract, or 'historical compromise', between capital and labour so beloved of political theorists where Sweden is seen as the archetypical case. (It was in this tradition that Esping-Andersen's work developed.) However, these political theories are gender blind, and Hirdmann shows how a compromise between men and women was just as important to the development of Swedish society as the capital–labour compromise. The former also set rules and expectations for divisions of labour and power. It was just that the capitalist compromise – being carried out in a dominant male discourse of the economy and public politics – completely overshadowed the parallel patriarchal compromise over gender divisions of labour and power, where the discourse about families, children and women was politically peripheral (cf. Acker 1992). However, as with labour in capitalism, although women in the gender system may be structurally subordinate, nevertheless they have substantial influence and room for action. For example, by the early twentieth-century in Sweden women had gained the vote, were increasingly entering the formal labour market and were relatively well-organised politically, as well as retaining more traditional bases of social power in families and households. So too, any given contract will leave numerous less defined, grey areas which become the site of new conflict and, possibly, the origin of transition to another overall contract. The gender system will therefore show major variations in space and time, both with regard to the nature of the gender contract and to its rigidity.

Hirdmann (1990) develops this notion empirically for Sweden since the turn of the century. A *housewife contract* emerged in the 1930s and lasted into the 1960s as a response to an inter-war crisis between the sexes. While traditional family forms had been eroded, the position of women *vis-à-vis* marriage, domestic life and paid work was not established. The housewife contract was one attempt to resolve the competing demands for time, resources and roles made by men, married women and unmarried women. These conflicts, and the compromise – or gender contract – they led to, were pursued in 'political' institutions, preeminently political parties, the institutional expressions of labour (such as the union movement) and capital (such as the employers' federation), and the 'people's movements' in general (for example the cooperative movement). This housewife contract was in turn challenged by the circumstances of the 1950s and 1960s, leading to a *transitional phase* where women and men again voiced competing demands. A reinforced housewife contract (rather like the 'Bismarckian model' in west Germany) was not possible given the position and demands of Swedish women and eventually an *equality contract emerged* from the late 1960s onwards. While this allows women substantial gains, it too has its unsolved problems, heightened by the economic recession of the 1990s and the new political power of neo-liberalism . Another transitional phase may now be emerging. (See Duncan, 1994a for a more detailed review.)

Hirdmann does not develop her analysis with reference to geographical differences at one time. However, it is clearly possible to use it in this way; for example, judging from the positions of women vis a vis men (Duncan 1996) former west Germany shows a continuing housewife contract, Britain may be in a transitional phase from this contract, the former GDR may be returning *to* a housewife contract, and so on. Unlike the other models reviewed so far, it is more possible to conceptualise transitional forms, where these are an explicit part of the explanatory account. See Figure 7.3 (this replaces Hirdmann's 'transitional' contract by a 'dual role' contract, in recognising that the situation where women are formally positioned as different to men, in combining both mother and worker roles, can be less transitional than was the case for Sweden). As can be seen, if we were to translate

Figure 7.1 (lone mother poverty rates) into the gender contract categories of Figure 7.3, then a rather good fit would be achieved. Transitional cases, such as The Netherlands and Norway, can be more easily accommodated while the splits in the conservative and liberal regime types are resolved.

None the less, the problem of origins reimposes itself. If lone mothers' lives are so fundamentally affected by the gender contract of the country they live in, then how do these different gender contracts arise, and why do they differ between different countries? This is not so much a problem for Hirdmann's work on Sweden, where she

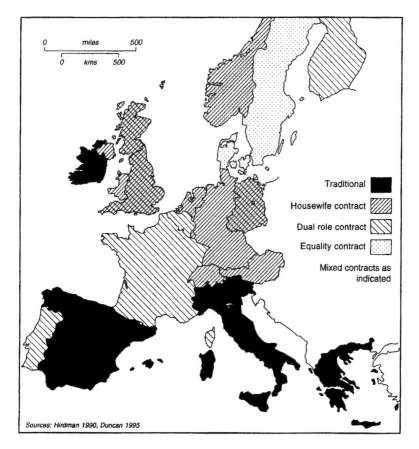

Figure 7.3   Gender contracts, western Europe, 1990s

follows a specific historical evolution and concentrates on outcomes which can be more easily 'traded off' in political systems, such as labour market participation and day care. It is not clear, however, how this can be generalised for other, less institutionalised, countries – especially for gender issues which are harder to 'trade', like domestic responsibility or control through male violence (Duncan 1994a). It is to this problem that Birgit Pfau-Effinger (1994, 1998) turns in explaining national variations in female labour market participation.

In developing the concept of gender contract (which she renames *gender culture*) in order to explain comparative differences in women's participation in paid work, Pfau-Effinger places considerable emphasis on dominant social norms and values about the nature of families. She identifies three long-standing 'family/gender models' in western Europe (rather than assuming a single 'traditional' family). In the *agrarian* family/gender model, men and women cooperate in a family economy in farm holdings or small businesses. This model can be seen to correspond, historically and geographically, to petty commodity production where women were both involved in production and in the public sphere (although gender relations were unequal and sometimes deeply exploitative). Children were also socialised as members of the family economic unit and the notion of childhood, as an institutionalised period, did not really exist. The *bourgeois* family/gender model is based on the ideal of a male breadwinner family and the separation of male public and female private, subordinate, spheres. This corresponds to Jane Lewis' 'strong' breadwinner regime, and to the widespread, but in fact historically inaccurate, understanding of the 'traditional family'. Children and childhood belong in this private sphere and 'motherhood' emerges as a specific, unpaid gender role. This model is fundamentally self-contradictory, where male and female citizens are equal in theory but unequal in practice as men and women. Historically, this family form developed with mercantalism and the industrial/capitalist transformation. Lastly, an *egalitarian–individualistic* family/gender model is based on the idea of men and women as individual breadwinners. While childhood is also constructed as a long phase of life with its own worth, caring for children is now seen as much more a task for the welfare state. Historically, this emerged during the twentieth century through the contradictions in the bourgeois family and the emergence of social democracy and the service economy, especially in those countries and areas where the bourgeois family form was only weakly established, and where the 'agrarian' tradition of women as producers in the public sphere survived. Throughout Pfau-Effinger places emphasis on the notions of childhood inherent in each form rather than, as in the other models reviewed in this Chapter, considering only the relations between men and women. This is important where, arguably, much feminist research has neglected parenting, and in particular mothering (cf. Ribbens 1994), or merely seen this one-dimensionally as just part of a patriarchal exploitation. The notion of gender cultures as expressed in this way, with an emphasis on moral ordering and responsibilities, also fits in better with the way the interviewed lone mothers accounted for their own behaviour as discussed in Chapters 3 and 4.

Pfau-Effinger then uses this approach to account for the employment position of women in the contrasting cases of Finland, the Netherlands and west Germany. In Finland, women are seen as independent full-time paid workers, who may also be housewives and mothers, while in former west Germany women are seen as dependent mothers and housewives, who may have supplementary jobs (often part-time jobs) at particular times. In The Netherlands, women (especially mothers) are even more likely to be at home or in part-time work, although here women are not seen so much as dependent on individual men. Most women in Finland express a preference for full-time work, but even if they want part-time work they would find little social or institutional support for doing so while (for married women and mothers especially) the opposite is true for west Germany and The Netherlands. The origin of these contrasting gender cultures lies in the particular historical route from agrarian into industrial society, the role various social groups played in this transition and, consequently, the dominant model of the ideal or 'normal' family and childhood. These alternative means by which women are integrated into society (primarily via the labour market and through their role in families) are long-established and enduring, even if they may be 'modernised' in various ways. For example in west Germany married women often take on part-time work, even though it can be economically 'irrational' given prevailing tax and benefit systems, which allows them some social independence from husbands or fathers. The latters' overall social position is not challenged however, and indeed this modernisation through secondary and supplementary women's paid work may help maintain it.

One important conclusion is that 'the state' is not the determinant actor – in contrast to the assumptions of most social policy research, including the theories of welfare state regimes and breadwinner states. Rather, different welfare state systems will reflect pre-existing gender cultures. For example, a pervasive day care system has been developed in Finland, but this works to support the pre-existing norm of women as full-time workers in both the agrarian family model and the succeeding equality model – it was not the development of day care that created the norm. Similarly in west Germany, part-time child care is most common, and this developed in support of a pre-existing dependent motherhood role where the ideal of the bourgeois family remains institutionally dominant. This returns us again to the issue of fetishizing 'the state' (see Chapter 1). Echoing Fernand Braudel (and indeed Marx), while the 'longue durée' of social institutions tends towards a stability in gender arrangements, at times of rapid and fundamental social change the gender order of institutions may no longer correspond with the norms of the gender culture. Former east Germany may be a current example. Overall, the notion of gender contract cultures is particularly useful in directing attention to where alternative ideas about male and female roles come from, how they are put in place, and how they are maintained. This concept, then, can more successfully place gender into welfare state regimes.

Combining Gender Contract and Capital–labour Contract – the 'Genderfare' Model

The discussion so far points to one fundamental conclusion about variations in welfare states – they reflect variations in *both* the capital–labour contract and the gender contract (or gender culture). The former is represented by Esping-Andersen type models, including the various feminist inspired critiques and developments, the latter by the work of Hirdmann and Pfau-Effinger. Naturally, one 'contract' will affect the other. For example, the nature of capital–labour relations in particular welfare state regimes will position women both in relation to social policy (as with the provision of day care) and in the workplace (thus women's wages are closer to men's in states with corporatist labour markets: Perrons 1994). Much less appreciated, however, the process works the other way round. The 'equality contract' between men and women in Sweden does not only require particular welfare state provisions, but also acts against the peripheralisation of women in the labour force and hence also affects the strategies that can be taken by employers and unions. Similarly, west Germany's housewife contract has necessitated the widespread use of 'guest worker' labour (where women are less available) and hence eases both peripheralisation as a management strategy (cf.

Friedman 1977) and the maintenance of a status driven social policy where 'standard', German, male workers can be treated as the core.

This means that in order to properly locate and account for variations in social policy it is necessary to combine both capital – labour (state welfare regimes) and male–female (gender contract or gender culture) spheres of analysis. This is especially so for those policies, such as those about mothering, which are not in themselves 'gender blind' (unlike, for example, Esping-Andersen's original exemplars of pensions, sickness and unemployment benefits). In the terms of critical realism, the position of women in welfare states is a concrete outcome of two 'necessary relations', not just one – the state welfare regime and the gender contract . We have named this combination the 'genderfare' model.

We can illustrate the utility of this combination by reference to the positioning of women in three countries within Esping-Andersen's 'conservative' welfare state regime – France, The Netherlands and west Germany. As we have seen, despite their identical regime location, the economic position of lone mothers varies considerably between these countries (Figure 7.1). There are similar discontinuities in other gender overt social policies, such as the provision of day care (Duncan 1996). However, this regime location is in each case combined with a different gender contract (Figure 7.3). In west Germany, which remains an archetypical case, the conservative regime is combined with a housewife contract, resting on a strong idealisation of the bourgeois family model (Pfau-Effinger 1998). Women are firmly positioned in a homemaking role in traditional families, public daycare is residual and lone mothers do poorly in economic terms. The family ideal in The Netherlands is also derived from the bourgeois model, but here the housewife contract is overlaid by a developing equality contract (ibid.). While daycare provision is also low, the social wage for homemaking is higher than in Germany, and men are encouraged to take part, for instance through the expansion of part-time work. Lone mothers fare better, economically, than in Germany, as Figure 7.1 shows. Finally, in France the bourgeois family form was never socially generalised, where the agrarian model remained pervasive, and has been modified by the development of a 'dual role' contract in line with pro-natalist objectives (Lefaucher and Martin 1997). Child case provision is highest and lone mothers do best economically. None the less, despite these differences in gender roles and relations, all three countries share conservative forms of 'mainstream' social expenditure as described by Esping-Andersen.

Figure 7.4 generalises this argument in terms of welfare state regimes and gender contracts, producing a relative set of national 'genderfare' positions. The next section applies this combined model to examine how social policy positions lone mothers, with particular reference to our four case-studies of Germany, Sweden, the USA and Britain.

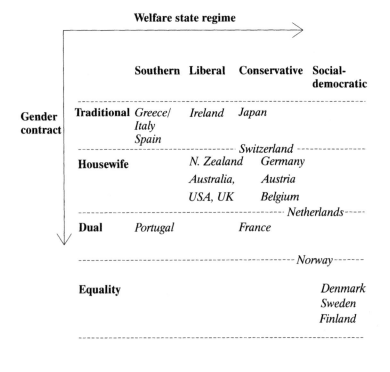

Figure 7.4   Genderfare in developed countries.

7.3 GENDERFARE AND THE POSITION OF LONE MOTHERS

Lone Mothers' Economic Position – Benefits, Maintenance and Employment

In a recent article Jane Millar (1996) summarises the policies of different advanced countries towards lone mothers. In order to do this, she uses a framework which differentiates between the level and nature of state policies towards three potential sources of income for lone mothers – social security benefits, maintenance from the fathers of their children, and employment. Millar's work is exemplary in going as far as it is possible in developing categorisations of policy based on empirical description. Furthermore, her work is most usefully based on up to date policy and statistical material from a number of sources (especially the work of Jonathan Bradshaw and colleagues, see Bradshaw 1996). Millar goes on, in the same article, to discuss her descriptive categorisations in relation to Esping-Andersen's welfare state regimes and Lewis' breadwinner state models. However, rather than repeating this discussion (see pp. 216–30), we employ her work here as a starting point in understanding the positioning of lone mothers through social policy. We do this by relating her empirical categorisations to our genderfare model (see Figure 7.4).

Benefits

Millar begins with a discussion of social security benefits for lone mothers. She notes that the most common, and chief, way of providing benefits to lone mothers is through the provisions that exist for all families with children: 'it is their claims as mothers, not as lone mothers, that are important' (Millar 1996, p. 102). (Mirroring what we discovered in Chapter 4, that it is largely lone mothers' moralities as mothers, not as lone mothers *per se*, that are important in their uptake of paid work.) As Millar notes, this normally means that non-employed lone mothers will receive social assistance benefits, while employed lone mothers will receive in-work means-tested benefits. Both will use universal family allowances. It follows that social security support for lone mothers is highest in those countries where support for all families with children is highest, and lowest where this general support is low, and this conclusion is generally supported by the available evidence.

Using Millar's 'league table' of relative generosity as a source, we can relate this finding to genderfare location. As Table 7.1 indicates, the 'generosity' of child benefit packages (Millar's summary measure of support to families) for lone mothers is high in those Scandinavian countries falling within the social-democratic welfare state regime. This is as expected where benefits are universalised at relatively high levels. In contrast, those countries within the liberal regime are much less generous, as is also to be expected, where most benefits are both residualised and means tested, and where universal benefits (such as child allowances) are either paid at a low level or are lacking altogether as in the USA. The level of the child benefit package is particularly low in Ireland, where the welfare state regime combines with a gender contract which has, until recently, assumed and enforced traditional families (Mahon 1994, McLaughlin and Rodgers 1997). In the other liberal regimes this package is a little more generous, especially where there has been both a past flirtation with social democratic concepts of the welfare state (as in Britain.) The development of a 'housewife contract' (if at a weaker level than in west Germany or Sweden in the 1950s) also requires more specific support for mothers at home. Lone mothers in Britain, Australia and New Zealand can therefore better survive on benefits than in the USA, although still at a level near the poverty line.

Welfare state regime theory would predict that the child benefit would be at a medium level in the conservative regime. This situation is further buttressed in those countries with a housewife gender contract (such as Germany). Here a concern to use social policy to maintain status differentials (including those of gender) would encourage generosity, but at the same time a reliance on families to provide welfare in the first instance (the subsidiarity principle) would militate against this. In this regime unemployment, sickness and retirement are covered by social insurance, which acts to replace earnings, and needs based social assistance is set at low levels. This obviously discriminates against mothers who will usually have less entitlement through paid work, but whereas married mothers can depend on their male partners, lone mothers will either exist in poverty (see Figure 7.1) or be be forced into paid work. In Germany this situation is recognised to some extent through relatively generous social assistance for mothers with children under two years (Klett-Davies 1997).

However, considerable differences are produced as the conservative welfare regime combines with different gender contracts. In France the gender contract stresses dual roles for women, with both high female employment rates and pro-natalist family policies (Lefaucher and Martin 1997). The child benefit package is at a generous level. Similarly, Belgium and The Netherlands are moving away from, or modernising, the housewife contract (for example in encouraging dual roles for both men and women in the the Netherlands, Pfau-Effinger 1998), and child benefit packages are relatively more generous. Finally, in the Southern Model, the patchy development of the welfare state is combined with gender contracts assuming women's central – but private – role in traditional families. While relatively strong feminist movements have developed, for instance in Italy, these are focused more on social definitions of female identity and criticise dominant discourses of 'equality' arguing that these are male biased and attempt just to to turn women into men. However, despite manifestoes on what action should be taken, this position has left the current needs of women as mothers politically peripheralised (Simoni 1996). The child benefit package remains at a low level, therefore.

Millar notes that designated benefits for lone parents (where eligibility depends on lone parent status) are much less important than the general child benefit package, and indeed are only developed in three countries – Ireland, France and Norway (see Table 7.1).[2] As Millar goes on to show, these designated benefits are intended as wage replacement benefits, to allow lone mothers to stay at home as fulltime mothers looking after their children (up to age three in France, to age ten in Norway, and 16 in Ireland). In each case the prevailing welfare state regime is combined with a gender contract emphasising the importance of motherhood – if in different ways (see Mahon 1994 and McLaughlin and Rodgers 1997 for Ireland; Lefaucher and Martin 1997 for France; Leira 1992 for Norway). Britain also has a pale reflection of these schemes where lone mothers have received a 'top-up' to the universal child benefit ('one-parent benefit'). This reflects the fact that, given an overall housewife contract, lone mothers were also traditionally seen as mothers at home (Lewis 1989b; Millar 1989). This top-up has been abolished for new lone mothers from 1998.

Maintenance

Millar turns next to income from fathers through maintenance. The basic position in western capitalist societies – predicated upon private ownership, the bourgeois family norm and legal contract – is that maintenance is a private contractual matter between equal parties, which can be legally enforced if necessary. The trouble with this is that

Table 7.1   Policies towards lone mothers by genderfare

	Child benefit package	Designated lone parent benefit	Maintenance system	Employment rate of lone mothers: partnered mothers
Social Democratic equality contract (Denmark, Finland, Sweden)	High	No	State advanced	Equally high
Social Democratic / transitional (Norway)	High	Yes	State advanced	Equally high
Liberal / housewife contract (Australia, New Zealand, UK, USA)	Medium-low	No	Private/ child support	Lower (except USA equal)
Liberal / traditional contract (Ireland)	Low	Yes	Private	Equally low
Conservative/ dual role (France)	High	Yes	Mixed	Equally high
Conservative / housewife contract (Austria, Germany)	Medium	No	Mixed	Higher
Conservative/ transitional (Belgium, Neths)	Medium-High	No	Mixed	Lower

Table 7.1   (Continued)

	Child benefit package	Designated lone parent benefit	Maintenance system	Employment rate of lone mothers: partnered mothers
Southern model / traditional contract (Spain, Portugal Greece, Italy, Japan?)	Low	No	Private	Higher

Sources: adapted from Millar, 1996; Duncan and Edwards 1997.

the parties are rarely equal; normally lone mothers will have far less bargaining power – they will usually be in more straightened circumstances and left in a position, with dependent children, where something is better than nothing. For example Sørensen (1994) calculates the amount of household income that married mothers stand to lose, if they became single. (This is a heuristic calculation of course, as economic calculation is rarely the main point in marital breakdown.) For Sweden, they would lose around 60–70 per cent of income, depending on the number of children, in the USA between 65 and 80 per cent, and in Germany as much as 75–85 per cent. For fathers losses would be only 20 per cent, 10 per cent and 1 per cent respectively. (This is just one specific instance of the inadequacy of the contract assumption, as critics working from both class and gender perspectives have pointed out, for example Marx 1976, Pateman 1988.) Combined with a situation where many fathers are unwilling to make maintenance payments, this basic maintenance system rarely provides significant income for lone mothers therefore. In Britain, for instance, on average lone mothers received only 9 per cent of their income in this way in 1993. Hence, in many countries social policy has been used in the attempt to enforce or increase maintenance payments by fathers.

Millar distinguishes between two categories of state intervention in maintenance – child support schemes and state advanced maintenance. With child support schemes, which vary substantially in rules and procedures, the principle is that the state acts 'to set and enforce family obligations between parents and children' (Millar 1996, p. 103). The level of maintenance awards to support children is no longer left as an individual contractual matter, but is set by the state according to a standard formula, where collection and enforcement is also undertaken centrally through a state agency. (Awards to support ex-partners, rather than children, are left in the private contractual sphere.) However, while direction is centralised in the state, this remains secondary to an emphasis on the private responsibility of parents (mostly fathers) for their children. Indeed, this emphasis is reinforced precisely through the state's enforcement role, and proponents of child support schemes often explicitly see this reinforcement of paternal responsibility as one of their objectives. As various critics have pointed out, child support schemes also act to sustain the financial dependency of individual women on individual men, and in this way maintains the traditional family 'in absentia'.

For state advanced maintenance both practice and underlying principles are quite different. Again, procedures vary but in essence the state advances the maintenance payments if they are not being made, and then subsequently seeks to recoup the costs from the absent parent. In effect, the maintenance obligation becomes a flat-rate benefit for children living with one parent. As Millar points out, this system places more emphasis on collective responsibility for children where the state plays a primary role in guaranteeing income through maintenance. This also breaks the link between lone mother and separated father, where the income of the former does not depend upon the actions of the latter. The traditional family model is replaced, in this way, by the state (whether this is 'women-friendly', or merely represents 'state patriarchy' remains a moot point, see Langan and Ostner 1994, Duncan 1994b). Certainly the state advanced maintenance system is superior in terms of generating income for lone mothers and their children. This is for two main reasons. First, collection rates for child support schemes remain low, for instance the relatively long running US system only collects 40 to 45 per cent of awarded payments. Secondly, and fundamentally, even with 100 per cent compliance few men actually earn enough to support more than one household, especially if they have become fathers or stepfathers in another family. State advanced maintenance avoids both these problems, although of course this requires additional state expenditure.

Turning to Table 7.1, we can see that the distribution of these different maintenance systems is explained in the same way as child benefit packages. Again, as would be expected, the social democratic regime countries have developed state advanced maintenance systems, and this can only be reinforced by combination with gender contracts emphasising women's equality. Until recently, as would also be expected, countries in the liberal regime relied on private, contractual enforcement. This fits in best with social assumptions of personal responsibility in a contractual market system, supported by a housewife contract where a husband's duty was to support his separated wife and children. However, in the USA, and most recently in Australia and Britain, this has been supplemented by child-support schemes. As we have seen, these also act to emphasise and support personal responsibility and, where the housewife contract is still an ideal, to also support the traditional family concept even where it has broken down in practice. In Ireland this sort of intervention is inappropriate where, in a traditional contract, divorce was not even legally possible until 1996. Hence the reliance on the designated lone parent benefits discussed above, such as the indicitively named 'deserted wives benefit' and 'deserted wives allowance'. The countries in the conservative regime show 'mixed schemes'; there is some development of restricted state advanced maintenance, but the emphasis remains on private responsibility. Again, the preservation of gender status differences through social policy dovetails with the preservation of the traditional family. Finally, in the Mediterranean countries of the Southern Model maintenance officially remains a private and contractual matter. In practice, this means that maintenance paid by fathers is rarely significant. Rather, where the traditional, matrifocal family plays an important welfare role, lone mothers are usually supported by – and often absorbed within – the mother's own maternal family (Gonzalez-Lopez 1997).

Employment

Finally, Millar turns to the third income source for lone mothers – paid employment. As we discussed earlier (pp. 212–16), there is considerable national variation in lone mothers' uptake of paid work. Millar asks how far these differences can be explained by national differences in tax and benefit systems, where some countries might provide financial incentives for women to enter the labour market, while others may discourage this. The answer – drawing on a range of recent research using both survey data and simulated model families – is 'not much'. Thus some countries, like Sweden, have high 'replacement rates' (that is the wages that have to be offered to equal benefit income) but, paradoxically, most lone mothers take paid work. Similarly, other countries, such as Britain, have relatively low replacement rates but only a minority of lone mothers are in employment. Rather, Millar concludes it is the overall policy regime – and in particular the relative ease with which women can be both mothers and workers – which influences lone mothers' ability to take up paid work. Policies concerning day care, parental leave and parental employment rights (such as leave to look after sick children) will be particularly important. It is also important to note that the ability to gain the replacement rate is also a function of the wages offered in the labour market, although as we discussed in Chapter 6 the social policy literature usually neglects this. In this context Sweden is a higher wage economy than Britain, particularly for women.

Millar's mention of the 'overall policy regime' brings us right back to the issue of categorising welfare states. Millar undertakes this descriptively, using the ratio between the employment rates for lone mothers and partnered mothers a a distinguishing criterion. We can reinterpret this material in terms of our combined genderfare model (Table 7.1). It is also useful, however, to expand Millar's data base by distinguishing between full-time and part-time work, where the latter can often be inadequate in providing a household income. Figure 7.5 presents this information, where the light diagonal line represents a ratio of one, that is equal employment rates for lone and married mothers. For countries above the line lone mothers have higher employment rates than married mothers, whereas they have lower rates in countries below the line, and the distance from this line represents the deviation from a ratio of one.

Again as expected, the Scandinavian countries with a social democratic welfare regime, combined with an equality contract, exhibit high employment rates for both partnered and lone mothers, with approximate equality between the two. Rates are especially equal for full-time work. Note, however, the lower than 'expected' rate for lone mother's total employment in Norway (and for all mothers working full-time). Here the gender contract retains more elements of the housewife contract, including policies such as the designated lone parent benefit which will increase the replacement rate even more than in the other

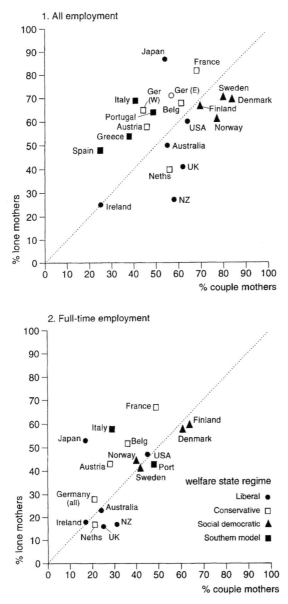

Source: adopted from Bradshaw et al 1996, Millar 1996, Duncan & Edwards 1997

Figure 7.5   Employment rates for lone and couple mothers: developed countries early 1990s

Scandinavian countries. (The apparently low full-time rate for Swedish mothers is, in a sense, a statistical anomaly. Most part-time work in Sweden is 'long part-time', often undertaken by parents exercising their right to a shorter working day, and in 1994 only 4 per cent of mothers with dependent children worked less than 20 hours per week: Björnberg 1997.) As we would also expect by now, France also fits into this group, although again not surprisingly more lone mothers hold jobs than partnered mothers – in the conservative welfare state regime replacement rates are lower, while 'pro-natalist' family policy will be less cogent for lone mothers.

For countries with liberal welfare state regimes and a housewife contract, lone mothers have lower employment rates than for partnered mothers. The liberal state regime, buttressed by expectations that women are primarily homemakers, does little to support mothers in employment. Both lone mothers and partnered mothers, therefore, have low rates of full-time working – which, paradoxically, is the most likely to offer a full household income. However, partnered mothers are better placed to take up part-time paid work in this environment, partly because of their generally superior access to informal child care, although this is not infrequently 'short 'part-time below 20 hours per week with particularly low returns. This is reinforced by the need and expectation that they fit paid work around their domestic responsibilities. Lone mothers are less able to take up these jobs but, even if they did, rewards would often not even exceed the low replacement rate. In Ireland, where the emphasis is more firmly placed on mothers as homemakers, employment rates are particularly low for both groups of mothers. In employment terms the Netherlands joins this group. As we have mentioned, an emerging emphasis here is that fathers should share domestic responsibilities and part-time work. State support for this dual role, and hence also replacement rates, are high.

An exception in this liberal group is the USA, with relatively high employment rates for both lone and partnered mothers (although below levels for Scandinavia and France, especially for full-time work). If we were to take the quality of work into account this anomaly would be reduced, where many of these jobs are badly-paid (de Acosta 1997). In addition, the weak development of the welfare state in the USA means not only that support for working mothers is low, but also that replacement rates are particularly low. Japan, with very high employment rates for lone mothers (but with high poverty rates, see Figure 7.1), with little support for either working mothers or mothers outside conjugal families, and a strong concept of the traditional mother (Peng 1997), takes this to an extreme.

In this respect the USA and Japan resemble the Southern Model countries. In these countries support for mothers taking jobs is low, while the gender contract strongly positions mothers in the role of homemakers. In many cases their role extends beyond domestic and caring work to include a sort of 'family preservation' welfare role. Many young adults, even when married, still live in the parental home for instance (Gonzalez-Lopez 1997). Many lone mothers find support in this way too (although statistically, without an autonomous household, they will rarely be recorded as such). There is little state support for lone mothers living autonomously, replacement rates are very low, and they are pushed into employment by the lack of an alternative. Consequently, lone mothers employment rates are substantially higher than those for partnered mothers, at least in the formal labour market. The exception here is Portugal (although we have tried to represent this in Figure 7.4). This is partly a statistical anomaly where farmers' wives, in an economy with a large agricultural sector, are recorded as workers. However, this in itself reflects a rather different version of the 'traditional' gender contract in Portugal, where a surviving agrarian family model sees women as engaged in productive work.

The remaining countries in the conservative regime, including Germany and Austria where the housewife contract is more strongly institutionalised, show employment patterns tending towards the Southern Model and for the same general reasons. Both state support and social expectations emphasise mothers' role as homemakers; lone mothers are weakly positioned on both counts but, where replacement rates are low, they are pushed toward paid work. Welfare systems are of course strongly developed in this regime, in contrast to the Southern Model, but the nature of this development helps to fix married mothers in a housewife role (perhaps working part-time) and to push lone mothers into the labour market. For in conservative welfare regimes unemployment, sickness and retirement are covered by social insurance, which acts to replace earnings. This obviously discriminates against mothers, but whereas married mothers can depend on their male partners, lone mothers will be forced into work – those divorced and separated, as well as many single mothers who are relatively young, will not have amassed adequate insurance. This strategy is only viable, however, if adequate day care can be found. In practice many lone mothers cannot take up paid work and for these mothers, depending on low levels of needs-based social assistance, poverty rates are especially high (see Figure 7.1). In Germany this situation is recognised to some extent through relatively generous social assistance for mothers with children under two years, and consequently the replacement rate is higher for these mothers (Klett-Davies 1997).

Genderfare and Lone Mothers in the Four Case-study Countries

In this section we bring together the information presented above, together with a brief account of current social policy, in order to understand the contrasting position of lone mothers in our four case study countries: Germany, Sweden, the USA and Britain.

Germany (more particularly former West Germany) is the archetypical conservative welfare state with a housewife gender contract based on the bourgeois family ideal. Social policy positions married and cohabiting women primarily as mothers in traditional male breadwinner/female homemaker families. For partnered mothers the most rational economic decision and the most socially legitimate are the same – to become a housewife (possibly 'modernised' by part-time work, even though this may be economically 'irrational'). Family wages, and the tax and benefit system which compensates for loss of income through social insurance based on previous employment history, leave women women dependent upon men. In addition, the child care and school system (with varying hours and no meal provision) leaves little choice (Klett-Davies 1997). The economic risks of partnership breakdown will also be high.

As Hobson (1994) points out, this strongly gendered logic to the German welfare state leaves lone mothers (apart from widows) in a residual position: they are neither the wives of working men nor male breadwinners. Single (never married) lone mothers are particularly vulnerable, but divorced/separated women also fare badly – not only are the economic risks of divorce particularly high (Sørensen 1994), but neither do they have a social right to income maintenance. Rather, family members are in theory obliged to provide support for children, not only fathers but also grandparents, although practice (dependent on court rulings and subject to income criteria) is less certain. Although replacement rates are low, day care is not easily available for the whole working day, and many lone mothers depend on minimal social assistance. This is especially severe for those with children over three years old, when benefits become less generous and there is an obligation to seek paid work. Consequently, relative poverty rates for lone mothers are especially high (Figure 7.1) even though there is a relatively high percentage in paid work (above the rate for partnered mothers, Figure 7.5). While the increase in lone motherhood clearly provides a problem for German social policy (how is the absent breadwinner to be put in place?), its residual position in social policy is likely to reinforce the legitimacy of the traditional breadwinner/homemaker model.

In *Sweden*, the archetypical 'social democratic' welfare state is combined with an 'equality' gender contract. In contrast to Germany the tax, benefit and welfare system treats all adult women as autonomous citizens and workers, and their economic dependence upon men is lower. These citizen-workers may also be parents, and hence the development of a pervasive day care system, together with rights to paid parental leave, paid leave to look after sick children and reduced working hours. Other child support benefits are high and universalised. Lone mothers share in these benefits because of their status as citizens, parents and workers. The state does, however, also recognise their status as lone mothers, in that they will usually receive preferential access to day care. In addition, the state advanced maintenance system acts as a flat-rate benefit for lone mothers, but in a way that reduces dependence on an individual man and enhances their autonomous status. Swedish state policy does not position lone mothers as a particular social category, although those who are seen as socially irresponsible (for instance, if they do not seek training or paid work) may attract regulation from social work agencies. As Leira (1992) remarks, Scandinavian welfare states privilege waged work – however useless – over unpaid care work – however useful. Lone mothers' employment participation rates are very similar to those of partnered women, with most in full-time or 'long' part-time paid work of 20 hours a week or more (Figure 7.5). Most lone mothers find the bulk of their income from paid work, with incomes near those for two parent families, and relative poverty rates are very low (Figure 7.1). In this way lone mothers in Sweden are integrated into a 'women friendly' state welfare regime (see Sørensen1994; Björnberg 1997). Lone motherhood does not pose any overall social problem, let alone a threat, to this regime – as long as female employment levels remain high.

The *USA* is generally regarded as the type case of the 'liberal' state welfare regime, combined with a gender contract emphasising that childrearing is a private matter to be undertaken in traditional families. Children are not seen as a social good, there is no system of child benefits, non-maternal child care is often frowned upon, and in any case its public provision is not sanctioned by liberal economic theory.

Consequently, conservatives can appeal to the primacy of 'the family' 'as the keystone of our civilisation' (President Richard Nixon in his 1971 veto of proposals for public day care subsidy) or portray daycare as the 'sovietisation' of American children (see de Acosta 1997). But at the same time, the powerful women's movement has similarly not shown much interest in pressing for public day care provision, focusing more on establishing legal equality between men and women as individuals, for example in employment, rather than considering the problems of women as mothers (Hewlett 1988) – in contrast to the Swedish women's movement for example. This 'privatisation' of motherhood is compounded by the welfare system where public assistance programmes both provide low levels of benefit and stigmatise recipients. The provision of 'food stamps' can be seen as an epitome of this residualised stigmatisation. Lone mothers become especially labelled as undeserving and benefits for low-income mothers have become the core of what is pejoratively known as welfare.

This reaches an extreme form in the Aid to Families with Dependent Children (AFDC) programme and its successors, the Personal Responsibility and Work Opportunity Reconciliation Act (1996) which introduces time limited benefit support for lone mothers and Temporary Aid for Needy Families (TANF) where ADFC is replaced by lump sum grants for states to run their own programmes. It is evident that most states will lower benefits still further (the value of food stamps was also lowered towards an extreme minimum) and impose tight time limits on the receipt of benefits. Even those more liberal states will be constrained by TANF requirements that they put recipients to work in two years. As 'work' is operationally defined as as dropping mothers from the benefit rolls or, in a bizarre return to the early nineteenth century, farming them out to 'workfare' employers in exchange for their benefits, it is evident that this legislation will further depress wages and increase lone mother poverty. As Linda Gordon presciently noted:

> The stigmas of 'welfare' and of single motherhood intersect: hostility to the poor and hostility to deviant family forms reinforce each other. The resentment undercuts political support for the program, and benefits fall further and further behind inflation. (Gordon 1994, quoted in de Acosta 1997)

This stigmatising process is especially marked for African-American lone mothers, who historically were often marginalised in public assistance programmes, and where a high proportion of African American families (partly because of poor employment prospects for males) do not fulfil the ideal family form. Overall, the low value of benefits means that lone mothers must supplement their income through paid work – but because of a lack of affordable day care, and because of fears of losing their right to benefits, they often end up in poorly paid and insecure jobs (Figure 7.1). Maintenance is regarded as a private responsibility, and although this is ameliorated through the state legally enforcing payment by fathers, collection rates are low and in any case many cannot afford much. In summary, lone mothers in the USA are not only poor, but are seen a 'a trope for dependency or family breakdown' (Hobson 1994, p. 176).

Finally, in *Britain*, the 'liberal' state ostensibly gives mothers a 'choice' on whether to take up paid work or not. On an underlying level, though, traditional motherhood is assumed in terms of the lack of day care provision, which is amongst the lowest in Europe, but not in terms of a family wage. Thus it is difficult for mothers to participate on equal terms in the labour market, but paradoxically they need to. Policies thus reinforce mothers' uptake of part-time paid work, which is often short-term, low paid, insecure and sometimes even without employment rights and protection (Chapter 6). This positioning is reinforced where the gender contract sees mothers' prime responsibility as unpaid domestic and caring work. Lone mothers are particularly disadvantaged, with as many as 50 per cent having no access to any sort of child care (Popay and Jones 1990; Bradshaw and Millar 1991). Mothers are therefore implicitly dependent on a male breadwinner or, if this fails as with lone mothers, on increasingly minimal and stigmatised state benefits. The proportion of British lone mothers in paid work is not only low (Figure 7.5), it is also below levels for partnered mothers and is actually decreasing over time. Few find the bulk of their income from paid work, and the majority consequently exist at minimum income levels (as defined by social security criteria) considerably below the average for two-parent families.

The 1990s saw a major attempt to shift the prevailing balance of lone mothers' income away from the state, towards maintenance and paid work. Prior to this, British governments had treated lone mothers as non-working mothers supported by the state, albeit experiencing dilemmas over this (Bradshaw 1989; Lewis 1989b; Millar 1989). The 'top-up' to the universal Child Benefit, 'one-parent benefit' recognised these additional needs – although only symbolically as the level of benefit remains low and, equally symbolically, is to be progressively abolished from 1998. Maintenance from fathers was seen as a matter for the courts and for parents themselves.

The 1991 Child Support Act (CSA), however, requires the biological fathers of lone mothers' children – termed 'absent' parents – to support them according to a fixed formula, enforced by the state through the Child Support Agency. The Agency formula does not take account of a man's need to support any non-biological children he may live with in another family, presuming they are supported by their own 'absent' father. Subsequent biological children are included in Agency calculations. Thus biological, rather than social, parenthood is posited as the relevant factor. Implicit is the idea that men will be attached to families (financially) by the state, even if they choose to remove themselves physically. The mothers of their children thus are rendered privately dependent on men in their rightful breadwinning role, even if 'absent', rather than publicly on the state as breadwinner. Thus traditional familial and gendered divisions of labour are reproduced, rather than there being adaptation to the changes in family forms.

The CSA also seeks to manipulate financial incentives so that paid work, especially part-time, is attractive for lone mothers. The Act extended eligibility for Family Credit – a top-up benefit – for low income parents in paid work and those paying for professional day care. Employed lone mothers who do not claim in-work benefits can keep all of any maintenance from 'absent' fathers (and Child Support Agency involvement is voluntary in their case). However, lone mothers who do not move into, or continue, employment and are living on Income Support – the state 'safety net' benefit for those with no other source of income – gain nothing from the child support paid by the father, as is also the case (bar a £15 'disregard') for those claiming in-work benefits. More punitively, lone mothers claiming state benefits who do not reveal the name and, if known, the whereabouts of the 'absent' father can suffer financial penalties to their already minimal benefit payments unless they can demonstrate 'good cause' to withhold this information. In addition, lone mothers on Income Support receive slightly less in one-parent benefit than do working lone mothers. In an effort to further lure lone mothers on Income Support into the labour market, the British government put forward plans to have a deferred £5 per week credit against their child support which lone mothers can claim as a lump sum if they subsequently take up 16 hours or more of employment, while the one parent benefit is currently to be abolished for new lone mothers after 1997. The CSA has been the subject of much criticism, with calls either for changes or its abolition. Arguments include that it is driven by a desire to save state expenditure rather than a concern with children, pushing women into low paid insecure jobs and reducing their entitlement to support for bringing up children (Wages for Housework and Payday Men's Network 1993); that the interaction of the CS Agency, Family Credit and other benefits is complex and insecure (Millar 1994); that the day care offset meets only minimal costs, excludes those who use informal child care (the source for the majority of working mothers, including lone mothers – Popay and Jones 1990; Bradshaw and Millar 1991) and does not address the actual lack of provision itself; that enforced financial dependency means that lone mothers are enmeshed in patterns of control by their former partners (Clarke et al. 1993); and that changes in family structure and employment make the idea of a 'family wage' obsolete, so increasing numbers of men cannot support even one family on their own (Millar 1994).

In Britain it is no longer clear if women are integrated into the social order as workers in the labour market (as in Sweden) or as mothers and housewives in families (as in Germany). If the state provides sufficient day care support and other welfare measures to integrate lone mothers into the labour force, then it implicitly takes the position that all mothers are primarily workers. It would hardly be politically feasible to deny partnered mothers access to public day care provision, and the category of 'lone mother' is not an empirically sustainable day care rationing device (see Edwards 1993). On the other hand, treating lone mothers as primarily mothers and homemakers makes heavy demands on Treasury expenditure, even at minimum levels – a cost the British government is currently balking at. This strategy also flies in the face of demands from all angles of the political spectrum that women should both be economically and socially independent. Both policy courses, therefore, are fraught with political implications *vis-à-vis* the relations between men and women, and the nature of 'the family'. This situation helps explain why lone motherhood in Britain provides a particularly powerful symbolic role for social expectations and conflicts about gender roles and relations (see Chapter 2). It leads to lone mothers in Britain being regarded as, at best, a social problem or, at worst, a threat to the social order.

7.4 COMPARING WELFARE STATE REGIMES AND
GENDER CONTRACTS: LONE MOTHERS' VIEWS

So far in this chapter we have taken a 'top-down' perspective in comparing social policy in different welfare states, taking the perspectives of social science theorists and policy researchers. However, it is lone mothers themselves who are faced with the varying structures of opportunities and constraints set up by various social policy regimes in various countries. In this section, therefore, we turn to the views of lone mothers themselves as revealed in the interviews we conducted in Britain, Germany, Sweden and the USA.

We did not ask the interviewees to directly compare conditions, as they saw them, in different countries. (In retrospect, it would have been interesting to do so.) When the majority of the lone mothers made comparisons these were either between themselves and other 'types' of lone mother (as discussed in Chapter 2) or between what it was like to be a lone mother living in their own and other areas or neighbourhoods (as discussed in Chapter 3) – in other words, within one national welfare regime. However, amongst the British lone mothers, two made references to what it must be like to live as a lone mother under different welfare regimes. Pippa, a White middle class lone mother living in the suburban area of Brighton, had a sister who was living in France. As discussed in Chapter 2, this group of mothers held a 'primarily mother' conception of motherhood although in some cases, as with Pippa, this led to the repression of personal desires to follow a career. Because of her sister's experience of life in France Pippa was aware that it was far easier to find day care there, and that most mothers worked – a situation she observed with some envy. On the other hand Sasha, a white working class lone mother living in the stigmatised council estate in Moulescoomb, not far away, had a father who lived in the USA. Following a holiday at his home, Sasha had speculated on moving out there. In contrast to Pippa (with whom she shared a 'primarily mother' conception), Sasha drew unfavourable comparisons with her alternative location:

My father lives in America and single parents don't survive out there, he said. There's no such welfare like we get here. Cos I was going to live out there once, but I wouldn't be able to do what I am doing here [that is stay at home on benefits and care for her children herself]. So it's better in this country, I think, being a single parent

More dramatically one of the Swedish lone mothers had lived under two welfare regimes: as a married mother with two children (and no paid work) in Britain and as a lone mother with her children (and full-time paid work) in Sweden. One thread running through her account was a comparison between the policies and gender cultures in the two countries. She had explicitly chosen Sweden as the country in which she wanted to live as a lone mother, as opposed to remaining in Britain, because she felt the welfare regime would support her in building an independent life. As she said when asked why she had agreed to take part in the research:

> I thought it was so exciting, this comparison between England and Sweden. If you hadn't done it I would have (laughs). No, it's really exciting ... Oh yes, [the questions] were very relevant. Some are, since it's an English survey. I heard you say that if it had been a Swedish survey then it would have stressed how one manages on one's own. I think the basic English question is that you don't manage on your own. There's a totally different viewpoint there.

Beata has two children (aged 6 and 4) and works full-time in a high status administrative position, while her children are in a 'sibling group' in a local authority nursery near to where she lives. (Her oldest child is soon to start school and will attend a local 'after school' club before and after school.) Beata married a British man and lived with him in Britain, before leaving him when her youngest child was about six months old and returning to Sweden. She drew an unfavourable comparison between the parental leave opportunities (or lack of them) available to mothers in the two countries:

> This thing that we have had one and a half years to be able to stay at home, you don't realise how much it's worth if you can't compare with other countries. When you have to go out to work after six weeks, you're not back to normal even yourself. Really you ought to be on sick leave for three months after the delivery. But there's nothing that's called that abroad. It's six to eight weeks or three months, and then you have to go back again. And there we are struggling and trying to breast feed for three months up to six months, and then to know that after a month you begin to feel stressed because you have to go back to work again. But a year is the minimum I think to stay at home. You need to stay at home not least for your own physical health if nothing else. It takes a long

time to adjust back. That's how I felt. One year of real peace and quiet, after that I need to get out and work.

After she returned to Sweden, Beata 'put her name down' at the local job centre, found a nursery for the children and then started work. In her account this process appeared to be accomplished with remarkable ease, from a British perspective at least.

Beata linked the difference in the services and support available to mothers in Britain and Sweden with the contrasting gendered expectations and moralities around the roles of women and men, and childrearing, in the two countries, and which she felt had led to the breakdown of her marriage:

> It was because of the attitude in England, this thing that you can't be yourself, you can't do what you want because others think you shouldn't. And we arranged a housewife life in England, not this that you have maternity leave and then go back to work. I felt terribly split, it was horrible, just that. I didn't even have to bother about the money. I didn't even have access to the bank accounts and so on. But I had to do the shopping and I had to do this and that, and the food should be on the table. There was a lot of you should, you should. And that thing about the English mentality that the men should always have to do something together, it's never the family. So on Sundays I could come to the pub before Sunday lunch, and it had to be in the oven then for an hour. So you had to fix everything. And then everything, meat, potatoes and vegetables, is cooked in the same fat. And that was something I couldn't cope with. So I never came to the pub on Sundays because I couldn't cook such food. So it became a bone of contention. I became bitter, I missed my old life. I felt it was difficult for me to stay there any longer ... No, I thought it was really nice when he went and sat down on the sofa with the paper. No, I felt go away, let me fix it ... On the whole I think we have a very different attitude to children [in Sweden]. [In Britain] you have children and you love your children, but they grow up in a totally different way. It's the mother. The father is out earning money and has a social life. The woman stays at home with the children and keeps quiet. To me that's totally incredible. I think it's very strange, I'll never get over it. It's idiotic that I fell for that.

She was also scathing about the different attitudes to ensuring fathers paid maintenance in Sweden and Britain:

No [my ex-husband doesn't help financially]. I've just been to court about that, the Swedish DHSS foreign department against him, that he should pay maintenance according to English law and at the English level not Swedish. I don't think it's even half of what we get here. Yes, this has taken four years ... He doesn't want to [pay] because you don't have to in England. There hasn't been a proper law for that. But the law came in 1992 I think, but it hasn't been implemented ... I think it's incredible. How can you as a parent not take responsibility for your own children? It's not like that in Sweden.

What does this case study illustrate? Briefly, it goes some way to showing the effects, for an individual's experience, of different national welfare state regimes and the related dominant gender cultures and moral rationalities. In Sweden Beata was able to follow a high – status career and be a mother, and pursue her own objectives as an independent person. In her account, her life as a lone mother in Sweden was far superior to that as a married women in Britain, where both social policy and gendered expectations pushed her into a dependent homemaking role. It is also interesting, in terms of the genderfare model we use in section 7.3 to account for national social policy differences, which combines both welfare state regime and the gender contract concepts, that Beata also combines both in her explanation of preferring lone motherhood in Sweden to marriage in Britain.

However, in theory at least, return to Sweden was not the only alternative available to Beata. Her British ex-husband worked in a well-paid job in the finance sector and, in her account, she alludes to having lived with him in a high status suburban neighbourhood. While the unsupportive British welfare system may have remained the same had she moved to another type of neighbourhood (say, the gentrified area that the Brighton 'alternative' lone mothers lived in), she may have found expectations about the relationship between motherhood and paid work, at least, to be more conducive. Like other lone mothers in that area (see Chapter 3), she may have been able to find the material and ideological support to regain her independence. We should also recognise that not all Swedish lone mothers are so satisfied with Swedish conditions. (Beata might well respond that they had not tried the alternatives!) We refer in Chapter 4 (pp. 132–3) to a Swedish lone mother who preferred to stay at home with her children, at least when they were young, and who did not want full-time paid work. This mother experienced both the Swedish welfare state and local interpretations of the 'equality' gender contract as oppressive. Both expected her to want full-time work and to place her children in day care, and judged her as either disturbed or deviant in that she did not agree.

7.5 CONCLUSION: NAVIGATING THROUGH NATIONAL STRUCTURES

This chapter has demonstrated how lone mothers are positioned in different ways in different countries, paying some particular attention to the effects on their employment position and standards of living (section 7.2). In so doing, we have developed a new analytical account of national social policy differences, genderfare, which combines the concept of the welfare state regime with the concept of the gender contract (section 7.3). As the discussion established, the effects on lone mothers' economic activity and standards of living can be profound. However, lone mothers are not the prisoners of either welfare state regimes or gender contracts; lone mothers are not simply positioned, they also position themselves. The example of Beata, who preferred lone motherhood in Sweden to marriage in Britain (section 7.4) is a particularly graphic example of this. In this respect it is more accurate to see welfare state regimes and gender contracts as producing just another set of structures which, together with those produced in local labour markets and neighbourhoods, contribute to the formation of opportunities and constraints through which lone mothers socially navigate. Different lone mothers, from different social groups, may well conduct this navigation in different ways. Their gendered moral rationalities, as discussed in Chapter 4, will be a major means of conducting this navigation. The implications of this for how we understand choice and rationality is the subject of the next chapter.

NOTES

1. Expressing these differences in the form of a map again exposes the problem of fetishizing the national state.
2. In Australia separate means-tested benefits are available for different categories of claimants, including lone parents, but these are less distinctive as a 'designated' benefit and are excluded here.

8 Economic Decision-making and Moral Rationalities

8.1 INTRODUCTION: SOCIAL PROBLEMS, POLITICAL DISCOURSES AND RATIONAL ECONOMIC MAN

In previous chapters we examined discourses about lone mother-hood (Chapter 2), lone mothers in neighbourhood social networks (Chapter 3), in local labour markets (Chapter 6), and in different welfare state regimes and gender contracts – 'genderfare' (Chapter 7). These social structures and practices form opportunities and con-straints for lone mothers, and all are influential on whether they do, or do not, take up paid work. However, lone mothers are not simply the prisoners of these social structures and practices; they are not simply positioned, they also position themselves. As we showed in Chapters 4 and 5, there are various 'gendered moral rationalities' through which lone mothers think about, and socially negotiate, their position on how paid work and motherhood should be combined.

Considering lone mothers' agency in this way, as well as the struc-tures in and through which they act, introduces the twin concepts of motivation and rationality. This is a rather important stage to have reached in this book for, as Julian Le Grand has recently written in an article commenting on current changes in the welfare state, 'assump-tions concerning human motivation and behaviour are the key to the design of social policy' (1997, p. 153). He goes on:

> Policy-makers fashion policies on the assumption that those affected by the policies will behave in certain ways and they will do so because they have certain motivations. Sometimes the assump-tions concerning motivation and behaviour are explicit; more often they are implicit, reflecting the unconscious values or beliefs of the policy-makers concerned. Conscious or not, the assump-tions will determine the way that welfare institutions are constructed. (ibid., 153–4)

Le Grand continues to discuss these assumptions in terms of 'knights, knaves or pawns' (the title of his article). Knights – middle class policy-makers and professionals – act altruistically, embodying the Fabian idea of a benevolent state, and control the distribution of state largess to largely passive recipients – the pawns. More recently, according to Le Grand, assumptions have changed and both knights and pawns are now more commonly seen as actively acting like knaves – that is purely in their own self-interest. The problem for Le Grand is that people – both policy-makers and recipients – can act as either knights or knaves, or indeed both, depending on their own motivations and the circumstances they find themselves in. This overall point is reflected in Chapters 2–7 in this book where we have described in detail how lone mothers do indeed behave differently in different circumstances, although in our terms more in line with what they believed to be morally right rather than as knights or knaves. The same conclusion applies, however. Policies based on the assumption that people exhibit consistent behaviour can go badly wrong or at the least would lead to inefficiencies.

A key moment in Le Grand's argument is that we have no way of actually determining if people will behave as knights, knaves or pawns in welfare situations. Moreover, he claims, there does not seem to have been much research on how people actually are motivated in different situations and still less on testing such theories against empirical situations. Hence the necessity for 'robust welfare policies' that perform equally well however people behave.

Looked at more broadly, this is an extraordinary assertion. There is a whole range of theories accounting for human motivation and behaviour, from psychoanalytic theory, to sociobiology, to psychology, to structuralist and deconstructionist sociology, to organisation theory, to neo-classical economics. What is more, these research traditions have been avid in testing their theories and showing how the theoretical parameters work in practice. In response to the perceived inadequacies in these applications several hybrids have resulted, including a whole range of economics/sociology mixes as we will see later in the chapter. Indictively the only theory that Le Grand does mention is public choice theory, which attempts to use a neo-classical economics perspective in understanding political and bureaucratic decision-making. Ironically, as we shall see, this approach does assume that people behave consistently.

In the neo-classical perspective people act as individual 'rational economic man' in maximising personal utility, which (in theory at least) can be psychological just as much as monetary. The net sum of all these decisions, however, will be in the overall public interest – or at least that is how the theory goes. Clearly, Le Grand's knights, knaves and pawns are particular versions of rational economic man. In implicitly incorporating into his analysis the assumptions of neo-classical economics, Le Grand follows a long tradition of social policy as a discipline, especially the male-dominated, institutionally powerful 'public policy research' tradition.[1] In turn, this tradition has been strongly influential in British public policy-making, especially in the Fabian-like mixed economy governments from 1945 up to the advent of Thatcherism and marketisation in the 1980s – when it was outflanked by the new right, the Institute of Economic Affairs, and a more explicit version of rational economic man. (Or as David Donnison, another leading personality in the public policy research school, and erstwhile director of the Supplementary Benefits Commission, put it: 'it became clear that no one in power would be interested in any help I could offer' (1997, p. 9).) How 'New Labour', following its 1997 electoral landslide, will play these two strands is as yet unclear (but see Chapters 2 and 9 for some first thoughts). What does seem clear, however, that ideas of rational economic man are still central. As Frank Field, at the time of writing Minister for Welfare Reform, put it in his recent book *Making Welfare Work* (1995):

> the starting block is a willing acceptance of the fundamental role self-interest plays in human motivation. The job of welfare reconstruction is to plan a series of benefits reforms which allow self-interest to operate in a way that simultaneously promotes the public good.   (Field 1995, p. 20, quoted in Le Grand 1997)

This is of course a restatement of the assumption of rational economic man.

There is, however, a serious *non sequitur* to these arguments. We may accept that people act rationally, and in their own self-interest. This does not then mean, however, that they act like rational economic man – for he is just one possible model of self-interested rationality, and indeed one which is heavily criticised. Hence, a basic (if often unacknowledged) assumption of the public policy research tradition may well be incorrect. The central questions remain of what is rational and how self-interest is defined and arrived at. The task of this chapter is to pursue these questions in the light of what we have discovered in previous chapters.

First, in section 8.2, we examine the inadequacies of conventional economics, and in particular the model of rational economic man, in explaining economic decision-making. The importance of this model is greater than its ostensible status as a rather bizarre economic theorisation would suggest because it extends far outside neo-classical economics, if often implicitly, into the realms of social policy and everyday politics. Section 8.3 continues by assessing the various reactions to this failure of conventional economics. As we shall see the attempts to to reform this approach, and to move beyond it, lead to conclusions rather like our own where how people act in social networks, and how this constitutes their economic behaviour, becomes a central economic question. In section 8.4 we examine the application (explicit or implicit) of conventional economic models – and their limitations – to research about lone mothers and paid work. We conclude that any successful explanation of economic behaviour needs to embody an operationalisation of 'culture' and 'morality'. This is what we attempt with the idea of gendered moral rationalities.

8.2　THE PROBLEM OF ECONOMIC SCIENCE

In the neo-classical approach it is assumed that individuals, as separate economic agents whose 'preferences' or 'tastes' are already given, make selfish cost–benefit type analyses in order to maximise their personal utility. People act, in other words, as 'rational economic man'. While on occasion the 'taste' for 'leisure', 'welfare' or 'pleasure' more generally is included in the definition of utility, this is usually operationally defined in monetary terms. Preferences are assumed to be consistent and stable, with consistent ranking of alternative preferences, independent of the behaviour of everyone else. Using these assumptions, mathematical models based on differential calculus and the technique of constrained maximisation can symbolise rational actors working on the principle of marginal utility. In turn, this mathematics is seen to allow the natural-science like prediction of economic behaviour. Neo-classical economics is thus claimed as a universal theory potentially applicable to most of human life. On the one hand 'theory' predicts behaviour, while the econometric and statistical manipulation of data sets can measure this behaviour in practice. While other social science disciplines may be interesting and useful enough in describing the outcomes of this economic behaviour, or even in accounting for the origin of tastes and preferences, they remain essentially peripheral to the explanation of social behaviour. Thus Nobel prize-winner Gary Becker, an avid exponent of the universality of neo-classical economics, can use this model in his latest book *Accounting for Tastes* (1996) to explain why people take drugs, give money to beggars and fall in love. The decisions of lone mothers to take up paid work, or to live on benefits, is a comparatively trivial explanatory problem seen in this light therefore, and indeed as we discuss in the section 8.4 there is a burgeoning econometric literature on this theme.

There are a number of levels of criticism of the neo-classical view of social life, some of which are well-rehearsed (see Hollis and Nell 1975, Ferber and Nelson 1993a, Ormerod 1994, Lawson 1997 for review). Even for 'homo economicus' (who springs from who knows where, with no childhood, no family, no relationships, no community, no responsibility, but simply maximises satisfactions according to self-interest) the concept of 'rationality', and what factors are relevant to and constitute it, are not neutral, and there are several alternative conceptions as to what 'rationality' actually is (Hargreaves-Heap 1992). Rationality will often be different over the long and short terms, choices are often interactive, with varied expectations, outcomes are often uncertain, or themselves uncertainly constitute future choice. Choice, particularly a social one, is rarely a discrete, one point in time decision. Not surprisingly, preference consistency and transitivity – essential assumptions in most neo-classical formulations – in fact rarely exist. Hence people end up taking decisions where imagination often plays a larger role than probability (or why should homo economicus play the lottery?) and they make economic choices using rule-of-thumb heuristics, which are often sub-optimal and sometimes quite misleading. (The recent history of the British housing sector is a spectacular example, where both consumers and producers took grossly inefficient, wasteful and damaging decisions, Barlow and Duncan 1994.) It is for all these reasons that the tenets of rational economic man are consistently falsified when people's choice behaviour is tested in experimental – and we should add real life – situations (Hargreaves-Heap 1992, Taylor-Gooby 1997).

Indeed, some social theorists like Ulrich Beck (1992) argue that modern society is characterised by the risks and uncertainty created by the breakdown and and withering away of traditional and ascribed social structures and relationships. Who can be sure that marriage is anything but temporary, that motherhood is a stable and valued role, or that BSE, the greenhouse effect or economic chaos will not make all this academic? From this perspective, neo-classical economics has no sense of social time. The problem is that for neoclassicists there is no need for a sense of time. The theory is perceived as a fundamental universal beyond time and place.

If we widen the focus beyond this framework, to include people living in socially negotiated, collective and temporal worlds, then what is a rational choice for any individual becomes even more contested and contextualised. Homo sociologicus, who does inhabit a social world of families, communities and relationships, plays the lottery because he wants to be included and have collective fun with others. It is not only that 'preferences' or 'tastes' (to use conventional economic terms) determine what is rational. In addition, these preferences and tastes change according to the social context. Neither are social decisions, like the demand for education, getting married or becoming a criminal, based purely on individual considerations at one point in time. Externalities abound, where these decisions will affect both 'who I should become' as well as the lives and even the identities of friends, relatives and associates (Akerlof 1997). These sorts of questions are also moral ones. Preferences and tastes, and the decisions they inform, are thus collectively negotiated, modified and changed. Parents' choice of a secondary school for their children, for example, is often shaped long prior to the overt choice and is largely based on mothers' social interactions and impressions developed in a variety of different social networks including those of the children themselves. This choice is usually also highly gendered where mothers make most of the decisions in a social environment stressing the responsibilities of motherhood (David et al. 1994). Nor is 'rationality' split off in some way from emotions and feelings; these too have their rationality, but expressed around different 'utilities', such as children's needs for example as we saw in Chapter 4. If rational economic man really did exist, we would probably label him autistic. Economic rationality is better seen as just one form of emotional feeling; it is just that, as Paul Ormerod (1994) says, neo-classical economists have scored a great propaganda coup in labelling their version of behaviour as 'rational' – leaving other versions implicitly 'irrational'.

In this social world some people also have more power than others, and are able to impose their 'tastes' on others, either directly or indirectly. The power relations of gender are one, major, example (see Walby 1990). These may often be 'unseen' so that women are socialised into, and internalise, a less powerful position in their 'tastes', for instance in terms of particular biographical expectations of motherhood. (At least in terms of dominant conceptions of what is powerful.) Thus Alan Carling (1991) shows how women's gendered understandings can prevent them from taking economic advantage from a man, even if they are in a position to do so; indeed, they may often act in a more self-sacrificing way (doing even more housework for example), apparently to confirm that these understandings have not been breached. The notion of leisure is particularly problematic in relation to women, therefore (Wimbush and Talbot 1988). At other times these gendered power relations may be directly expressed, as with male aggression and violence – although even here this can remain socially unrecognised or devalued. Survey information shows that domestic violence, for instance, is common and repetitive, and is most often associated with conflict over the allocation of labour, monetary or sexual resources (Smith 1989; Browne and Herbert 1997). Similarly, the incentives for paid work are as much 'social' as 'economic' (for example to gain respect, make friends, find power, confirm social status or gender identification), while consumption is often as much about conveying social meanings (think of clothes, housing, or even food) as it is about satisfying individual wants (Weale 1992). Both are also subject to coercion of various sorts. In like fashion the public sphere of markets could not operate without collective social behaviour in the form of mores, norms, informal rules of thumb, formal rules, rights, duties and sanctions (Hodgson 1988). Again, some groups and institutions, dominant firms for example, have more power than others and can control markets and coerce the behaviour of others.

Unsurprisingly such collective, and socially derived, frameworks for individual behaviour in the 'public world' are also gendered. As well as depending on understandings and expectations (private sector managers must act 'macho', for example, see McDowell and Court 1994), this gendering is also institutionalised (as in the welfare states we described in Chapter 7) and can be directly enforced through coercion, as the many forms of male harassment in the workplace show only too well. Hence men and women are differentially positioned in various sorts of markets, firms, states and families (rather than there being one version, as conventional economics usually has it, of 'the market', 'the firm', 'the family' or 'the state').

As our examples have suggested, women, families and children have traditionally been absent from conventional economic study. For example, the first edition of Samuelson's best-selling introductory tome *Economics* (1948) contained only two references to 'females', included in the 'minorities' section. (The early, almost heroic, work of Margaret Reid on the 'women's realm' of the household was usually ignored or forgotten.) Even today, this disregard continues (Ferber and Nelson 1993b). Paid work is generally seen as central, households are seen in terms of consumption rather than work, and issues like care and poverty – which usually affect women and children more directly – are neglected (compare with the attention given to unemployment). It is not just that these subjects are judged peripheral in themselves, but given the concept of rational economic man and rational choice then gender, as a social relation, is removed to the periphery of exogenous conditions. It is indicative of this approach that when neo-classical economics was finally extended to include families and children, it did so in the form of a separate specialism, as a discrete object of study rather than a development of approach. First, unpaid work at home was introduced as a third alternative to paid work and leisure in models of individual choice (Becker 1965) and subsequently, a neo-classical model of household behaviour was developed to include exchange between men and women (Becker 1974, 1981). The elaboration of this model constitutes the 'new household economics'.

According to Becker the major gain to marriage accrues out of the mutual dependence between spouses that results from each specialising in those functions in which they can best capitalise on their human capital – women in domestic work, men in market work. An individual's utility maximisation will be greater than if either partner remained single, and could not specialise so fully. Marriage then involves trading in the fruits of these different skills. Economic self-interest, therefore, will tend to both further enhance the development of specialised human capital and also create the 'traditional family'. Only when, as recently, women's market earning power increases, because of technological and economic change, does it pay women to become more independent. The marriage rate will then decline, fertility will decrease, and both divorce and lone motherhood will increase. The current crisis of the so-called 'Second Demographic Transition' of the developed countries (Lesthaeghe 1995) is thereby explained through neo-classical theory.

Criticisms of this approach reflect the criticisms of neoclassical economics as a whole. The starting point is socially simplistic, and hence leads to preposterously naive results (Bergmann 1995, Wooley 1996). For example, why is it that men and women develop 'tastes' for market work and domestic work respectively? This is especially a problem when new household economics must make the assumption that tastes are exogenous even to interactions in one's family. The only alternative is to accept that gender roles are naturally determined. Becker et al. also assume that male heads of households act like 'benevolent patriarchs'; they are altruistic in making decisions that are in the best interests of all the family – the utility functions of a family members become subsumed into the male utility function. This replicates the fiction that market life behaviour is perfectly selfish, and in family life it is perfectly altruistic – where men get credited with the altruism! (Although Becker claims he only uses male and female pronouns as a convenient way to distinguish the altruist from the beneficiary, 1981, p. 173.)

Nor does Becker discuss differential power within the family, and while the model stresses the advantages of traditional marriage for women, possible disadvantages are not included. If we were to include emotional and sexual work, as well as a proper value for caring, then within this model women must normally be economic losers – a point well appreciated by some radical feminists. It then becomes more logical to appeal to male violence and ideological power to understand both the creation of the traditional marriage and its current weakening (Delphy and Leonard 1992). The definition of rationality will be affected by social norms, for example women often take a longer-term, more cooperative view (Scott and Perren 1994, Seguino et al. 1996) and alternative notions of rationality are possible. Thus over-specialisation may reduce flexibility and can leave specialists in a vulnerable position if circumstances change, it may therefore be more rational in the long term for women to take up paid work. This is especially the case if a life course perspective is taken, where individual needs and risks change over time. Certainly, there is little empirical support for Becker-type marriage trading models, and the happy congruence between 'theory' and 'traditional' family patterns only applies for a historically quite exceptional period – the 1950s (Oppenheimer 1994). After all, this traditional family was historically created and exists over the longer term more as social ideal than social practice (Lewis 1992a; Pfau-Effinger 1998). Similarly, women's specialisation in domestic work can result from coercion, or gendered social expectations, more than from 'rational' trading. Carling (1991) shows how 'gender ideology' is relatively autonomous from the exchange model of partnership. Economic pressures rarely translate into changed behaviour if gender understandings work against this, and women's gender understandings mean that they will rarely take full economic advantage of men, even if they are in a position to do so. As Carling adds in a more sociologically informed aside, this self-sacrifice might well be seen as self-preservation. This is presumably not only preservation in terms of the women's own understanding of her identity, but also in terms of the often aggressive or violent reaction of men. Not only is the 'Second Demographic Transition' a collective social and cultural phenomenon, it is also inevitably deeply gendered (Solsona 1998)!

Why is it then, as Valerie Oppenheimer (1994) asks, that given the poor empirical support for Becker type models, they have become so firmly entrenched? The cynical answer, following on from our discussion of economic science in general, is that these models allow the world to be corrected so that it fits into neo-classical discourse. This also fits in with how those with social power would like the world to operate. For our purposes new household economics has one further limitation. Lone mothers have no resident partner with which to trade or bargain. Hence, in these terms, lone mothers and their children do not constitute a family. But of course, families and households involve much more than rational exchange of labour and lone mothers are, in fact, mothers. As we showed in Chapters 4 and 5, they share gendered expectations and moral rationalities about what motherhood involves.

There are much more realistic accounts which can better point towards an understanding of women's behaviour in combining motherhood with paid work. Thus Joan Tronto (1989) and Selma Sevenhuijsen (1991) have shown how caring, including mothering, is not a purely instrumental task, nor is it a natural activity that springs from a innate differences between the sexes; rather it is a socially negotiated ethic rooted in practical activity. Although motherhood has specific material consequences for those who undertake it, the emotional commitment which it entails goes beyond a purely labour related concept of work. As Bren Neale (1995, p. 16) puts it, motherhood 'involves the development over time of a moral commitment to an ongoing, interpretive relationship with a child ... invariably it involves interweaving children into the life plan and life style of the primary carer'. Moral situations are not defined in terms of economic exchange, but in terms of the preservation of relationships, meeting emotional needs, and the avoidance of harm. This implies that women's family based understandings are rooted in a concern with process rather than goals; with activities and ways of being which are regarded as valuable in their own right, rather than as simply means to ends (Edwards and Ribbens 1991). The 'rational' practice of motherhood, therefore, may involve establishing an emotional equilibrium between connectedness and empathy on the one hand, and the feeling of autonomous self on the other. In turn, the definitions of these moral poles is created through participation in the web of relationships ('social capital') which make up the real world. This also means that parenting, and household arrangements more generally, will be carried out in a variety of ways in different kin and community networks.

However, all this should not be taken to imply that women, or mothers in particular, are 'irrational' while men and women in the public world of paid work are 'rational' in a means–ends sense. While conventional economic theories have traditionally seen rationality as a mode of thought and behaviour that does not incorporate emotions and morality (which are implicitly defined as 'irrational'), all rationality requires the existence and use of emotions of some sort. This is why, as we discussed above, 'economically rational' behaviour in the pubic world of paid work is best seen as one sort of multi-rational and emotional behaviour. Intriguingly, Becker (1996) himself has recently introduced concepts of 'personal' and 'social' capital into his own framework in an attempt to deal with what he recognises as the substantive inadequacies of traditional economics in this respect – although unfortunately this attempt is stymied by the confines of his traditional methodology.[2]

In short, neo-classical economics holds a seriously distorted view of economic behaviour. This is damning from the point of view of those interested in explaining real-world social phenomena, although the economics discipline has been avid in finding ways of shrugging off this 'external' critique (there is nothing better, the model conveys the essentials, it is elegant, it is simple yet powerful, it allows mathematical extension, and so on). After all, this critique is most often mounted by sociologists, economic historians, anthropologists and the like who – according to many economists – simply 'tell stories'. In a male-dominated profession, maybe alternatives are just 'touchy-feely economics for softies' to quote from one review of Marianne Ferber and Julie Nelson's *Beyond Economic Man*, in which feminist economists call for a complete restructuring of the discipline (Jenkins 1995). Much more serious from the point of view of the conventional economist is that mathematical economics – the 'Imperial Guard' of the discipline as Paul Omerod describes it – actually shows that the model breaks down 'internally'. In the attempt to rescue neo-classical theory from the external critique by introducing more realistic mathematical parameters (representing market power, market complexity and uncertainty) the model ceases to be mathematically sustainable (see Ormerod 1994). Surprisingly, mathematical economics shows that there is, after all, something called society.

8.3 SEARCHING FOR THE 'INVISIBLE HAND' – REVIVING A SOCIAL ECONOMICS

At this point some economists, especially those who have already made their name in the discipline, have abandoned conventional economics either wholly or partly. (For initial fame and promotion still derives from developing yet another mathematical model, or in fitting a data set to algebraic functions.) Wassily Leontief, Nobel prize winner in economic science, concludes that his discipline is not providing understanding of real economic systems, Robert Sugden (1991, p. 783) comments that 'there was a time when ... the job of the economic theorist seemed to be one of drawing out the often complex implications of a simple and uncontroversial set of axioms. But it is becoming clear that these foundations are less secure than we thought, and that they need to be examined and perhaps rebuilt'. George Akerloff (1997), in his presidential address to the Econometric Society, sees the introduction of 'thick description' from ethnography and biography as a means of accomplishing this rebuilding. Tony Lawson (1997) calls for economists to recover reality, and blames the decline of school and university enrolments, and the disappearance of postgraduate students, on the fact that they can more realistically study economic issues in other subjects. Ormerod (1994) goes so far as to announce the 'death' of economics. Rather than announce death, a few intrepid pioneers have even asked for a postmodern economics (McCloskey 1985, Brown 1994a,b). Economists are essentially persuaders, using mathematical models and scientific jargon as rhetorical gambits, economic research is a particular reading of the economy, using a canonised discourse to do so, and economic theory is a language game (see Manion and Small 1997). Why not base economic theory on the idea of 'femina economica' , who cares and acts in solidarity with others' needs (McCloskey 1993)? Ironically, then, it is economists who tell stories.

The trouble with a postmodern economics, like postmodern theory in general, is not only that it is better at critique than providing alternatives (although the critique of positivism and structuralism is not as new as some postmodernists believe), but that it implies a whole series of epistemological non-sequitors (see Sayer 1993). Just because we apprehend reality through discourses does not mean that all discourses are equally useful, that it is impossible to make judgments between them, and that social life only consists of discourse. Ironically, the postmodern deconstruction of neo-classical economics can serve as a justification for those who go on using it just because the 'honorific scientific aerosol' of economic modelling can make less conventional conclusions (for economics) more acceptable. For example, Siv Gustafsson (1997) reviews the work of' female' neo-classical economists who show that, contrary to the usual account, equal opportunity policy will not distort the market and that women are not better off specialising as housewives. However, rather than an argument for feminist neo-classical economics this is really, as Gustafsson implies, a case of rhetorically exploiting the social weaknesses of the model to produce the desired result. Rather than the 'add women and stir' response to the limitations of conventional economic science, in the light of our review so far it is surely better to start from somewhere else.

Sandwiched between the death of economics, and continuing as though the critique did not count, are a number of attempts to formulate more realistic alternatives to neo-classical theory. The 'new institutional economics' sits closest to the neo-classical account in trying to incorporate criticisms of conventional economics while keeping the discipline intact. In this view, institutions, rather than the Robinson Crusoe figure of rational economic man, are central to analysis. The 'invisible hand' of the market is not necessarily able to operate efficiently and institutions substantially influence, even govern, market relations between individuals and groups, and hence how they make economic choices. This governance may be accepted 'voluntarily', through custom, tradition and shared expectations, or it may be coerced. (Management theory spends some considerable effort in trying to get the mix right.)

This new institutional economics in part reflects the 'old' Institutionalist School, developed from the turn of the century onwards, which also criticised the simplistic neo-classical notion of rationality and its neglect of social behaviour and institutions (Ormerod 1994). As critics of neo-classical economics often cite, Adam Smith, the supposed intellectual discoverer of rational economic man, in fact gave considerable importance to morals, values and institutional frameworks. But where the 'old' institutionalists saw themselves in opposition to the neo-classical school in developing

Adam Smith's 'social' side, the 'new' institutionalists aim to provide a positive critique; the claim is to 'broaden the mainstream toolkit and then to use this analytical framework to explain phenomena that had previously been impenetrable' (Nabli and Nugent 1989, p. 1336). Both sides of Adam Smith's inheritance, the social and the economic, would be put back together. Institutional hierarchies may be more efficient allocators of resources than markets in conditions of uncertainty, especially where information is incomplete and asymmetrical, where only a few actors are involved, and where the 'atmosphere' of particular morals or values is important (Williamson 1975, 1985). Contract setting therefore becomes a central economic issue, and institutions are seen primarily as transaction cost-minimizing arrangements, as mechanisms for internalising externalities via property rights, and as systems for dealing with incomplete and asymmetrical information. In these conditions 'bounded rationality' is a more realistic model of economic behaviour.

This 'markets and hierarchies' tradition, as it is often called, has become important to the idea of quasi-markets and to the marketisation of state provided services where institutionally set contracts are central, as in the British National Health service for example. Other work focusses more on collective action; on how cooperation is achieved, or breaks down, why some groups might express institutional dissatisfaction through 'exit' (that is by leaving) or by 'voice' (by protesting). For example, while the 'taste' for discriminating against women in the labour market cannot survive in the neo-classical world (unless women do 'naturally' offer inferior labour – in which case this is not discrimination), in the institutional world various types of transaction and opportunity cost not only allow discriminating behaviour to survive, but to be profitable. Women's bounded rationality then leads them to make the best of accepting this situation. Consequently, in this view, feminist strategy can be informed by determining what combination of exit, in leaving the labour market, and political protest might reduce the market for discrimination (Krug 1997).

New institutional economics does provide something of a more socially real rational economic man, one who makes institutionally bounded decisions in imperfect markets, where the 'atmosphere' can be important to how these decisions are made. This is still a rather limited view of economic decision-making, however – as it is meant to be, in the attempt to complement mainstream economics. We are still very much in the territory of methodological individualism and individual utility maximisation, where exchange and markets are seen as covering the essence of social life. Women's 'bounded rationality' does not include alternative views of what is rational for example, even though, as we saw in Chapter 4, these prefigure decision-making. In essence institutions only arise to 'correct' the real world so that the neo-classical model can properly operate.

One consequence is that more fundamental Marxist and political economy critiques of markets are not addressed (cf. Polyani 1967, Robinson 1971, Sayer and Walker 1992). Markets, which are just one – and extremely variable – social institution, will often fail. Dominating firms and groups can effectively control markets, capitalist accounting systems are unable to take account of externalities or public goods, and price signals are simply inadequate in making economic and social choices (Barlow and Duncan 1994). Markets are also rather poor at satisfying needs (as opposed to demand), and give some people considerable power over the lives of others. This more real political economy is better reflected in comparative, historical developments from the new institutional approach. Alfred Chandler's famous study *The Scale and Scope of Industrial Capitalism* (1990) shows how it was the institutional and social behaviour of 200 of the largest manufacturing companies in Britain, Germany and the USA – absolutely central to these countries' economic fortunes – that determined their economic success or failure. Similarly Lazonick (1992) explains why Britain, the first industrial power, was overtaken by the USA in the early twentieth century, which in turn has been overtaken by Japan. According to Lazonick, this was preeminently a matter of the institutional character of different, socially derived, capitalisms. Business firms developed different organisational capacities in interaction with different social structures and state forms. Ironically, but indicative of the claims of this variety of institutional economics, Chandler's preparatory study was entitled *The Visible Hand* (1977). Institutions have now become social actors rather than simply arrangements to compensate for the inadequacies of the real world in living up to economic theory.

This more social form of institutional economics still leaves us with a major problem, however – where does this' visible hand' come from? While institutional economics may have shown that it is not markets that coordinate the economy, but institutions, the same objection applies. How, exactly, do they do this? Mary Douglas, in approaching institutions from the viewpoint of cultural anthropology, is able to provide some answers in *How Institutions Think* (1987). She begins with small scale 'communities', a telling example just because they have so often been seen as exceptional in rational choice theory; it is here that personal, 'irrational' factors can be seen to dominate decision-making. Hence, in part, the extraordinary vitality of the concept 'community' – for there is something there that we all recognise even while we can show communities do not exist as social entities (see Bell and Newby 1971). This is why the concept never really disappears, and periodically re-emerges in different guises like that of 'locality'.[3] This 'something' is what we were exploring in Chapter 3, for lone mothers, through the idea of social networks. Douglas however, echoing Thomas Kuhn's theorisation of paradigmatic shifts in science, shows that once the exceptions become general then paradigmatic theory (in her case rational choice theory) is 'laid bare' (Douglas 1987, p. 21). For all institutions act, in general, like small-scale communities – they develop systems of knowledge on 'how to act', and maintain themselves through particular 'thought styles'. These thought styles encode, legitimate and rank information in various ways, and set standards on how people interpret the world and act within it. They also depend on collectivities to exist at all.

It is in this sense, then, that institutions 'think' and remember – and forget. Strictly speaking, as Douglas points out, it is not institutions in themselves that act, but the people that make them up. ('States' for example are in reality different collectivities of people with particular powers, who among other things act in different ways in relation to lone mothers.) People choosing rationally, then, are not choosing from private preferences but through social institutions. This conclusion is of some interest in the context of this book, and in Chapters 4–7 we described how lone mothers do just this in deciding how to combine motherhood and paid work. The point is, however, that the whole is greater than the sum of the parts. We must leave methodological individualism. In this light, the idea of rational economic man is quite bizarre. As Douglas puts it: 'Only by deliberate bias and an extraordinary disciplined effort has it been possible to erect a theory of human behaviour whose formal account of reasoning only considers the self-regarding motives' (ibid., 128).

The need to understand the social origins of the 'invisible hand' that informs economic behaviour places disciplines concerned with the social and collective, like anthropology and sociology, in a more central role. They can no longer be regarded just as a means of providing data for econometrics, or peripherally agonising about where preferences come from. Again, Adam Smith can be cited to legitimate this claim, where he was as much sociologist as economist not only in

The Wealth of Nations but also in his other bestseller, indicatively entitled *The Theory of Moral Sentiments*. Much the same can be said of Ricardo or Marx. In taking this on board the 'new economic sociology' of Granovetter (1992) and others argues that the 'economic imperialism' of both neo-classical and institutional economics (where the latter is an extension of the former) has erected an enormous superstructure on a fragile and narrow base. A more solid foundation is provided by recognising that economic goals incorporate non-economic goals such as approval and sociability, that markets and other economic institutions (like all institutions) are socially constructed, and that economic action – just one form of social action – is embedded in developing networks of social actors. The key to explaining economic behaviour then becomes a matter of tracing social networks and explaining how these networks support and influence particular choices and decisions (Granovetter and Swedberg 1992). Again, this is not unlike what we described for lone mothers in Chapters 3 and 4. It then also becomes important to understand how notions such as trust, reputation and morality are socially constructed. The discourses about lone motherhood that we described in Chapter 2 are not just a type of 'imperfect information' therefore, which distort state policy-making and lone mothers' economic decisions in combining of motherhood and paid work; rather discourse should be seen as central to economic rationality itself.

The conclusions of the new economic sociology have recently been developed in an influential body of work which places the concept of 'social capital' at the centre of economic behaviour (Putnam 1993a,b; Fukuyama 1995; see also Chapter 3). In this view, economic success is dependent – not on economic rationality in itself – but on the nature of society in which it is embedded. Robert Putman takes his cue from the stark contrasts between north and south Italy (and between different regions in each). In the north, communitarian and democratic traditions foster high levels of participation in a wide variety of social institutions, from bird-watching societies to political parties. This engagement then fosters collective norms of trust, recipocrity, mutual aid and sanction, as well as more institutions to put these into effect – most notably in the case of north Italy high quality local and regional government. In turn all this better allows economic entrepreneurship. In the terms of institutional economics, transaction costs are lower, risk taking is easier, information is better. The opposite occurs in south Italy, where anti-democratic, clientilist traditions lower trust and recipocrity, and so produce a vicious circle of economic failure.

Essentially, according to Putnam, these contrasting development paths were set up in the twelfth century with the emergence of republican and feudal systems of government in the different regions. Francis Fukuyama gives this account a more pointed political relevance in drawing out its wider implications, especially acute given his new right credentials. The individualism and prosecution of self interest, as advocated by neo-liberal politicians and conventional economics alike, is actually an economic dead-end. Trust reduces the cost, and increases the efficacy, of economic activity and distrust operates as both tax and disincentive. Rather than participation in civil institutions, however, Fukuyama concentrates more on the nature of families; inclusive families, as in China, restrict trust to small kinship groups whereas looser family structures, as in Japan, allow trust to spread to larger groups.

Interestingly, these accounts are paralleled by political economy work in urban and regional studies, where Emilia-Romagna (Putman's top social capital region) has been elevated to the status of an economic paradigm for regional development. Mutually supportive flexible specialisation, by interacting small firms in this post-fordist 'Third Italy' (distinguished from both the first Italy of fordist car factories in Turin, or the backward second Italy of the south) is seen as a model for regional development (see Scott 1998). Benneton is the emblematic firm of this 'Third Italy'. Again, the success of this model depends on the social embedding of firms in collective social networks, as facilitated by local traditions of government, although in these accounts current participation in radical politics (where Emilia-Romagna has been communist voting) is given more prominence (Cooke 1984, 1988). Participation does not only foster experience of democratic leadership, management, and following, but also develops visions, parables and ideologies about what is collectively possible. Rather than 'free' – non-social – enterprise by individual entrepreneurs or firms, this more collective model is seen as underlying most examples of successful economic development, from Silicon Valley to Japan (Sayer and Walker 1992). In the case of Japan, as echoed by Fukuyama, the different place of families in social structure has long been discussed as a key to its startling economic growth. The direction and success of economic decision-making is a question of the level and nature of social capital.

As we discussed in Chapters 3 and 4, the same general message about social capital as the 'visible hand' can be applied to lone mothers' decisions about how to combine paid work and motherhood.

Relative levels of social support, recipocrity and mutual aid – and also different ideas about what is possible – are produced by engagement in different sorts of social network. Lone mothers will then come to make economic decisions on the basis of what is socially accepted and possible. Subsequently, as we described in Chapters 6 and 7, these visions and decisions are variously supported, maintained and qualified by conditions in different local labour markets and state 'genderfare' regimes.

There is, however, a problem with this account, which we also raised in Chapter 3. How, exactly, is social capital produced and maintained, and what sort of social capital has what effects? This is not just a matter of historical research, where Putnam's account of historical development in Italy has been criticised as over-simple – many southern Italian regions have strong traditions of collective and democratic recipocrity for example (Sabetti 1996). Similarly, the link between Japanese family structures and business practices is certainly not direct (Sayer and Walker 1992). As Margaret Levi (1996) points out, Putnam's idea of social capital is at the same time both rather general and romanticised. Almost any sort of participation in dense local networks is seen as creating prosperity, but local networks can promote distrust and parochialism as much as trust and innovation. Presciently in view of our discussion in Chapters 3 and 4, Levi uses the neighbourhood as an example. Thus suburban lone mothers were often constrained by the type of social capital available to them in such neighbourhoods. Social capital is not simply a 'good thing'. It can have, different forms, different effects and different people will be affected in different ways. Even in Putman's Third Italy, women workers, housewives and unskilled labourers seem to have been systematically exploited by communist voting male artisans and employers (Cooke 1994). We might also add that the way the concept has been applied to date has been largely gender blind; the social capital of mothers' networks and associations for example is rarely in the picture. This sort of social capital, which helps support the unpaid economy of households and community care, is equally important to socio-economic efficacy. But women largely disappear once they leave the more formal world. While the idea of social capital may have pinned down economic's invisible hand, we still do not know how it works.

What the concept of social capital does do is to capitalise and codify one aspect of the critique of conventional economics that we have been following in this section; namely that economic rationality depends upon the social context. It is not just that what is rational depends on the context, but rational behaviour needs a social context to develop at all. But the social capital idea is still weak on the content and nature of rationality. This is, in part, because rationality is seen in narrow economic terms (even if the context is seen more broadly). This is perhaps especially true for Fukuyama who, as Will Hutton (1996) observes, believes free market economics 'to be 80 per cent right'. However, the critique of conventional economics also shows that economic rationality contains moral and emotional visions – not simply because people are moral and emotional ('tastes'!), but because this is how people make sense of the world. For this we need to return to Mary Douglas and her notion of how institutions think. As she concludes, 'each kind of community is a thought world, expressed in its own thought style, penetrating the minds of its members, defining their experience, and setting the poles of their own moral understanding'. In turn this means that individuals 'have no other way to make the big decisions except within the scope of the institutions they build' (Douglas 1987, p. 128). This is very much as we described for lone mothers taking up, or not taking up, paid work in Chapters 3 to 7. Personal decisions are set within socially variable 'gendered moral rationalities' which are collectively generated in different sorts of social networks and social contexts.

8.4 LONE MOTHERS' ECONOMIC BEHAVIOUR AND CULTURE AS THE MISSING LINK

How has this debate affected research on lone mothers' of economic decision-making? The answer, unfortunately, seems to be 'hardly at all', and most research continues, implicitly or explicitly, to follow the precepts and assumptions of conventional neo-classical economics. However two bodies of research, that of comparative social policy and new right underclass theory, do begin to move away from this in implying the importance of culture. In this section we shall briefly assess this work in relation to our conclusions so far.

As we have seen lone mothers disappear from the new household economics, presumably by definition because, having no male partner, they are unable to trade domestic work for a male market income. This is is perhaps why the econometric literature treats lone mothers as individual rational economic men seeking paid work. In this return to an even more conventional neo-classical position, lone mothers are seen as simply suffering from a higher level of constraints (the cost of child care for example) and/or lower levels of human capital (poor educational levels for instance). Motherhood as a quality disappears from the equations. As rational economic men, lone mothers then seek to use their human capital to secure the highest possible wage in the labour market, subject to constraints and the competing level of the 'reservation wage' of staying at home. Through statistical analysis of large data sets (taken in Britain, for example, from the General Household Survey or the Labour Force Survey), the aim is to measure how far, and in what ways, these individual attributes predict lone mothers' potential wage levels and hence their propensity to participate in the labour market. It would then be possible to estimate how social policy alterations (for example, changing benefit levels) would affect relative participation rates.

For all these reasons, econometric work on lone mothers and paid work reaches an explanatory cul-de-sac when cultural and moral definitions of rationality become apparent. For instance Jane Murray (1997) finds that lone mothers in Australia are 'relatively unresponsive' (that is, their modelled participation in paid work hardly changes) to simulated changes in the wage rate or benefit levels. Stephen Jenkins (1992) relates the greater propensity of African-Caribbean lone mothers in Britain to take up paid work to their higher rate of educational achievement; they possess higher levels of human capital which command higher wages. But why are African-Caribbean mothers high achievers in education in the first place? That African-Caribbean mothers, as a social group, are more likely to see motherhood and paid work as integral, rather than contradictory does not enter the econometric picture. Similarly, Yannis Georgellis and Harry Papapaagos (1995) find that their econometric model predicts hardly any increase in the uptake level of paid work by lone mothers even if universal, affordable child care was provided. This, they speculate, must be because 'for many mothers, and especially lone mothers, the priority is to be with their children rather than to work even when child care and other costs to working are fully covered' (ibid., 15). But how is this 'priority' created, and why does it vary between, for instance, African-Caribbean and White lone mothers in Britain, or between lone mothers in different countries?

This explanatory cul-de-sac is compounded by the correlative nature of econometric work. Correlation between variables is given greater prominence than establishing cause, and in practice the two are often confused. This conflation has of course been much criticised, both for economics in particular and positivist social science in general. (See for example Hollis and Nell 1975, Sayer 1976, 1992; Lawson 1997.) Evidence on social process – on how and why things happen – which will often be qualitative and taken from in depth case study, is rarely used. In addition, theorisations of social process (except for a general notion of rational economic man) are usually lacking. Econometric work becomes heavily data driven, therefore, rather than informed by causal evidence or theory. Rarely is there any theoretically or conceptually informed guide to what the empirical material means (cf. Sayer 1992). It is data that is explained, not the events and processes that create the data. Thus in research on lone mothers and paid work different modellers include different sets of variables in estimating the wages commanded by various individual attributes, depending on the particular data set used. The statistical results vary substantially, and sometimes in contradictory ways, in each account. (And given all the problems of using regression based techniques on what is often non-normal and sometimes highly auto-correlated data, statistical results may not be as robust as proponents like to think). So John Ermisch and Robert Wright (1991) emphasise the labour market in explaining lone mothers' declining employment in Britain, Ian Walker (1990) emphasises the benefit structure, and Jenkins (1992) stresses the age of youngest child and child care costs. In one sense econometric work on lone mothers and paid work spends a lot of time 'proving' the obvious – what is already known about patterns of behaviour. What it is poor at doing is explaining why these patterns have arisen (and hence its policy recommendations will remain oblique).

It is important to note that the model of rational economic man extends far outside econometric work, although its use is often implicit. This is especially true of Fabian social science tradition and the social policy discipline as a central product of this, although compared with economics the focus is more squarely on national social policy as providing the framework for individual utility maximisation. One example is the body of work advocating an expansion of day care in Britain so as to allow lone (and other) mothers to take up paid work (for example, Cohen and Fraser 1991; Holtermann 1992). Here, cost–benefit analyses are employed to estimate the financial results for both state expenditure and lone mothers' incomes, and thus the suitability of the proposed policy. This work is perhaps an exception in using cost–benefit analysis in a formal way, but most work in this tradition informally assumes this calculus. The technique of 'visual correlation' through cross-tabulation is commonly employed. For example type of economic activity (full-time paid work, part-time etc) is commonly cross-tabulated against type of lone mother in terms of civil status or some other characteristic like educational level or class. So too cultural and moral definitions of rationality show through the cracks. For example Bronwen Cohen and Neil Fraser (1991) also have to acknowledge that some lone mothers will not make 'economically rational' decisions even with expanded and affordable day care provision. But they are unable to say why this should be so.

The visual correlation method commonly employed in social policy work should not be seen as just 'dumbing down' from econometrics, however, where economists might see 'proper statistics' as superior. Looked at from the viewpoint of what is actually explained, as opposed to what is claimed, then visual correlation is superior in being more openly descriptive and less analytically pretentious. (As we noted above inferential regression based techniques are often mathematically suspect in any case.) It is probably a superior means of presenting survey material, confirming for instance that the better educated lone mothers and those with older children are more likely to be in paid work, or that child care is an important constraint for many (for example McKay and Marsh 1994: Ford et al. 1995). Rather, the problem is that this social policy tradition is also (if more openly) descriptive, concentrating on outcomes rather than investigating social and behavioural processes. This descriptive limitation depends on a similar confusion between correlation and explanation, and social cause is not established – except by implying rational economic man. This is why the emphasis is on the individual characteristics of lone mothers. Lone mothers' social relations and understandings rarely enter the picture.

One recent example is the study by Jonathan Bradshaw and colleagues (1996) of cross-national variations in lone parents' and married mothers' employment rates in 20 countries – in many ways a milestone in this tradition. The 'visual correlation' method is used to asses various explanatory factors for the national differences observed – demographic, labour markets and training, child care provision, tax and benefit policy, and – also using model family data – financial incentives to work As well as providing a lot of useful cross-national information in one place (which we have benefited from in Chapter 7), the cross-tabulation generally supports the reformist case argued. But the study also shows the limitations of this tradition. We still do not know how lone parents act in different contexts, and why they do so. The same explanatory impasse reached by econometric work is replicated where unexplainable but apparently crucial 'socio-cultural' factors (as Bradshaw et al. call them) remain lurking in the background. Evidence on social process and social context – on how things happen- cannot be appreciated. In other words the analysis concentrates on taxonomic associations rather than substantive causes (see Chapter 1). 'Culture' has escaped again. It has only re-emerged at the boundaries of social policy research.[4]

The emergence of comparative theory in social policy, following Esping-Andersen's pathbreaking work *The Three Worlds of Welfare Capitalism* (1990), has allowed some recognition of cultural differences (see Chapter 7). The Fabian tradition assumed that national social policy followed some preordained evolutionary development, resting on economic development and overseen by more or less benevolent states (if subject to the vicissitudes of particular governments – not least Thatcher's in Britain). But Esping-Andersen showed that there are in fact quite different types of welfare state, resting on different social and political conceptions of the relations between individuals, families, states and markets. In turn these regimes find their origins in collective political and ideological views of society. If anything, divergence is more likely than convergence. What is economically rational, therefore, becomes different in different welfare state regimes. (Interestingly, the notion of rational economic man fits best into the ideology of liberal state welfare regime where markets are most prioritised.) This 'cultural' implication is taken up more fully in feminist developments of welfare state theory. The original theorisation saw the male norm of standard workers as universal, and welfare regimes simply respond to the breakdown of this norm in different ways. The position of women, however, has been much less of a norm and varies considerably between regime types. It is most rational for mothers in Sweden to take up full-time (or long part-time) employment; correspondingly, it is more rational for German mothers to remain at home. Lone mothers, as we saw in Chapter 7, become a 'litmus test' of gendered social rights in different welfare regimes.

This addition of a type of cultural difference is limited, however. While welfare states may be socially and collectively created, lone mothers are posed as still simply responding. Different national policies provide lone mothers with different economic choices. Implicitly, then, lone mothers are still rational economic men – they simply respond in the context of differently gendered welfare state regimes.

Again, this cuts out lone mothers' own, collectively realised, understandings of their situation.

Ironically, in view of their insistence on rational choice, it is the new right which has most taken up the issue of 'culture' in the debate on lone motherhood. (This political appropriation of culture which perhaps helps explain the reluctance of traditional social policy to engage with the issue.) As we discussed in Chapter 2, the 'social threat' discourse identifies lone motherhood as central to the development of a dangerous underclass. This underclass has developed, the argument goes, because the welfare state has perverted the incentive structure for making rational economic decisions. It is no longer rational for some individuals to live in nuclear families or to take up paid work. Subsequently this changed behaviour is justified and reproduced by a deviant underclass culture both within lone mother families and within communities in underclass dominated ghettos. Thus Charles Murray (1994) takes us through the decision-making of a (fictitious) couple, Ross and Stacey who are 'keeping company'. Stacey finds she is pregnant. She and Ross sit down, discuss their situation, and Stacey decides she is better off not marrying Ross or working, but becoming a lone mother and taking income support. Ross and Stacey are clearly rational economic men here, where it is the welfare state which is culturally deviant in discouraging marriage and paid work. Murray (apparently) also meets a real person, 'Scully', who systematically defrauds the welfare state to provide for himself, 'his woman' and their kids. (Scully also appears to be the product of a lone mother family.) Not only has Scully no financial incentive to work, but his cultural understandings and those of his friends in the 'new rabble' allow him to justify his behaviour (Murray 1994, pp. 22–5). Alternative definitions of economic rationality (in this case not to seek a wage, but to live off the state, the unofficial economy and even crime) are culturally reproduced in the everyday life of underclass ghettos. The way to remove this deviant rationality, according to Murray, is not only to reinforce the liberal welfare state regime – for example by cutting state benefits still further, but also to reinforce culturally traditional values. In this way, culture – seen moralistically as deviant culture versus traditional culture – is used as a sort of conceptual and political qualification to notions of rational economic man.

The 'ethical socialists' like Norman Dennis, also discussed in Chapter 2, take the 'conceptual qualification' of culture a stage further. 'Cultural circumstances' become central to how individuals act and in this way outdo any perverse rationality. Dennis argues, for example, that if the young males who are trapped in poverty in British inner-cities and peripheral estates are 'victims', then they are:

> victims not of defects in the cash benefit system but of their cultural environment. They are the products of a cultural environment within which the messages of responsibility, striving, self-help and self-improvement have been progressively weakened.   (1997, p. 89)

For Dennis it is not increased poverty or inequality, or the financial balance of work versus welfare, that produces an underclass. Rather it is the erosion of a working-class culture of respectability under the 'relentless assault of liberal elites in the government, the media, education and the criminal justice system.' (Deacon and Mann 1997, p. 3). Most important of all has been the release of young men from 'the expectation and requirement that they should make a permanent home with their children and the mother of their children – whether it suited them or not' (Dennis 1997, p. 152). The cultural transition from moral control to individual licence has brought about both the collapse of the (married) two parent family and changed attitudes towards paid work.

The views of both neo-liberals like Murray, and the ethical socialists, therefore come to mirror Putman's idea of social capital discussed in section 8.3 – although now the accent is on the negative effects of the 'cultural embedding' of economic behaviour. We would suggest that both negative and positive views are each, in their own way, somewhat caricatured and one-sided. Rather, it is necessary to investigate the nature and forms of social capital in particular situations, and to assess how 'culture' in this sense actually does influence economic decision-making. This is what we undertook for lone mothers in Chapter 4. It would then be possible to find a theoretical vocabulary which more appropriately condenses how social capital works in practice without overly resorting to a political discourse. The concept of gendered moral rationality, which we introduced in Chapter 4, attempts to do this.

8.5 CONCLUSIONS

The critique of conventional economics shows that any successful explanation of economic behaviour needs to embody an operationalisation of 'culture' and 'morality'. It is therefore necessary to move away from a focus on individuals as separate selves, towards an understanding of gendered institutional and social processes, and the expectations and beliefs shared by social groups that produce different notions of 'rational' courses of action. As the feminist economics movement has shown, conclusions like these imply that the whole structure of how economists think and conduct their research needs to be redefined (for example Blank 1993; England 1993; Strassmann 1993). Research and practice in social policy will also remain inadequate when based on implicit notions of rational economic man. The process of lone mothers' uptake of paid work is much broader and deeper than an apparently self-evident concentration on individual variable-based correlations and national policy can allow.

One common response to this from conventional economists, public policy researchers and policy-makers alike has been that the rational economic man model is the 'least worst' and 'best practical' theory. Whatever the insights offered by the critiques, the argument goes, they do not provide a practical alternative, and at least the neo-classical approach gives both a basic behavioural theory and 'solid' quantitative research evidence upon which policy-makers can act and make decisions. At the most neo-classical economics needs softening round the edges, in the recognition that institutions are important for example, and in this way continues to be used extensively. The recent 'quasi-marketisation' of the British national health service is a good example (Lunt et al. 1996). In this book we have sought to offer something of a 'more better' and 'just as practical' alternative. Our concept of gendered moral rationalities focusses on collective negotiations and understandings about what is morally right and socially acceptable. Calculations about individual utility maximisation, and in particular perceived economic costs and benefits, will be important once these understandings are established, but are essentially secondary to such social and moral questions. The concept of 'gendered moral rationalities' may provide a better starting point for analysis.

NOTES

1. A first version of Le Grand's paper was given as his inaugural lecture as Professor to the London School of Economics Social Policy department.

2. Becker defines personal capital as 'the relevant past consumption and other personal experiences that affect current and future utilities' and social capital as 'the influences of past actions by peers and others in an

individual's social network and control system' (1996, p. 4). However, while recognising the problem for mainstream economics in 'accounting for tastes' (the title of his 1996 book), in tackling it Becker is unable to see outside the predetermined framework of rational economic man.

3. See Duncan 1986, 1989b; Duncan and Savage 1989, 1991 on why locality does not exist either!

4. This is perhaps not so surprising where conceptual breakthroughs most often start on the less hidebound intellectual peripheries or mixtures; see Kuhn 1970.

9 From National 'Welfare to Work' to Local 'Welfare and Work'

In this final chapter we will not provide a summary and overview of the book's contents; this is available in Chapter 1 (pp. 20–2), while each chapter also contains a summarising conclusion. What we see as the book's longer term contributions to research are discussed as appropriate in each chapter: we would point to the elaboration of a basic framework for analysing discourses about lone motherhood and new family forms (Chapter 2); the identification of gendered moral rationalities by which lone mothers make decisions about combining motherhood and paid work (Chapters 3 to 5); the reminder of the importance of the 'demand side' for labour, and of the geography of employment, for lone mothers' uptake of paid work (Chapter 6); the development of the 'genderfare model' as a means of accounting for variations in national state policy towards lone motherhood (Chapter 7); and, not least, the implications of all this for rationality and economic decision-making as distinctly social, moral and contextual processes (Chapter 8).

Rather, in this conclusion we want to pick up one of the reactions to our work in seminars and presentations of various sorts – what are its implications in terms of current social policy initiatives? This issue is particularly appreciated in the British context where the political agenda is seemingly completely changed by the landslide election victory of a 'New Labour' government in 1997 and its espousal of 'Welfare to Work', including a 'New Deal' for lone mothers. For more than a decade social science research in Britain was largely ignored by government, or even vilified – unless it came from the new right perspective of 'one of us' (as Margaret Thatcher, Conservative prime minister during the period, is supposed to have said). One response by many social scientists was to recoil into the realms of abstract theorising or 'issue less' research, where the indignity of producing policy relevant research, only to be defined as irrelevant, could be avoided. Now, at last, there is a feeling that social science research can make a difference, even if this is indirect (and possibly subject to the

281

constraints of New Labour's supposed vetting procedure – being 'on message').

This development has more than a purely British dimension. The 'Blairism' of this New Labour government is heralded as showing a third way between the old, supposedly unrealistic, agenda of social democracy and the 'old left', and the now discredited new right agenda of the 1980s. The dramatic electoral success of New Labour in Britain, and its apparent discovery of fresh, new policy agendas between and beyond old left and new right, has made it an exemplar for renewal and survival for social democratic parties across Europe. For a time, at least, the new British prime minister Tony Blair was the darling of the European left, as party leaders rushed to take on something of his mantle. Blairite slogans popularising this third way, like 'tough on crime and tough on the causes of crime' , were soon appearing in translation all over western Europe. President Clinton even joined Blair in a 'wonkathon' in February 1998 (where 'wonk' is apparently US slang for policy expert) in order 'to craft and define centre-left philosophy for the world of today' (Blair, quoted in *The Guardian*, 7.2.98), with a major conference for all European centre-left parties planned for the autumn of 1998. At a deeper level, behind this sloganising and conferencing, the political philosophy of communitarianism is taken to provide a base for this new way forward.

NEW LABOUR'S COMMUNITARIANISM

Modern versions of communitarianism start off from the critique of liberalism, especially its concept of individualism and its universalistic claims. First, as we have shown for lone mothers in this book, individuals are not asocial creatures but become what they are, and act, through their contextual social experiences and relations. Stephen Driver and Luke Martell (1997, p. 29) call this the 'descriptive and explanatory' communitarian level of criticism. Secondly, there is an ethical level of communitarianism, more normative in tone, which sees community as a 'good thing'. Individuals are not autonomous and will not properly develop if their communities are fragmented or dysfunctional, and hence the community as a set of institutions should be fostered and supported. The theories of social capital we discussed in Chapters 3 and 8 use both these levels in attacking free market theory. Third, there is a philosophical level of criticism which tends to say that it is not possible to find universal foundations for human behaviour –